THE NEW TECHNOCRACY

Anders Esmark

BRISTOL
UNIVERSITY
PRESS

First published in Great Britain in 2020 by

Bristol University Press
University of Bristol
1-9 Old Park Hill
Bristol
BS2 8BB
UK
t: +44 (0)117 954 5940
www.bristoluniversitypress.co.uk

North America office:
Bristol University Press
c/o The University of Chicago Press
1427 East 60th Street
Chicago, IL 60637, USA
t: +1 773 702 7700
f: +1 773 702 9756
sales@press.uchicago.edu
www.press.uchicago.edu

British Library Cataloguing in Publication Data
A catalogue record for this book is available from the British Library.

Library of Congress Cataloging-in-Publication Data
A catalog record for this book has been requested.

ISBN 978-1-5292-0087-4 (hardback)
ISBN 978-1-5292-0088-1 (paperback)
ISBN 978-1-5292-0091-1 (ePub)
ISBN 978-1-5292-0090-4 (ePDF)

Cover design by blu inc
Front cover: VitalyEdush/iStock
Printed and bound in Great Britain by CMP, Poole
Bristol University Press uses environmentally responsible
print partners

Contents

List of Figures

1

Rediscovering Technocracy

Forget left and right. The real divide is technocrats vs. populists.

(Freeland, 2010)

Technocracy is back (it was never gone)

Not so long ago, technocracy was largely forgotten. Then a wave of populism swept across the Western hemisphere. First came the realization that the rise of populist parties and movements in Europe was no longer contained, but a growing political force to be reckoned with. Then came Brexit in the summer of 2016, and roughly half a year later the election of Donald Trump. Since then, politicians and political scientists alike have been scrambling to make sense of the populist challenge to democracy. In the course of these events, technocracy has increasingly been invoked as the principal reason behind the current surge in populism. Taken to its radical conclusion, this link between populism and technocracy means, as summarized by journalist, author and (at the time of writing in 2019) Deputy Prime Minister of Canada Chrystia Freeland in the epigraph to this chapter, that technocracy vs populism is now the defining political conflict of our era. This is of course a rough outline of recent events, but there is certainly a current resurgence of interest in technocracy driven by the widespread search for causes and responses to the success of populist movements and parties in recent years. However, this resurgence also follows decades of relatively sustained silence on the topic of technocracy, roughly since the beginning of the 1980s, meaning that technocracy plays an increasingly vital role in attempts to come to grips with *the* political challenge of the foreseeable future, while at the same time being rather poorly understood. The purpose of this book

1

is to provide some measure of improvement of this situation and take a step towards a better understanding of technocracy.

In other words, the book reverses the current rediscovery of technocracy as an explanation for populism. Rather than arriving at technocracy through the question of populism and its causes, I will arrive at populism as a corollary to the question of technocracy only in the concluding chapters of the book. To be clear: this is not a matter of dislodging technocracy from populism or exonerating it from culpability in current challenges to democracy. On the contrary, I fully agree that technocratic policy and politics is one of the principal reasons for the current resurgence of populism. Indeed, technocracy and populism are diametrically opposed but structurally identical approaches to the business of government and politics, currently caught in something of a death spiral, and the question of how to break out of this spiral is one of the fundamental challenges in global politics today. However, any attempt to meet this challenge will come up short without an adequate understanding of technocracy.

This is all the more so because we are dealing with a new type of technocracy that is different from what technocracy used to be in important ways: technocracy has undergone a transformation from an earlier form of technocracy, which is reasonably well understood, to a new form of technocracy that is not. On one level, this emergence of 'The New Technocracy' can be understood as a transition from the original form of technocracy shaped by industrial society to a form of technocracy coinciding with the arrival of post-industrial society and its subsequent development into a fully fledged network society, risk society and knowledge society. However, the new technocracy is not merely an effect of the broader societal structures and dynamics of post-industrial society. The new technocracy is a form of governmental rationality and practice operating in an ongoing back-and-forth between state transformation and the evolution of post-industrial society. The most important expression of this governmental rationality and practice, I argue, is 'The New Governance' paradigm and its core idea of a transformation from government to governance. At the heart of the new technocracy, then, we find the idea of substituting traditional government for new governance, brought to bear on policy and politics through the intersecting principles of connective governance, risk management and performance management during the last three to four decades.

The book explores the broader set of changes in state–society relations and the policy–politics nexus involved in the arrival of the new technocracy and its operational programme of new governance.

While these changes cover a wide array of new governance practices, they can also be subsumed under an overarching reversal of the original technocratic compromise with bureaucracy against democracy in a new technocratic compromise with democracy against bureaucracy. Clearing up the considerable confusion concerning the relationship between technocracy and the competing regimes of bureaucracy and democracy in this way is essential if we are to come to terms with the particular challenges of the new technocracy. I do not, however, and this is probably worth emphasizing to clear away potential mistakes from the outset, propose that technocracy has simply displaced bureaucracy or democracy. In fact, a technocratic regime has never existed in its pure form in the history of government (although it has perhaps come close). Technocracy has only been partially realized in a context of ideas and institutions associated with bureaucracy and democracy. Nevertheless, technocracy has had deep and significant impact through its continuous competition and compromises with these other regimes.

Nowhere is this impact more pronounced than in the group of countries that, differences notwithstanding, constitute the most consolidated liberal democracies, advanced post-industrial societies and ardent adopters of the new governance: Western and Northern Europe, the United Kingdom, the United States, New Zealand and Australia. Although the argument in the book pertains first and foremost to this group, however, the relevance of the new technocracy does not stop at the doorstep of the Western hemisphere. Singapore is often seen as a sort of global exemplar of democratically tempered technocracy, and in a particular radical version of that argument, the Singapore style of technocracy is hailed as 'Asia's future', gaining ground in countries such as South Korea, Malaysia, Vietnam, Thailand and India, home to Prime Minister Modi's rendition of the good governance credo: 'minimum government, maximum governance' (Khanna, 2017: 19). Asia may indeed be the next frontier for the new technocracy, just as the Soviet Union and Maoist China were once seen as the frontier of earlier technocracy (Hoffmann & Laird, 1985; Andreas, 2009), but the heartland of the new post-industrial technocracy, as well as its industrial predecessor, is still 'the West' in the apparent Eurocentric and colonial meaning of the term.

Technocracy at a glance

Available definitions tell us that technocracy is a 'political system in which the determining influence belongs to the technicians of the administration and the economy' (Bell, 1973: 348), or a 'system of governance in which technically trained experts rule by virtue of their specialized knowledge and position in dominant political and economic institutions' (Fischer, 1990: 17). What does such a political system look like? In 1819, the ideational forefather of technocracy, Saint-Simon, proposed a government composed of a Chamber of Invention populated mainly by engineers or practical scientists, a Chamber of Review composed of theoretical scientists and a Chamber of Execution representing various industries according to their importance (Rossides, 1998: 86). A century later, Veblen proposed the creation of an industrial directorate, composed of a small council of engineers and technical experts, supported by a broader administrative structure providing intelligence and advice (Veblen, 1921: 89). Around the same time, the text that gave technocracy its name laid out a similar 'National Council of Scientists as Managing Directors' (Smyth, 1921: 15). The closest thing to a comparable popular manifesto for the new technocracy calls for the introduction of a 'cabinet executive committee' in order to curb the purported failures of American politics (Khanna, 2017: 98).

Understood as a form of government in the formal and institutional sense, then, technocracy is associated with the creation of institutions designed for political decision-making based on technical and scientific expertise, typically in the form of councils, committees, cabinets or independent agencies, and meritocratic appointment of experts to these and other political institutions. While these are indeed important indications of technocratic regime formation, my approach involves two amendments to prevailing definitions. For one, my use of the term 'regime' is *conceptually broader* than the institutional approach to forms of government. Rather than specific political institutions and procedures of meritocratic appointment, I focus on governmental rationality and practice in a wider sense, which is to say technocracy as an 'art of government'. In contrast to the image of a form of government 'as old as time', second, I understand technocracy in more *historically specific* terms as a distinctly modern regime, arising from industrial society and 'doctrines formulated in the industrial era' (Meynaud, 1968: 195). Taking these amendments into account gives us the following five dimensions of technocracy, which will be central throughout the book.

First and foremost, technocracy involves the exercise of government, or political power more generally, as *(post-)industrial management*. Setting aside the finer points about the concrete organization of political institutions, Saint-Simon and his then assistant Comte also advanced the claim that a government acting in accordance with the principles of the emerging industrial society would simply replace the government of men with the administration of things, meaning that a government capable of developing a social order based on the logic of industrial production to its fullest capacity can simply reduce politics to efficient administration. Since a properly developed industrial society will inherently do away with ignorance, strife and conflicts of interest, there will be no need for traditional government preoccupied with domination, containment and mediation between irreconcilable factions. Hence, the idea of politics as a particular domain, arena or form of life with intrinsic value to society is brushed away for a vision of political decisions completely submitted to the logic and demands of industrial production: 'politics, to sum up in two words, is the science of production, that is, the science which has for its object the order of things most suitable for production' (Saint-Simon, quoted in Hayek, 1955: 127). The first rough outline of technocrats as a social group, correspondingly, is the class of *industriels* viewed by Saint-Simon as being most fit to manage society in this way.

This embryonic version of industrialism as a form of political rationality, in the context of the first industrial revolution, is the ideational and material birthplace of technocracy. From this starting point, technocracy has developed along with the transition to the current post-industrial society (at least in certain parts of the world). Technocracy has always been inherently linked to the process of industrialization, and the major revolutions in technocratic history are the four industrial revolutions we have experienced so far. While the features of post-industrial society are very different from those of industrial society, the basic technocratic logic of governmental managerialism remains the same: traditional government should, in one way or another, be replaced by efficient administration of the social order in accordance with the demands and opportunities of the techno-economic system. Technocracy is not, however, a mere effect of techno-economic development or other determining historical forces, but always and everywhere a project that aims to reshape the relationship between state and society in the image of the most recent industrial revolution.

This preoccupation with the demands and opportunities of new innovations and modes of production, second, imbues technocracy with a deep-seated *technological progressivism*. Although (post-)industrial systems of production are assemblages of many and heterogeneous factors of production, the principal factor is always technology. In the technocratic view, society is first and foremost a techno-economic system defined by its constitutive technology, and at any given time it is the demands, limits and possibilities of this technology that set the basic parameters of technocratic governance: efficient management makes the most of technological capabilities and drives technological innovation further. More generally, technological progressivism involves the view that technological innovation is the key to economic welfare, social change and strong government. For the technocrat, there is a 'technological fix' for everything, including the problem of government.

This belief in the power of technology also comes with a more or less pronounced element of utopian thinking (Segal, 1985). The idea that technology holds the key to the realization of grander utopias such as the liberation of humankind from the toil of labour, production without degradation of natural resources, or a society without money has circulated widely in technocratic thinking. Progressivism is thus intrinsically bound up with utopianism and, at the margins, with the imaginary technological futures of outright science fiction. On occasion, this has led technocratic thinking to advance somewhat radical and partially obscure visions of societal development, sometimes resulting in outright ridicule and scorn. However, the new technocracy is still deeply immersed in techno-progressivism and utopianism proclaiming the emancipatory and empowering potential of digital information technology and/or the bioengineering technology at the core of the latest industrial revolution.

Building on the broader ideas of governmental managerialism and technological progressivism, third, technocracy is characterized by its pervasive pursuit of *social engineering*. On one level, social engineering means the comprehensive design, planning and management of society and citizens as an integrated system, or, with the favourite metaphor of industrial technocracy; as a social machine. On another level, social engineering also points to a more specific and historically vital link between technocracy and the engineering profession. Technocracy was originally an engineering project in a quite literal sense – an idea of government by engineers propelled forwards by the rise of the modern engineering profession nurtured by states in search of more efficient production and institutionalized innovation. Indeed, social engineering came about with a 'cult of the engineer' in industrial society: if society is understood as an industrial system of production, who better to run this system than the engineers in charge of its design and daily operations?

Industrial technology, machinery and production is basically mechanical, and the great social machine of industrial technocracy was (and to some degree still is) conceived in corresponding mechanical terms. By contrast, the social engineering of the new technocracy reflects the informational and digital nature of post-industrial production and innovation. In current popular usage, social engineering has come to mean cyber attacks, online manipulation and breach of information security. Although such activities clearly do not exhaust the field of social engineering, they reflect an important change in the nature of social engineering: it is no longer mechanical, but informational and digital. While this development has to some degree led to a new cult of the information engineer, technocracy has long since abandoned the idea of government by engineers. Social engineering in the information age may still include actual engineers, but their job is simply to keep the informational infrastructure running for the higher-order functions of economists, policy analysts, accountants, communication experts, managers and so on.

Moreover, the technocratic art of government is deeply informed by *scientism*. Indeed, technocracy and scientism are sometimes viewed as more or less interchangeable terms (Olson, 2016). It is a basic principle of technocratic rule that political decisions should, to the greatest extent possible, be based on technical and scientific expertise and knowledge. In other words, technocracy is based on the 'assumption that human problems, like technical ones, have a solution that experts, given sufficient data and authority, can discover and execute' (Kuisel, 1981: 76). Taken to its radical conclusion, this vision of scientific government and politics suggests that scientists and other experts are supremely equipped to take on positions of political authority. In reality, however, the influence of scientific and technical expertise on decision making is still mediated by compromises with traditional political institutions and politicians. In practice, technocracy thus means government by scientists as little as it means government by engineers, but it remains firmly committed to the objective that political decision-makers should simply stick to implementing scientifically correct solutions to technical problems.

On one level, technocratic scientism is rooted in Enlightenment ideals about scientific rationalism and the broader 'scientific and technological worldviews of the modern Western tradition' (Fischer, 1990: 59). In a more specific sense, however, the premium placed on scientific expertise and knowledge can reasonably be called scientism in the sense of a belief that physics, chemistry and related sciences united by the formal language of mathematics and logic – including 'hard' social science – constitute a universal form of knowledge that can be applied technically to solve any problem, regardless of its origin or nature (Sorell, 1991). In a more critical vein, the term also suggests potential scientific overreach, narrow interpretations of scientific method and unwarranted claims to certainty and objectivity (Hobbs,

1953; Haack, 2003). In his thorough (albeit unsurprisingly critical) analysis, Hayek described Saint-Simon's and Comte's legacy as a 'Counter-Revolution of Science' in relation to the French Revolution, and deemed it far more influential than is 'commonly realized' (Hayek, 1955: 156).

Last but not least, technocracy consistently aims to *depoliticize* political decisions and the political system in general. For technocrats, 'progress can be achieved only by the "depoliticization" of problems' (Ridley, 1966: 43). The technocratic pursuit of efficient management of the social order based on technical and scientific expertise means that technocratic 'reasoning finds interference from vested interests, ideologies, and party politics intolerable. Its antithesis is decision making through the weighing of forces and compromise' (Kuisel, 1981: 76). While this rejection of political ideology and the normal machinery of politics is stark and confrontational in principle, it also implies a high degree of ideological flexibility in the world of real politics. Technocracy has thus shown a historical ability to compromise with different ideologies and their organized representatives. In particular, technocracy has been able to migrate between the two great modern ideologies of liberalism and socialism in the pursuit of rational solutions 'beyond' ideology. This is of course a position often associated with 'Third Way politics', and there is little doubt that this position represents something of a sweet spot for technocracy when forced into the realm of political ideology and factional politics.

Technocratic depoliticization also seeks to curb public involvement, practical experiences of ordinary citizens, extensive deliberation, and the discretion and leadership of elected representatives. Together with the particular technocratic brand of scientific elitism, depoliticization is thus the source of an inherent conflict between technocracy and democracy, at least beyond the most minimalist definitions of electoral/representative democracy. Although observers of technocratic rule have always been acutely aware of this, the new technocracy has to some extent clouded the conflict: whereas industrial technocracy was loudly and even aggressively anti-democratic, the new technocracy has situated itself firmly within the constitutional and institutional framework of democracy and often lays claim to democratic legitimacy in its own right. The new technocracy thus presents itself in a new alliance with democracy, as expressed by popularized terms such as 'techno-democracy' and 'direct technocracy' (Khanna, 2017). The problem with the new technocracy in this respect is that, intentionally or not, it glazes over the inherent conflict between technocracy and democracy.

Setting the agenda: the new technocracy in context

As mentioned, the recent resurgence of interest follows a long period of relatively sustained academic silence on the topic of technocracy. This is not to say that technocracy has ever been a subject of heated academic debate. Rather, it has enjoyed a somewhat marginal and cross-disciplinary existence in various fields such as public policy and administration, elite research, party politics, parliamentary studies, democratic theory, historical sociology, and science and technology studies. Nevertheless, it is possible to identify a number of key debates central to the argument developed in the book. First among these is, of course, the relationship between technocracy and populism. However, the emerging debate on this issue has also been characterized by a rather indirect approach to technocracy, which often remains an ethereal phenomenon alluded to as a generic explanation for populism. Even in more focused and astute analyses of the relationship between populism and technocracy, the problem of populism still defines the parameters of the inquiry (Bickerton & Accetti, 2017; Caramani, 2017). Although it is certainly my hope that the book will contribute to this debate, I take the liberty of setting it aside until the final chapters. The road that takes us there relates more immediately to the following research traditions and agendas.

First and foremost, my approach builds on the *historical sociology of technocracy*, meaning a relatively distinct group of literature that has analysed the technocratic regime under the viewpoint of broader transformations in the relationship between state and society. While the specific contributions from this tradition will become readily apparent throughout the book, a few contributions should be highlighted upfront. First among these is Daniel Bell's *The Coming of Post-Industrial Society: A Venture in Social Forecasting* (1973), and his lengthy reflection on the accuracy of his forecasting in the introduction to the latest reissue (1999). The importance of Bell's forecasting lies not only in having provided the first comprehensive outline of post-industrial society (alongside Alain Touraine), but more specifically in his claim that post-industrial development leads to an increasingly technocratic form of rule. Bell thus hypothesized that the structures of post-industrial society would lead to a realization of technocratic government that had hitherto failed to make their full impact. I consider this the baseline hypothesis in the study of technocracy, and my argument is part support for and part revision of this hypothesis.

Bell's outline of post-industrial society can be considered the core monument in a series of more or less contemporary contributions making similar observations. In the European context, a series of essays by Habermas, compiled and published in English under the title *Toward a Rational Society* (1971), gave technocracy a prominent role in the embryonic version of what was later to become the fully fledged theory of communicative action, deliberative democracy and the conflict between 'system' and 'lifeworld'. In an even earlier contribution, Meynaud provided the first systematic attempt to outline the basic dimensions of the technocratic regime and its impact on state institutions in terms of personnel, channels of influence and methods of intervention (1968). Although eyeing developments in the United Kingdom and Germany, Meynaud's focus was the French case, which has always stood out as an exemplar of European technocracy in sort of ideational and historical interplay with the American version of technocracy mapped out by Bell (Ridley, 1966; Kuisel, 1981; Porter, 1995).

Most of the vital contributions to the historical sociology of technocracy, however, either appear in or reflect on a historical period, roughly speaking from the 1950s to the 1970s, which I shall generally refer to as the golden years of industrial technocracy. Presumably, the reason for the prolonged silence on the issue after this period is the assumption that technocracy disappeared together with a number of things abandoned or at least significantly weakened in the 1980s: extensive social planning, Keynesian political economy, managerial capitalism, welfare state expansion and so on. My argument, by contrast, is that the 1980s mark a turning point from advanced industrialism to post-industrialism and a corresponding new form of technocracy. On the one hand, this line of argument suggests that Bell's original version of the belated realization actually holds much better for the golden years of technocracy during the period of advanced industrialism rather than post-industrialism proper. On the other hand, my analysis remains firmly rooted in the original correlation between post-industrial development and technocratic rule introduced by Bell: the arrival of the new technocracy has been shaped by the deepening and widening of post-industrial society along the trajectories of the network society, the risk society and the knowledge society.

There are of course exceptions from the general rule of silence on the subject since the golden years of industrial technocracy. Of particular importance here is Fischer's analysis of the broader social and political epistemology of technocracy and 'the politics of expertise' in US public policy (1990), which continues a productive tradition of bridging between the historical sociology of technocracy and the analysis of policy making and implementation (Meynaud,

1968; Straussman, 1978). Moreover, Fischer's critical approach to public policy involves a keen eye for the conflict between technocracy and deliberative democracy (Fischer, 2000). A particularly germane idea advanced by Fischer is the notion of a 'quiet' and 'faceless' technocratic revolution beginning roughly at the end of the golden years of industrial technocracy (1990: 19), carried through by a new and modest technocratic pose presented in a 'subdued and pragmatic language addressed to organizational and technical "imperatives"' (Fischer, 1990: 110). Although this is an important indication of a significant shift in technocratic policy and politics, which also provides some further explanation for the increasing academic silence on the subject, my argument deviates substantially from Fischer's insofar as the new technocracy is neither particularly quiet, faceless, subdued nor pragmatic, nor technocratic in quite the same way as earlier technocracy.

Science and technology studies has also maintained an interest in technocracy as part of its broader interest in the social role of technology and scientific knowledge. From this perspective, notable contributions have been made on the diffusion of scientific management (Olson, 2016) and the potential conflict between techno-scientific expertise and citizens (Bucchi, 2009; Dusek, 2012). Technocracy has also been the subject of studies in organizational culture and organizational theory more broadly (Clegg, 1990; Burris, 1993; Parkin, 1994). This approach has helped identify the schism between bureaucracy and technocracy at the level of individual organizations, more or less directly based on earlier ideas about the importance of the 'technostructure' in modern organizations (Galbraith, 1967). In general, this approach corroborates the belated realization thesis insofar as it points to an increased organizational impact of technocracy with the advent of post-industrial society and production. However, this group of literature also has limited relevance for the matters at hand here, as it deals mainly with scientific institutions and business organizations, and only marginally with technocratic policy and politics.

By linking the new technocracy to the new governance, second, the book is also situated firmly in the domain of *governance studies*, broadly meaning the extensive body of literature concerned with the sources, dynamics and effects of the transformation from government to governance. While this transformation is more or less universally seen to have taken off in the 1980s, systematic reflections on the development only started appearing during the 1990s. As noted in an early landmark observation of this process, the transformation from government to governance does not necessarily mean no or even less government, but rather a 'change in the meaning of government; a new process of governing; a change condition of ordered rule; and a new method by which society is governed' (Rhodes, 1996: 652). The material expression of this development, according to this early inventory, is six more or less distinct trends: pursuit of the minimal state; the prominence of corporate governance ideas; New Public Management (NPM) reforms; diffusion of Good Governance concepts; interactive social-political forms of governing; and proliferation of 'self-organizing networks' (Rhodes, 1996).

While these trends remain visible today, the new governance has become increasingly structured around two constitutive paradigms: the market-based approach of NPM and the network-based approach now predominantly labelled New Public Governance (NPG). NPM is generally associated with a wave of reforms taking place in the 1980s in the United States, United Kingdom, New Zealand, Australia and, to some extent, continental Europe and Scandinavia (Peters & Pierre, 1998; Kuhlmann, 2010; Pollitt & Bouckaert, 2011). Although the differences between specific national reforms remain a matter of debate, the core idea of NPM is that the creation of public quasi-markets through organizational disaggregation, management by incentives and changes in budgeting and accounting practices will drastically increase governmental efficiency. NPM has been declared both dysfunctional (Hood & Dixon, 2015) and dead (Dunleavy et al, 2006), but it is viewed by others to be alive and kicking (De Vries, 2010). Either way, the perceived flaws of NPM became part of the reasoning surrounding the emergence of network governance as an alternative avenue of reform sometime in the 1990s (Christensen & Lægreid, 2007). Sometimes labelled 'joined-up government', 'whole of government' or 'holistic governance', the core idea in this avenue of reform is the extensive use of networks as means to ensure the internal coordination and collaboration of state institutions, as well as involvement of external stakeholders (Koppenjan & Klijn, 2004; Stoker, 2006a; Rhodes, 2007; Ansell & Gash, 2008; Goldsmith & Kettl, 2009; McGuire & Agranoff, 2011; Bevir, 2013). Roughly since the turn of the millennium, the network approach has increasingly been redefined as NPG (Osborne, 2010; Pollitt & Bouckaert, 2011).

Although the ideational and practical schism between NPM and NPG is very much at the centre of public sector reform, the transformation from government to governance has also spawned a long list of variations on the basic theme of new governance. A recent authoritative inventory counts 20 or so more or less distinct types of governance, including network governance, good governance, cybernetic governance, experimentalist governance, governance of complexity, regulatory governance, governance and learning, economic governance, climate change governance, e-governance, participatory governance, collaborative governance, democratic governance, European governance, global governance and so on (Levi-Faur, 2012). For some, such lists mainly testify to an indisputable lack of conceptual rigidity in the field of governance studies. Rather than theoretical sloppiness, however, the ongoing invention of new subdivisions and specialized areas of new governance reflects the dynamics of the transformation from government to governance rather accurately. The new governance is not a fixed system of thought or coherent political programme, but a loosely connected set of ideas and material practices used across the globe, albeit with a clear slant towards advanced liberal democracies.

Theories and empirical analysis of the new governance have come from the fields of public policy analysis, public administration, democratic theory, organizational research, sociology, law and economics. The technocratic nature of the new governance, however, has remained a non-issue for the majority of such contributions (Esmark, 2017). The key exception from this rule is a group of more critical contributions advancing the idea that the new governance operates through a 'politics of depoliticisation' (Burnham, 2001), which is in turn seen as a key reason for political disengagement and anti-politics (Stoker, 2006b, 2019; Fawcett et al, 2017), outright hatred of politics (Hay, 2007) and 'post-democracy' (Crouch, 2004). Although the fact that depoliticization is essentially an extension of technocracy has not gone unnoticed in the depoliticization literature, the implications have remained somewhat undeveloped. In this respect, my analysis fully shares the gist of the depoliticization debate, but it also provides a fuller exploration of the technocratic nature of new governance, which leads to a more cautious view of the potentials for repoliticization and the revival of democracy.

Third, the book relates to a strand of research concerned with the rise of *neoliberalism* and the potential existence of a neoliberal hegemony in global politics (Harvey, 2005; Plehwe et al, 2006; Braedley & Luxton, 2010; Chomsky, 2011; Centeno & Cohen, 2012). While the 1980s is more or less universally seen as a time of revival for laissez-faire and anarcho-liberalism, originating in the US, the UK and the broader Anglophone family tree, interpretations differ on whether neoliberalism has since been consolidated or halted, in particular since the global economic crisis of 2008. In one view, neoliberalism has lived through a rapid 'rise and faltering' on a less than fully global scale, with the crisis marking the 'great neoliberal recession' (Mann, 2013: 129, 322). The opposite view is that 'virtually everything' remains of the neoliberal hegemony after the crisis, understood here as the power of big corporations rather than laissez-faire market fundamentalism per se (Crouch, 2011: 179). While the aim of the book is not to answer this puzzle per se, the influence of neoliberalism on current politics, and its relation to the new governance in particular, is very much part of the argument.

It is largely uncontroversial to state that the NPM is to some degree informed by the broader neoliberal agenda. NPM reforms coincided with the surge in neoliberalism in the 1980s and, in its crudest form, took on a potential function as the 'the acceptable face of spending cuts' in the quest to reduce the public sector (Stoker, 1998). In its more refined and less apparently ideological form, NPM still exhibits a rather straightforward example of neoliberal market fundamentalism in its drive to create public quasi-markets and instate practices of corporate management. The argument can be extended to the various programmes of Good Governance that, as Rhodes originally put it, marries NPM to the advocacy of liberal political institutions and liberal democracy (1996: 656). The core formula of Good Governance programmes, propagated by institutions such as the World Bank, the International Monetary Fund (IMF) and the United Nations (UN), is thus a combination of democratic stability, institutional capacity and NPM ideas about governmental efficiency. In addition to such institutions, the formula is also visible in arguments about the importance of Good Governance by notable observers such as Francis Fukuyama (2004).

Whereas the link between NPM/Good Governance and neoliberalism is relatively straightforward, the case of network governance and NPG is somewhat more complex. On the one hand, advocates of post-NPM governance have routinely pointed to the neoliberal underpinning of NPM as a source of ideological bias and/or a cause of perverse effects. On the other hand, post-NPM forms of new governance can also be seen as an extension of neoliberalism in their own right, albeit a form of neoliberalism that rests less on the ideological force and simplicity of laissez-faire than the subtle mechanisms ingrained in governing technologies such as networks, partnerships and urban governance (Jessop, 2002; Fuller & Geddes, 2008; Bevir, 2013; Blanco, 2015). The latter argument has been developed with particular depth by 'governmentality' studies (Burchell et al, 1991; Rose, 1996; Dean, 2010; Dardot & Laval, 2013), based on Foucault's later lectures (2007, 2008).

Following this line of argument, the governmental impact comes of liberalism has less to do with laissez-faire than with the 'omnipresent' form of government based on the much more active and intervening form of liberalism rooted in German 'ordoliberalism' (Esmark, 2018). In this view, the neoliberal tenor of the new governance comes less from the apparent market fundamentalism of NPM than from the association between centrist Third Way politics and NPG (Burnham, 2001; Jessop, 2002). While broadly supporting this view, my analysis also deviates substantially from the focus on liberalism as ideology and/ or hegemony: the key to understanding the new governance is not a particular ideological affiliation, but rather the technocratic nature of its principles – of which Third Way politics is simply an extension.

A last area of debate central to the issue at hand is the growing number of critical reflections on the scientific and political status of economics, not least in the wake of the financial crisis of 2008 (Chang, 2010), and on the existence of an *econocracy* in particular (Davis, 2017; Earle et al, 2017). The term was originally coined to describe the influence of economic science on public policy (Self, 1975). In a more recent warning about the 'perils of leaving economics to the experts', an econocracy is defined as a form of rule where 'political goals are defined in terms of their effect on the economy, which is believed to be a distinct system with its own logic that requires experts to manage it' (Earle et al, 2017: 7). This rise of economic experts to this position rests on the near-universal commitment to the neoclassical paradigm within the economic discipline, which approximates the formal and mathematical language and standards of hard science in order to advance the field of economics, or more prosaically to gain political power, pecuniary rewards and/or academic prestige. The dominance of the neoclassical paradigm and the extensive use of mathematical models is thus seen as a debatable or outright damaging attempt to furnish economics with hard science status and control of a politically influential body of knowledge.

The results of this development include an invasion of economic language into political and social life, a reduction of political questions to technical issues removed from the public arena and, ultimately, that the majority of citizens are left incapable of real democratic participation (Earle et al, 2017: 19). Although this analysis largely disregards the broader history of technocracy and technocratic depoliticization, it makes a compellingly clear case for economic science and knowledge as the primary source of technocratic power and influence on current public policy, which are in turn seen as the source of populist reactions ranging from Trump to Sanders, from UKIP to Corbyn, and ultimately to

Brexit (Earle et al, 2017: 24). However, while parts of my argument will support the main tenets of this analysis, in particular when it comes to the question of the technocratic preference for quantification, measurement and calculation within the broader parameters of performance management, I take the conflation of technocracy and econocracy to be too limiting, both historically and in the case of the new technocracy.

Outline of the book

The book is roughly divided into three parts. The first part deals with the history and logic of technocratic regime formation more broadly. Chapter 2 is a historical analysis of technocracy and its major revolutions, from its original conception in the French Revolution to the latest and largely unexplored revolution from the 1980s and onwards. In this way, the chapter provides a historically informed understanding of the technocratic regime and establishes the core idea that the dynamics and structures of post-industrial society is the main driver of technocratic influence on policy and politics. Chapter 3 attempts to answer the question 'who are the technocrats?' Although I ultimately do not take this question to provide the best or most pertinent entry point to an analysis of technocracy, the actor-centred approach does raise the important issue of how to identify technocrats within the political system and determine the nature and extent of political influence. The chapter maps the available answers, from the most general idea of the 'technostructure' to the specific (and rare) occurrence of a fully technocratic government. Chapter 4 argues that technocracy should be viewed and analysed more generally as a distinct regime type. The chapter thus provides a more detailed discussion of the technocratic regime and provides an overall argument and model for the interplay between technocracy, bureaucracy and democracy (and by extension non-democratic, authoritarian regimes). In a final step, the chapter moves from the overall regime to the level of policy paradigms and provides an overall model for the ensuing part of the book.

The second part of the book offers a more detailed analysis of the new technocracy as it has developed in post-industrial society. Chapter 5 analyses the new technocratic pursuit of an imperative but difficult transition to a network state under the conditions of the network society and the informational revolution. Focusing on the interplay between technology and organization, the chapter argues that the new technocracy is defined by a new commitment to the power of networks, in stark contrast to the earlier preoccupation with large-scale and vertically integrated bureaucratic organization. Three types of new governance particularly invested in this development are discussed in more detail: communicative governance, collaborative governance and multilevel governance (MLG). Chapter 6 analyses the changes in technocratic rationality and practice brought about by the proliferation of manufactured, global and incalculable risk in risk society. In light of these risks, the traditional security thinking of industrial technocracy has been substituted by the internalization of risk and a new credo announcing the impossibility of insurance against dangers and uncertainty. This has, in turn, prompted important changes in technocratic regulation, expressed most directly in the preoccupation with the creation and management of resilient citizens, organizations, communities, societies and systems. The chapter concludes with two examples of this logic in the domains of ecological and economic governance. Chapter 7 returns to the technocratic preoccupation with quantification, measurement and objective scientific knowledge and the status of post-industrial society as a knowledge society. In spite of an apparent historical continuity with earlier technocracy, the principle of learning from evidence and continuous improvement of public policy that underpins the new technocracy nevertheless reflects important changes in the interplay between technology and knowledge. In particular, the rise of evaluation systems and evidence-based policy reflects an experimental agenda and a commitment to radical incrementalism and what works approach, which is rather far removed from industrial technocracy. The chapter concludes with a discussion of such experimental governance in the rather diverse cases of European Union (EU) policy coordination and nudging interventions.

The third part of the book takes up the question of the relationship between technocracy and populism. Chapter 8 discusses technocracy as an explanation for the new populist challenge. Following a brief overview of the current debate on the meaning and causes of populism, the chapter singles out the interplay between technocratic depoliticization and populist repoliticization as the key dynamic. Building on existing observations of this logic in the debates on populism as well as anti-politics, the chapter explores how the new technocratic preoccupation with network organization, reflexive risk regulation and experimental performance calculation have all contributed in particular ways to depoliticization, which in turn has led to populist counter-reactions and specific attempts at repoliticization. Chapter 9 discusses the possible contributions of this analysis to the broader quest for responses to the new populist challenge. This question is rephrased as a matter of how to rein technocracy back in in order to break out of the vicious circle in which the interplay of technocracy and populism is currently caught. Lack of attention to this problem is likely to exacerbate this problem and reinforce the current tendency to reinforce technocracy and fight fire with fire. Two general approaches to the question of reining technocracy back in are discussed: a short-term cordon sanitaire and a more long-term normative reinforcement of the decisionistic model of parliamentary democracy infused with elements of a pragmatic deliberative model.

2

Technocratic Revolutions: From Industrial to Post-industrial Technocracy

> A world run by engineers would be more planned, more strategic, more organised.
>
> (Chapman, 2016)

The invention of technocracy

The term technocracy was coined just after the First World War by the mechanical engineer William Henry Smyth. Born in Birkenhead, close to Liverpool, Smyth had emigrated to the United States in 1872 and spent most of his career practising as a consulting engineer in Berkeley, patenting devices such as a steam beer fountain, a racing boat oar and high-speed tractor. Smyth also wrote a number of contributions to the *Berkeley Daily Gazette*, which were later compiled by the University of California and published under the title *Technocracy: First, Second and Third Series* (1921). Smyth's basic claim in his founding technocratic manifesto is that the national direction and control of the economy during the recently concluded war had pioneered a new idea in the ancient art of government. Indeed, the management of the nation's productive forces under the 'period of national stress' during the war had amounted to a form of government with 'no precedence in human experience', due to 'the fact that we rationally organized our National Industrial Management. We became, for the time being, a real Industrial Nation' (Smyth, 1921: 13). For this unique experiment in government, Smyth goes on to state, 'I have coined the term Technocracy' (1921: 13).

Destructive as the war had been, management of the wartime economy had also led to the creation of various federal agencies in charge of production planning and distribution of munitions, food and fuel, near-complete mobilization of the workforce, new taxes, war bonds, comprehensive propaganda efforts and so on. Most importantly, engineers, inventors and scientists had been systematically involved in the efforts to direct the wartime economy. Building on these experiences, Smyth saw the conclusion of the war as a historical window of opportunity for a 'revolutionary' transition to national industrial management with the aid of 'our scientists, our technologists, our exceptionally skilled; let us commandeer, conscript, enlist, their loyalty, their devotion, their enthusiasm, their intelligence, their interests, their talents, their accomplishments for purposes of Peace and the realization of Noble National Purpose' (Smyth, 1921: 14). If national reconstruction and the future form of government were to take the direction of industrial management in this way, it 'would indeed make us an organized human aggregation – a unified social machine, capable of intelligent self-conscious national life' (Smyth, 1921: 15).

Although Smyth's claim to have coined the term technocracy is largely uncontested, his manifesto has lived a life in relative obscurity, presumably because it is rather messy and messianic (something not uncommon to the more utopian brand of technocratic writings). Moreover, Smyth was clearly recycling ideas expressed more eloquently by established intellectuals of his time, most notably those of Thorstein Veblen as we shall see. Nevertheless, Smyth's vision of national industrial management carried through by a mobilization of engineers, technical experts and scientists does capture the essence of American technocratic thinking at the back end of the second industrial revolution, which the First World War to some extent epitomized and concluded, with a certain aplomb. However, the history of technocracy started well before the term itself made its way to the stage. The origins of technocracy are to be found in an 'attack launched on the normal machinery of politics' that 'began with the advent of industrialization' and the new dynamics of 'rapid technical progress': under these conditions 'a whole movement, anxious to obtain the most from these innovations, believed that it was necessary to begin by modifying the system of political leadership' (Meynaud, 1968: 195).

The history of technocracy has, through and through, been shaped by the dynamics of industrialization, industrial revolutions and the intimate relationship between such revolutions and war. The exact nature, timing and number of industrial revolutions remain a matter of dispute. For the purposes of the argument here, however, we can distinguish between four industrial revolutions that are also *technocratic revolutions* in one way or another. Approaching the issue in this way is clearly not intended to produce a continuous and comprehensive analysis of industrialization and industrial revolutions in themselves, but rather an examination of critical junctures and defining moments in the history of technocracy, starting with the first industrial revolution. Contrary to what might be expected, however, this starting point does not take us back to the United Kingdom, but rather to France. As one observer states: 'the United States gave us the word "technocracy", but France seem to have some claims on the thing itself' (Porter, 1995: 114). That is somewhat of understatement. It would be fair to say that the French invented technocracy.

First revolution: French technocracy

The case for the French ancestry of technocracy can be summed up in the core idea that 'the French Revolution was also a technocratic revolution' (Alder, 1997: 20). In addition to everything else that has been said about the French Revolution, this line of argument suggests that it was also the original 'epiphany of technocracy', leading to 'the rise of the technocrats' (Armytage, 1965: 63). This interpretation rests on the more fundamental claim that the French Revolution was an industrial revolution as much as it was a political revolution. Albeit incomplete or failed, also as an industrial revolution, the French Revolution assigned political meaning and significance to industrial innovation and production in a way that provide the basic template for technocracy as a form of government (Alder, 1997: 66). In other words, technocracy was born of the French Revolution in its particular capacity as a political *and* industrial revolution, shaped as much by the more or less direct 'penetration of English ideas' associated with the industrial and scientific revolution as political ideas and conflicts (Armytage, 1965: 61).

The birth of social engineering

A possible point of departure in this history is the substitution of the Gribeauval artillery system for the Vallière system (both systems were named after officers who championed them) in 1765 (Alder, 1997). On one level, the choice of a new artillery system can be seen simply as a matter of military strategy following French defeats in the Seven Years War (1756–63), leading to the substitution of the light, mobile and unadorned Gribeauval cannon for the heavy and heavily ornamented

Vallière cannon. However, the Gribeauvalists not only championed the new cannon on account of military thinking and strategy, but also in an attempt to turn from artisanal production to an 'interchangeability' system of production. Although not a system of mass production by current standards, the interchangeability system was an industrial system of production based on uniformity and discipline applied both to products (through universally accepted standards of measurement and calculation, technical drawings, precision gauges and machinery and so forth) and to the production process (through reorganization of the workplace, division of labour and training and so on).

The Gribeauval system was in this respect one of the most direct and important expressions of a new 'social epistemology of Enlightenment Engineering' and a corresponding vision of 'technological life' instilled in Gribeauvalists at the newly formed French engineering schools, the first modern educational institutions committed to engineering in the service of the state (Alder, 1997: 57). *L'École des Constructeurs de Vaisseaux* had been founded in 1672 to train naval engineers, but two institutions in particular are central to the social epistemology of enlightenment engineering: *L'École Royale des Ponts et Chaussées* (founded in 1747 and charged with the training of civil engineers) and *L'École Royale du Génie de Mézières* (founded in 1748 for the purpose of training the officers of the royal army engineering corps). Based on Enlightenment ideals about empiricist natural philosophy and the mechanical arts, the schools sought to develop engineering as a distinct form of knowledge focused on the 'active manipulation of human instruments to purposeful ends' and 'institutionalized innovation' in the service of the state (Alder, 1997: 82). To accomplish this, the schools pitted meritocracy, standardized curricula, testing, discipline and competition against the hierarchy of the *ancien régime* and the aristocratic culture of honour and courage dominating the higher ranks of the infantry and cavalry.

More than just a new profession, the engineering schools ultimately sought to develop a distinct 'class' and the 'new men' of the future (Alder, 1997: 83). The engineers brought their skills to a variety of military and civil fields such as naval warfare, fortification and the construction of roads and bridges. However, the artillerists took up a special position as supervisors of 'the kingdom's largest industrial establishment' (Alder, 1997: 128). It was in their capacity as managers of the proto–military-industrial complex of state armouries charged with the supply of the entire weaponry of the French state that the Gribeauvalists sought to implement an interchangeability system of production. However, this was by no means a linear process. The system met with substantial resistance from craftsmen, guilds, merchants and political sponsors of artisanal production and had to some extent been rebuffed when the onset of revolution and Gribeauval's death coincided in 1789. Nevertheless, the interchangeability system remains the core of a broader 'engineering project driven by state bureaucrats following their own operational logic' in an attempt to 'replace the corporate order with a more innovative technological regime' and ultimately to reconfigure 'the relationship between society and the machine' (Alder, 1997: 66).

Technocrats in government and the invention of the technocratic 'pose'

The onset of the revolution provided a new window of opportunity for this project, and even propelled a selection of engineers into a position of political leadership. The first technocrats in parliament, on this account, were former students and professors from the engineering schools taking up seats in the Legislative Assembly and later the National Convention of the First Republic. During the most radical phase of the revolution, two fortification engineers (Lazare Carnot and Claude-Antoine Prieur-Duvernois) were furthermore appointed by Robespierre to take up seats on the Committee of Public Safety and thus to a position of de facto government. Between them, the two engineers were instrumental in the proliferation of the metric system (formally introduced in 1790), the establishment of *L'École Polytechnique* in 1794 (supplementing the specialization of the existing engineering schools with a more generalist approach and an emphasis on pure science, mathematics, physics and chemistry) and, not least, the supply of muskets to the revolutionary armies formed under the new principle of national conscription (Alder, 1997: 255).

The latter task provided an opportunity for a revitalization of the interchangeability system with the aid of Honoré Blanc. In contrast to the earlier attempts to reform existing armouries, the attempt to base the supply of muskets for the revolutionary armies on interchangeability production involved the creation of workshops in Paris under the auspices of a central 'Atelier' of perfection charged with the provision of standardized tools and measures. At the time of its creation, more or less *ex nihilo*, the Paris manufacture was the largest industrial project in Europe, and it 'belonged root and branch to the radicalization of the Revolution' (Alder, 1997: 262). Beyond the immediate military needs of the revolutionary armies, however, the engineers also saw the Paris manufacture as a stepping stone towards a more long-term guidance of 'the French Republic towards technocracy' and a form of technological life where the 'utopian community was a workshop' of skilled technicians and machinists 'devoted to a common program of innovation', and where 'social harmony would be achieved by mechanical routine' rather 'fraternal vows and organic consensus' (Alder, 1997: 257).

Long-term goal aside, the more immediate contribution of the first two engineers in modern government was their line of defence under the Thermidorian Reaction in 1794, directed at Robespierre, the Committee of Public Safety and its Reign of Terror in particular. Formally, Carnot's and Prieur-Duvernois's seats on the Committee were aligned with Robespierre's Montagnard faction of Jacobins that had orchestrated the Reign of Terror in response to the pressures of the populist revolutionary movement of the lower-class sans-culottes. The two 'Techno-Jacobins' thus appeared complicit in the Reign of Terror. Faced with the Thermidorian Reaction, however, they positioned themselves as purely technical and scientific members of the Committee that had merely been preoccupied with technological advances ensuring the military victories of the Republic, whereas Robespierre and other despot politicians had been responsible for orchestrating the Reign of Terror. This line of defence, in other words, involves a denial of any complicity in 'modern (interest) politics, a vast technocratic pose in which "Reason" was to speak with a single voice about the national destiny' (Alder, 1997: 301). This newly minted technocratic pose proved highly successful and allowed the two engineer-savants to escape the harsh fate of Robespierre and his allies. Indeed, Carnot went on to serve in the new de facto government of the Directorate that replaced the Committee of Public Safety, and later on as Napoleon's Minister of War. Prieur-Duvernois took up seat in the Council of Five Hundred.

This 'Thermidorian exculpation', based on a claim to represent pure scientific rationality and technical expertise without any complicity in politics at the highest level of government, constitutes something of an 'ur-event in the relations of science and politics in the modern era' (Alder, 1997: 301). There is thus a direct line from the technocratic pose adopted under the Thermidorian Reaction to the technocratic rejection of complicity in interest politics underpinning current politics of depoliticization. However, the extreme nature of the Reign of Terror also lays bare the inherent paradox of this claim to a position simultaneously inside and outside politics. By creating a space for purely rational and scientific decisions at the very heart of executive power exercised in its most extreme and violent form, the technocratic pose thus supresses the fact that:

the activities of the technocrats meshed with broader patriotic and social program that lay behind the Terror … Indeed, as the directors of a vast military and industrial program founded on republican fervour and state-sanctioned discipline, they possessed as much power as 'politicians' like Robespierre … One may indeed say that the technocrats were *central* to the state's arrogation of the Terror – and this involved them in political choice. (Alder, 1997: 301)

The Thermidorian exculpation of the first technocrats in government completes and finalizes the original template for technocracy developed during the French Revolution. In sum, the Revolution saw the emergence of a political programme of social engineering and social organization in accordance with principles of industrial production, rooted in the broader social epistemology of enlightenment engineering codified and institutionalized by the French engineering schools, and carried through by the ascension of the new group of engineers to the status of military officers and civil bureaucrats. These are, put briefly, the essential pieces of what was to become the French system of 'Grands Écoles' and 'Grand Corps', regarded to this day as the quintessential institutionalization of technocracy. Moreover, the Revolution propelled a number of engineers into the position of legislators and, in the case of the Committee of Public Safety, de facto executive power. The Thermidorian exculpation from the latter adds the technocratic pose and the claim to a technical and scientific position within the political system, from which it is possible to arrive at purely rational and depoliticized decisions.

The first political theory of technocracy

The interpretation of the French Revolution as the first technocratic revolution is also reflected in the more or less universal recognition of Saint-Simon (1760–1825 and formally Claude Henri de Rouvroy, comte de Saint-Simon) as the ideational forefather of technocracy, although the lineage is sometimes extended back to Francis Bacon. Saint-Simon is rarely considered a significant figure in the pantheon of political thinkers as he was 'neither noble, profound, consistent, familiar, nor provocative' (Wolin, 2004: 337). Indeed, there even seems to be general agreement that Saint-Simon was 'mentally unstable and at times quite mad': as Wolin goes on to say, however, his madness may have been a precondition for the one particular contribution he did bring to the table, namely an ability 'to perceive the future in an almost uncanny way' (Wolin, 2004: 337). Madness or not, Saint-Simon's foresight means that proponents and critics of technocracy alike have been haunted by the spectre of eternally recurring 'Saint-Simonism' ever since.

Saint-Simon was not an engineer, but associated himself with the professors and students of *L'École Polytechnique* and ultimately assumed the role of the 'self-appointed spokesman' for the new epistemology of enlightenment engineering and managed to inspire a cult of 'St. Simonians' who 'where the first technocrats; apostles of the religion of industry. Machines, according to St. Simon, eliminate human drudgery; and his followers become evangelists for the engineer' (Armytage, 1965: 66). Saint-Simon's ideas were clearly shaped by the events of the French Revolution, and the source of his foresight lay in the distinct idea that the 'revolution broke out in part because the old system had simply run out of authority ... at a time when the world had turned into one in which scientific intelligence, skill, and productivity were decisive' (Ryan, 2012a: 650). The failures of the Revolution, in Saint-Simon's view, had less to do with the arcane battle of republics and empires than the incomplete transition to a completely new authority structure grounded not in the political rhetoric of the revolution, but in the principles of industrial production and management. There are two key implications of this view.

For one, the revolution was a seismic shift in European history not as a contest of political principles per se, but because it had revealed that the constitution of political authority ultimately led back to the problem of social organization and integration. The question was not so much whether authority was conferred on leaders by God, family name or popular election, but rather that 'authority presupposed forms of social integration that it itself could not supply but it had to draw on' (Ryan, 2012b: 650). In other words, the problem of political authority was restated in quintessentially sociological terms: 'political sociology had been born, if not baptized' (Ryan, 2012b: 650). This view on the failures of the Revolution should not be accredited to Saint-Simon alone, but also to his then assistant, the young Auguste Comte. The latter would of course go on to overshadow his mentor and 'baptize' sociology, although as a freestanding positive science rather than a political science. Before that, however, the two came up with an immediate solution to the problem of social integration as the new foundation for political authority: bringing the latent 'miracles of productivity' of the embryonic industrial society to their full capacity through 'principles of organization according to which society's productive forces are employed in the most productive fashion' (Ryan, 2012b: 648).

The creation and management of society based on such principles of organization and integration, second, called for a new elite. Industrial society, in Saint-Simon's view, had created a new class of *industriels*, including manual workers, artists, engineers, scientists, managers and owners (Wolin, 2004: 338). The common denominator among the members of this class was their productive function within the new industrial order, as opposed to the idling class who either destroyed human and productive potential or 'squandered it in ostentation' (Ryan, 2012b: 650). The French Revolution had, in part at least, exposed and demoted the idling class by stripping away the royal and aristocratic prerogatives of the old regime, but it had failed to institute a new hierarchy of authority where 'those who exercised authority would do it because they were appropriately qualified to guide a productive and contented society', not because of their family name or military prowess (Ryan, 2012b: 648). In its full realization, however, the authority structure of industrial society would be a strict meritocracy and a mechanism for elite circulation ensuring that 'a rational society will be run by a hierarchical organization of managers and scientists' (Ryan, 2012b: 650).

Given this emphasis on changes in the mode of production, social structures and class, Marx is often seen as one of the more immediate heirs to Saint-Simon. Albeit Marx did take inspiration from Saint-Simon, or at least Saint-Simonians, the differences are more striking. Saint-Simon focused on industrial organization and production, not capitalism, as the preeminent characteristic of modern society. Second, Saint-Simon's distinction between *industriels* and the idling class has little or nothing in common with Marx's juxtaposition of labour and capital, and what Saint-Simon was advocating was certainly not the dictatorship of the proletariat, but rather meritocracy and elite circulation. Marx and Engels, and many with them, saw Saint-Simon as a utopian socialist. However, his ideas can be traced to anarchism, (neo)liberalism and fascism as well. In other words, Saint-Simon's industrialism is not aligned straightforwardly with any of the major established political ideologies, but rather displays a high degree of ideological flexibility, which has been an endemic feature of technocratic thinking ever since.

Moreover, the significant differences between Saint-Simon and Marx are essential because, according to one line of argument at least, the former was right and the latter was wrong (Wolin, 2004: 317). Saint-Simon's uncanny foresight, in this view, has to do with the fact that all the essential features the industrial society, as opposed to inevitable collapse of capitalism, 'have been faithfully reproduced in modern managerial society' and the 'age of organization' (Wolin, 2004: 318). On the very same point, Ryan contrasts Marx's view of capitalism and 'obsession with the proletariat' with Saint-Simon's more persuasive picture of industrial society and prescient announcement 'that the modern world was the product of a managerial revolution. At the time, nobody understood this; by the 1950s it was clear that Saint-Simon had invented the modern understanding of industrial society, and its organization' (Ryan, 2012b: 650). That point in time, however, came only after another industrial and technocratic revolution.

Second revolution: American technocracy

In political theory and history, the great American Revolution is of course a contemporary of the French Revolution. The interpretation of the French Revolution as the founding technocratic epiphany could also be pursued further along this line of inquiry: Honoré Blanc contacted and met Thomas Jefferson, who took a keen interest in the interchangeability system and imported it, with the approval of George Washington, as the new basis for the American military and its civilian contractors in effort to secure independence from European arms manufacturers (Hounshell, 1985). However, the major American contribution to the history of technocracy comes a century later with the second industrial revolution that ultimately lead Smyth to introduce the term technocracy after the conclusion of the First World War. In addition to the obvious fact of introducing the term itself, this second technocratic revolution is notable for two contributions: the theory and practice of scientific management and the rapid rise and fall of technocracy as a distinct political movement. At the centre of both developments, we once again find the engineer and the social epistemology of enlightenment engineering.

Smyth was typical, although certainly not the most prominent representative, of large swathes of engineers inspired by the broader sentiments of the progressive era in the United States. Taking on board broadly progressive ideas such as the need for social and economic reform, rationality, planning and a suspicion towards traditional politics, the engineering profession was essential to the formation of an operative bond between technocracy and the American Dream in the early decades of the 20th century (Akin, 1977). The guiding principle of this bond was the 'myth of the engineer' (Akin, 1977: 46), which is to say the claim that engineers and technical experts were uniquely qualified to develop and manage a new socio-economic order for the good of all, based on the full utilization of technology and the logic of industrial production. In other words, the myth of the engineer accurately reflects the broader social epistemology of enlightenment engineering and the sociopolitical importance ascribed to the 'new men' of the increasingly organized and self-conscious engineering profession, codified and institutionalized by French engineers and their schools. Whereas Saint-Simon had anointed himself spokesperson for the enlightened engineering of society a century earlier in France, this role was now taken on by Thorstein Veblen in the United States.

The technocratic bible

The immediate reason for this role is *The Engineers and the Price System* (Veblen, 1921), which was published at a point in time when the majority of the work that has earned Veblen status as a founding father of institutional economics was already behind him. Indeed, his late-career turn to more or less willing spokesperson for the progressive engineers is sometimes seen as an aberration in relation to his more scientifically validated work. On another reading, however, Veblen's later writings can be seen as fully consistent with the fact that his historical approach to the problems of social and economic development had always been greatly influenced by Edward Bellamy's utopian novel *Looking Backward* (1888), even to the extent that it had 'awakened him to his life's work' (Stabile, 1987: 36). *Looking Backward* is itself a founding text for the more utopian current in American technocracy, later represented in exemplary fashion by Harold Loeb's *Life in a Technocracy: What It Might Be Like* (1933). Moreover, the 'Bellamy clubs' rapidly forming and disappearing between 1888 and 1896 set a pattern later replicated by the technocracy movement (Segal, 1997: 12). Against this background, Veblen's penultimate book coalesced disparate ideas, analysis and suggestions for reform among the progressive engineers and movement into what has been called a 'foundation of technocratic thought' (Akin, 1977: 25) and a 'technocratic version of the federalist papers' (Stabile, 1987: 46). Indeed, a highly critical inquiry into the origins of the technocratic movement in the United States would later identify it simply as the 'Bible of Technocracy', although Veblen did not use the concept at all (Raymond, 1933: 120).

The key claim in the alleged bible is that the capitalist economy (the 'price system') had entered a state of conflict with the system of industrial production in the early decades of the 20th century, in essence because the system 'is forever in danger of turning out a larger product than required for profitable business' (Veblen, 1921: 36). This conflict had been partially avoided in the first wave of industrialization due to the lower capacity and sophistication of industrial production, now replaced by a complex system of production, based on the 'inclusive organization of interlocking processes and interchange of materials' between the main lines of industry 'shaping the conditions of life': transport and communication, the production and use of coal, oil, electricity and water power, steel and metals, building materials, rubber, industrial farming and so on (Veblen, 1921: 36). Moreover, the role of early industrial entrepreneurs ('captains of industry'), acting as industrial experts, financiers and business managers at one and the same time, had been replaced by increasing specialization and goal conflicts between shareholders ('absentee ownership'), business managers ('lieutenants of the vested interests') and production engineers (Veblen, 1921: 22).

Only the latter, in Veblen's view, were fully capable of operating the complex system of production, whereas business managers had been left increasingly estranged and incapable of comprehending the workings of the system (Veblen, 1921: 39). Profit-seeking shareholders, for their part, were even further removed from any real insight into industrial production. Building on his earlier critiques of capitalism in the theories of conspicuous consumption and the leisure class, management of the industrial system of production according to capitalist principles is thus seen by Veblen to result in waste and misdirection. The need to maintain a profitable price, coupled with increasing ignorance of technology, machinery and production (the 'industrial arts'), mean that capitalist business management will inevitably result in the unemployment of material resources, equipment and labour, the systematic dislocation of resource exchange and sabotage of information, as well as a focus on salesmanship and production of superfluities and spurious goods (Veblen, 1921: 67). Indeed, the mismanagement of the industrial system by 'ignorant business men with an eye single to maximum profits' led Veblen to suggest that 'if the country's productive industry were competently organized in a systematic whole, and were then managed by competent technicians with an eye single to maximum production of goods and services ... the resulting output of goods and services would doubtless exceed the current output by several hundred per cent' (Veblen, 1921: 75).

Veblen does little to substantiate the claim, opting instead for a concluding 'Memorandum on a Practicable Soviet of Technicians', suggested for 'mature deliberation' among the many technicians 'competent to initiate' the enterprise of taking over and managing the industrial system (Veblen, 1921: 86). Two of the principal ideas advanced in the somewhat unspecific memorandum are the substitution of absentee ownership for joint ownership and the creation of a central industrial directorate. The latter can be seen as Veblen's particular contribution to the historical list of institutional blueprints for technocratic government, initiated by Saint-Simon and Comte a decade earlier. In Veblen's version, the industrial directorate would hold supreme power in all matters of production and distribution, although based on consultation procedures with accredited spokespeople, sub-centres and local councils from the various branches and regions of the productive industry (Veblen, 1921: 89). Smyth's contemporary blueprint for the governmental infrastructure of national industrial management displays similar ideas (1921: 15).

Veblen's soviet of technicians clearly never materialized. On the contrary, mobilization around the myth of the engineer seemed to decrease with the return to normalcy after the war and the increasing prosperity of the 1920s: 'Engineers, after their spree of criticism, accommodated themselves to the business ideals of the decade' (Akin, 1977: 44). Veblen seemed to have expected this outcome: by 'settled habit, the technicians, the engineers and the industrial experts, are a harmless and docile sort, well fed on the whole and somewhat placidly content with the "full dinner-pail" which the lieutenants of the Vested Interests allow them' (Veblen, 1921: 83). Having rejected the idea of an imminent overturn of the capitalist system led by engineers in this way, however, Veblen also relinquished his well-developed cynicism and concluded his case for national industrial management with a hopeful 'just yet' (Veblen, 1921: 104). Although there were to be no revolutionary soviet of technicians, the wider circles of progressive engineers more or less directly influenced by or influencing Veblen's technocratic bible did provide two contributions: a theory and practice of scientific management, the influence of which can hardly be overstated, and an utterly failed attempt to turn technocracy into an overt political movement.

Scientific management

The efficiency movement, Taylorism and scientific management are more or less equivalent terms for a form of social engineering shaped through and through by the progressive era. Frederick Winslow Taylor was a mechanical engineer by training, and his attempt to reorganize industrial production essentially an extension of the new 'ideology' of the progressive engineers (Layton, 1976). On one level, Taylor's idea of maximizing output and efficiency through rigid measurement and standardization of tasks, work and production procedures were intended for the workshop and the engine room of the industrial system. However, Taylor was also clear that the principles of scientific management should be applied not only to the steel works where he had developed and implemented them, but 'with equal force to all social activities', including homes, farms, churches and governmental departments (Taylor, 1967: 2). Scientific management and industrial engineering were not merely intended for the factory floor, but ultimately for the government of society as such. Indeed, the progressive engineers found in scientific management the argument and method for a transferral 'of their occupational talents from the factory to the social macrocosm' (Akin, 1977: 8). Properly applied, scientific management would not only lead to more efficient production, but also economic abundance and social harmony in society.

Scientific management is clearly not an offspring of Veblen's technocratic bible. Taylor published *The Principles of Scientific Management* in 1911, and initially Veblen seemed to have placed the scientific managers and self-proclaimed efficiency experts firmly on the side of profit and business management (Stabile, 1987). However, a more affirmative and direct link between Veblen and scientific management was forged between 1915 and 1920 with attempts by the progressive engineers to politicize and reform the engineering profession, and the American Society of Mechanical Engineers (ASME) in particular, with the explicit goal of taking on a leading role in the engineering of society (Layton, 1962). Key figures in this development were Henry Gantt (yes, he of the Gantt chart), who worked with Taylor and contributed significantly to the development of scientific management, and fellow engineer Morris L. Cooke. Their attempts to reform ASME met with mixed success, leading Gantt to establish the 'The New Machine' in 1916, a group of engineers and other progressives advocating pursuing the pervasive implementation of scientific management throughout the industry at the hands of a body of selected engineers (Akin, 1977: 53). The group quickly dissolved due to the events of the First World War, but Gantt elaborated further on scientific management as an economic and political force at the hands of engineers in various writings compiled in the book *Organizing for Work* in 1919 (practically the same time that Smyth published his technocratic manifesto in the *Berkeley Daily Gazette*), which provides a broader social philosophy and framework for the social engineering of society according to the principles of scientific management.

During his development of this framework, Gantt had taken a good deal of inspiration from earlier writings by Veblen (Layton, 1962: 68). Veblen had, in turn, been acutely aware of the ideas and activities of the progressive engineers, which led him to organize a series of courses on 'The Social Function of Engineers', 'The Productive Use of Resources' and 'An Engineering Approach to Industrial Organization' at the recently opened New School for Social Research during 1919–20. There is thus a certain degree of circularity in the exchange between Veblen and the scientific managers: what Veblen saw in the progressive engineers advocating scientific management as the key to the rational organization and management of society was to some extent an echo of his own ideas (Layton, 1962: 66). Gantt saw scientific management as the key to the efficient utilization of the industrial system for the broader good of the community, in marked contrast to the waste and narrow self-interest of existing business management and the wider capitalist system of production for profit. Moreover, the governmental application of scientific management would substitute 'true democracy' for parliamentary democracy, which 'accomplishes nothing and leads nowhere' (Akin, 1977: 52). Gantt died before he could participate in the seminar at the New School, and a common agenda or mission never emerged. However, the seminars did provide a point of contact between the progressive engineers and the more academic and theoretical circles around Veblen, which led directly to the publication of the alleged technocratic bible.

Scientific management is the core of the American technocratic revolution during the progressive era. In its immediate context, scientific management had considerable influence on the booming disciplines of management, administration and policy studies (Haber, 1964; Fischer, 1990; Burris, 1993). The application of scientific management to government presented a solution that had substantial influence on planning ambitions from the New Deal administration and decades onwards (Graham, 1976). Indeed, scientific management made the second technocratic revolution a 'managerial revolution', even if some of the predictions attached to this claim turned out infamously wrong (Burnham, 1941). Robert Reich summed up the point while looking ahead to the 'next frontier' in 1983: scientific management emerged in the second decade of the 20th century and shaped American history 'for the next fifty years' (Reich, 1983: 49). In a more ambitious version of this argument, scientific management not only shaped American history, but history as such through the more or less global spread of the standards of scientific management, also well beyond the half-century outlined by Reich (Olson, 2016).

On the surface of things, the same cannot be said of the other major result of the second technocratic revolution: the rapid rise and fall of the technocracy movement.

Technocracy as a political movement

The technocracy movement emanated from the same circles of progressive engineers around Veblen, but took a different course. The origin of the movement is the formation of the Technical Alliance in 1919, which included Veblen among its 15 members. Formally, the Technical Alliance was conceived much as an reiteration of The New Machine: it was composed of engineers and other progressives advocating the rational reorganization and management of society by technical experts, and it was intended to take up Gantt's original idea of an energy survey documenting the capacity and wastefulness of the current system of production. Just as The New Machine, however, the Technical Alliance disbanded less than a year after it was formed. In spite of the apparent similarities, however, the Technical Alliance was different in one important way: it was formed and headed by Howard Scott, a bohemian from Greenwich Village with little or no formal credentials (although he claimed to be a distinguished engineer), nor influence among the leading proponents of scientific management and the efficiency movement. Nevertheless, Scott managed to participate in the discussions around Veblen at the New School and set himself up as 'chief engineer' of the Technical Alliance (Akin, 1977: 29). When the Alliance disbanded, Scott went on to serve as research director for the Industrialist Workers of the World.

Scott approached the issue of social engineering somewhat differently from the more established engineers such as Gantt and Morris. As he would later explain, technocracy

> never had any use for Taylor or any of the efficiency or scientific management crowd. They never realized that human toil is the last thing in the world you need to be efficient about; the only way to be efficient is to eliminate it entirely ... who in the hell wants to be efficient with a shovel, and what sense would there be even if you succeeded? (Scott, 1965: 8)

Reiterating Veblen's original assessment, Scott saw the efficiency movements simply as business management consultants and men 'so lame in their thinking and social outlook that they missed the boat completely' (Scott, 1965: 8). Personal squabbles and harsh terminology aside, the sentiment makes clear that technocracy was a project of radical techno-economic reform shaped in the image of society without labour, at least in the capitalist sense. However, the programme presented by Scott also remained unclear or downright incomprehensible in its reification of technology, consistently evading a clearly outlined vision, specific sociopolitical goals and even solutions to observed problems (Segal, 1985).

When the Great Depression presented a new window of opportunity for reformist thinking after the self-contended 1920s, however, Scott seized the day and formed the Committee on Technocracy in 1932, together with Walter Rautenstrauch, creator and head of the department of industrial engineering at Columbia University (the first of its kind in the United States). The name was apparently Scott's idea, albeit without any acknowledgement of Smyth's earlier publication of his technocratic manifesto, which in turn led the latter to restate his claim to the term (Akin, 1977: 184). The Committee picked up where the Technical Alliance and The New Machine had left, and set out to conduct the great energy survey of America. Following the now established pattern, however, the committee proved short-lived and Rautenstrauch left within a year. In marked contrast to its predecessors, however, the Committee on Technocracy managed to garner public and academic attention sparked by the search for answers to crisis of the depression: in a brief period from 1932 to 1933 technocracy was a matter of intense national interest. For the same reason, however, the committee did not quietly disband in the manner of its predecessors: it ended in public spectacle and ridicule.

As the committee started to present its energy surveys, various media and opinion leaders took a keen interest in the results and the broader technocratic agenda. Completely unprepared for such public scrutiny, however, the committee struggled to present a clear framework or methodology for the sparse results of the energy survey. Adding to the problem was Scott's use of the committee as a platform for his personal interpretation of the technocratic project, leading to the public perception that technocracy was Scott's 'child' (Raymond, 1933) and thus concomitant with his 'prophetic' and 'messianic' style of communication, clouding purported scientific analysis (Adair, 1970: 33). Moreover, a series of articles in the *New York Herald Tribune* concluded that Scott's personae was built on a largely fictional life story and invented academic credentials (Raymond, 1933: 100). The definitive blow came with a nationally broadcast speech to the

New York Society of Arts and Sciences in January 1933, in which Scott delivered 'a rambling, confusing, and most uninspiring address' (Segal, 1997: 9). The speech brought accumulating dissatisfaction among the more scientifically minded members of the Committee on Technocracy to a low point, and the committee broke up shortly thereafter. The national press swiftly declared the death of technocracy, relegating it to the dustbin of short-lived fads on the same level as mah-jong, miniature golf, pole-sitting and marathon dances (Adair, 1970: 28).

The technocratic movement did have a long afterlife, however, spread out across various regional factions and media outlets across the United States and Canada (Adair, 1970; Akin, 1977: 97). Following the public implosion of the Committee on Technocracy, a national convention in Chicago in 1933 was held to regroup the technocratic movement, but ultimately led to a split between two rival groups vying for leadership of the movement. The first group gathered around the Continental Committee on Technocracy (CCT), representing a utopian and largely cosmopolitan version of the technocratic movement, summarized by its leading figure Harold Loeb (1933). The second group, much less utopian in outlook, rallied around Scott and his new organization Technocracy Inc. (Segal, 1985: 123). Although initially the most successful, CCT fell apart in 1936. Technocracy Inc., for its part, increasingly became something more akin to a cult of Scott's persona with an increasingly militarist appearance, including strict hierarchical organization, a special salute, the adoption of a monad symbol as the insignia of the movement and the use of the official 'technocratic grey' on vehicles and uniforms. The mobilizing efforts of Technocracy Inc., by some accounts, remained significant until the immediate aftermath of the Second World War, at which point it faded decisively into the existence of an increasingly obscure educational institution dedicated to preparing the American population for the immanent collapse of the price system (Adair, 1970). In this capacity, Technocracy Inc. exists to this day.

Hence, the main legacy of the technocratic movement in the United States in the first half of the 20th century is the image of a social and political movement fading into obscurity, bordering on parody, in spite of clear ambitions and a certain window of opportunity. In addition to Scott's persona, prominent explanations for this development include the New Deal reforms, seen by some to absorb the demand for reform and undercut the more radical programme of technocracy (Schlesinger, 1957), poor leadership and failure to organize efficiently (Elsner, 1963), the lack of coherent political theory and programme (Akin, 1977), thinly veiled elitism or even fascist inclinations (Segal, 1985: 123). However, the apparent contrast between the success of scientific management and the failure of the technocracy movement can also be misleading. Although the technocracy movement remains a fringe phenomenon in the history of social and political movements, it also gave voice to more radical and fundamental ideas about the relation between the techno-economic system and the state, which to some degree overtook and incorporated the more limited objectives of scientific management with the ensuing steps in technocratic history.

Third revolution: the golden age of technocracy

Whereas the first and second industrial revolutions are well established, both in terms of their core technological innovations and approximate time span, the content and timing of the third industrial revolution is considerably more contested. The solution adopted here is a rather pragmatic one: I take the third industrial revolution to be defined first and foremost by the nuclear age announced in dramatic and tragic fashion towards the end of the Second World War. However, the nuclear age more or less coincided with the jet age and was quickly followed by the space age. In addition to the new capacities for energy production and transportation following in the wake of these technological leaps, the third industrial revolution is also defined by a new capacity for large-scale production and use of composite materials (as opposed to dependence on raw materials), as well as the embryonic version of the key innovation that would later come to define the fourth industrial revolution: the computer. More technologies and innovations could probably be added to the picture, but those listed are all essential to the creation of an advanced industrial system of production from the 1950s to the 1970s, a period of time defined by well-documented leaps in material prosperity and societal transformation, as well as the emergence of the military-industrial complex and the geopolitical world order of the Cold War and mutually assured destruction. This era of advanced industrialism also marks the golden years of industrial technocracy, due to a logic of belated realization outlined with particular zest by Daniel Bell.

The five dimensions of post-industrial society

Bell's venture in social forecasting announcing the coming of Post-Industrial Society tentatively located the birth years of this new social structure to the years 1945–50 (1973: 346). In addition to the arrival of nuclear power, major events in this short time span include the first carrier-based jet fighter (the FH Phantom) in operational service, although land-based models entered operational service earlier, the public unveiling of the first operational computer, the ENIAC in 1946 (followed by the MANIAC and the JOHNNIAC), the founding text (by Norbert Wiener) on cybernetics as a new science of self-regulating systems and mechanism in 1947. Beyond their immediate technological impact, these innovations also led to the institutionalization of a new framework of cooperation between government and science with the creation of the Atomic Energy Commission and the National Science Foundation in the United States. In the same period, the government and economic science also entered a new marriage. Gross national product was introduced in 1945, and standardized input/output tables used as planning grids for the entire national economy five years later. The US Council of Economic Advisers was established in 1946, linking technical economics inextricably with public policy. More generally, Bell abstracts five core dimensions in the ongoing transition from industrial to post-industrial society (1973: 14):

- economic sector: the transition from a goods-producing to a service economy;
- occupational distribution: the pre-eminence of the professional and technical class;
- axial principle: the centrality of theoretical knowledge as the source of innovation and policy formulation in society;
- future orientation: the control of technology and technological assessment; and
- decision-making: the creation of new intellectual technology.

Bell repeatedly emphasizes that these dimensions pertain directly to what he alternately calls the techno-economic system and social structure, and only indirectly to politics and the state. Nevertheless, the interplay between technological innovation, economic changes and political action permeates the analysis. In retrospect, it is clear that the list appears most successful as an inventory of the major trends under advanced industrialism, whereas it comes up short in certain respects as a forecasting of post-industrial society proper. For the same reason, however, the list is an indispensable reference point for understanding the emergence of post-industrial society out of the era of advanced industrialism.

Dimensions one and two concern modes of production, occupational patterns and associated changes in the educational system that have since become standard measures of advanced industrialism and post-industrialism. The most well-known expression is the distribution of the workforce across primary, secondary and tertiary sectors of employment, pioneered by economist Colin Clark. According to the so-called Clark's sector model, the switch from industrial to post-industrial society in the United States occurred just prior to the Second World War, after which the gap between the number of people employed in the secondary and tertiary sectors have only widened. Relying on cross-sectoral data from the International Labour Organization (ILO) and Organisation for Economic Co-operation and Development (OECD), Bell notes that only the only the United States had more than half of the workplace employed in the service sector, albeit Australia, New Zealand and Northern/Western Europe were at the verge of reaching the same tipping point at the time of observation. The rise of the professional and technical class invoked as the second post-industrial trend expounds on this development by mapping the increasing numbers of highly skilled white-collar workers and, in particular, scientists and engineers. Collection of data along the same dimensions have documented the continuation of the trends observed by Bell, although the post-industrial society has come to be associated more with the rise of the 'quaternary sector' of knowledge workers and the rise of the 'creative class' (Florida, 2012).

These newer developments are, however, still broadly in line with the economic and educational patterns mapped out by Bell, and even more so with their underlying dynamic: the increasing importance of theoretical knowledge for innovation, growth and socio-economic development at large. Whereas the expansion of the service economy and the professional and technical class are in the end extrapolated socio-economic trends, the increasing primacy of theoretical knowledge constitutes the more general and fundamental principle at the heart of post-industrial society in Bell's view. The primacy of theoretical knowledge is the so-called 'axial' principle of the entire social system of post-industrial society and the underlying process of 'fundamental social change' from industrial society to post-industrial society:

> Industrial society is the coordination of machines and men for the production of goods. Post-industrial society is organized around knowledge for the purpose of social control and the directing of innovation and change, and this in turn gives rise to new social relationships and new

structures which have to be managed politically. (Bell, 1973: 20)

In other words, the primacy of theoretical knowledge defines post-industrial society essentially as a knowledge society. In light of the many more popularized versions of this term that have followed since, however, it should be emphasized that the axial identified by Bell refers to the primacy of *theoretical* knowledge in a rather particular sense.

From being a process driven largely by individual inventors, entrepreneurs and 'talented tinkerers' (Bell, 1973: 20), largely indifferent to science and the fundamental laws of nature underlying their investigations, innovation comes to be viewed as a process of organized and systematic interaction between technology and science under the auspices of government. In effect, theoretical knowledge becomes the key 'strategic resource' and the 'university, research organizations, and intellectual institutions, where theoretical knowledge is codified and enriched, become the axial structure of the emergent society' (Bell, 1973: 26). It is thus the scientific codification, enrichment and institutionalization of theoretical knowledge in the pursuit of technological innovation and political management that constitutes the axial principle of society. Indeed, Bell's restatement of his original forecasting reaffirmed both the centrality of the axial principle and its particular emphasis on the theoretical knowledge vis-à-vis the trial-and-error empiricism that dominated industrial society: 'the change from "nineteenth century" technology to "twentieth century" technology arose from the codification of theoretical knowledge' (1999: 39).

Against this background, the remaining aspects of post-industrial society are seen by Bell mostly as ancillary methods to the axial principle. The fourth component, the pervasive orientation towards the future, refers in the most straightforward sense to the theory and methods of scenario planning, trend analysis, the Delphi method, 'futurology' and so on. More generally, however, future orientation refers to the conscious planning and control of technological innovation and growth in an effort to reduce uncertainty about the future. By the same token, future orientation also includes more or less developed forms of assessment, analysis and control of risks, including security risks, industrial risk and economic risks. As such, this dimension points towards the later development of post-industrial society into a fully fledged risk society (see Chapter 5), although this was barely visible to Bell at the time. The creation of new intellectual technologies, the fifth and last dimension highlighted by Bell, refers to the increasing reliance on formal methods for the management of organized complexity and rational decision-making such cybernetics, systems analysis and game theory (see Chapter 6).

The belated realization of technocracy

Having mapped out the five dimensions of post-industrial society in considerably more detail than the brief summary discussed, Bell goes on to ask 'who will rule?'. The answer hinges on the view that distinct societal forms ultimately 'depends on the extension of a particular dimension of rationality' (Bell, 1973: 342). Thus understood, the defining feature of post-industrial society is the dependence on the extension of *technocratic* rationality and the technocratic mode of rationalization: the axial principle and its antecedent dimensions constitute a fundamental shift in circumstances that places the already existing technocratic form of rationality and rationalization at the heart of society. This is the essence of the belated realization thesis, which can be summarized more straightforwardly in the idea that post-industrial society is defined through and through by the 'fundamental themes' of 'rationality, planning, and foresight – the hallmarks, in short, of the technocratic age. The vision of Saint-Simon seemingly has begun to bear fruit' (Bell, 1973: 348).

In one respect, the axial principle involves a consolidation and proliferation of the kind of institutionalized innovation already at the core of the social epistemology of enlightenment engineering during the first revolution. However, innovation still remained largely random and fortuitous in early industrial society. By contrast, the 'scientization of politics' and the advent of 'large-scale industrial research in postwar society', means that 'technological development entered into a feedback relation with the progress of the modern sciences', and that 'science, technology and industrial utilization were fused into a system' (Habermas, 1971: 104). This system, and the axial principle at its core, is essential to overcoming the limitations that had halted earlier technocratic revolutions. Whereas the window for technocratic influence only remained open during war and crisis under the first and second technocratic revolutions, the new axial principle of post-industrial society keeps the window open. The result, in Habermas' version of the belated realization thesis, is widespread 'technocratic consciousness' and reorientation of the social system to a logic of scientific-technical progress (1971: 111).

The axial principle, at one and the same time involves a change in 'the character of knowledge itself' and a shift from 'property or political criteria to knowledge as the base of power' (Bell, 1973: 343). Scientifically codified theoretical knowledge becomes a source not only of technological innovation and economic growth, but also of social and political power. As such, the axial principle provides ideal conditions for the old technocratic idea of government based on scientific knowledge. However, the new conditions posed by the axial principle and the fusion of science and technology also means that the mechanical engineers or production engineers so central to early industrial technocracy now come to play only a secondary role in this belated realization of technocracy. The technocratic elite of post-industrial society is made up first and foremost of those in possession of scientifically codified and enriched theoretical knowledge: 'the "new men" are the scientists, the mathematicians, the economists and the engineers of the new intellectual technology' (Bell, 1973: 344). Mechanical engineers are in this sense on the wrong side of the axial principle, and even if they do of course often join hands with the supreme commanders of theoretically codified knowledge in the pursuit of technological innovation, post-industrial society puts an end to their days as members of the technocratic elite par excellence.

This development is perhaps best illustrated by the most important institutionalization of advanced industrial technocracy: the RAND Corporation (named from Research ANd Development). Originally established in 1945 as Project RAND in a contract between the Department of Defense (then the War Department) and Douglas Aircraft Company, RAND was incorporated as non-profit organization in California with the purpose conducting research and analysis for the United States Armed Forces. RAND is deeply rooted in the military-industrial complex and military utilization of science and technology. RAND was thus involved more or less heavily in all major technological events of the time, including nuclear research, aviation and computer science. Moreover, RAND specializes in military strategy, scenario planning, risk analysis, game theory and other methods central to both the 'future orientation' and new 'intellectual technologies' of post-industrial society. However, RAND's interests have always extended beyond the military strategy and security to the use of applied science and systems analysis in economic policy and public policy more broadly, including healthcare, crime and social welfare programmes.

For decades, affiliates of RAND could be considered a who's who of prominent technocrats, including strategic analyst and futurologist Herman Kahn and mathematician John von Neumann (both of whom served, among others, as inspiration for the titular character in *Dr. Strangelove*, which also immortalized RAND as the 'BLAND' corporation), mathematician and godfather of game theory, John Forbes Nash Jr, co-developers of the ARPANET Barry Boehm and Paul Baran, futurologist and inventor of the Delphi method Olaf Helmer, and inventor of the neutron bomb Samuel Cohen, as well as political notables Robert McNamara and later Henry Kissinger. Today, RAND is home to the largest PhD programme in public policy in the United States and home to an accumulated 32 Nobel prizes (including the memorial prizes in economics that RAND helped create). Of course, other institutions could be added to the picture. In 1945, the *L'École Nationale d'Administration* (ENA) was added to ranks of the French Grands Écoles, and the existing engineering schools clearly changed significantly too. However, RAND stands out as the embodiment of advanced industrial technocracy under the axial principle of knowledge society.

Technocratic influence on public policy

However, Bell's belated realization hypothesis does not suggest a wholesale transformation to technocratic rule. The answer to the question 'who will rule?', simply put, is technocrats *and* politicians. The axial principle may provide those in possession scientifically codified theoretical knowledge with a source of power, but it also forces them to either 'compete with politicians or become their allies' (Bell, 1973: 13). Direct competition with politicians invariably involves a more or less direct attack on the basic principles of the democratic polity. Even where technocrats seek to become allies and avoid direct competition with the political leadership, however, a new and precarious balance of power between technocrats and electorally mandated politicians arise. In lieu of more pervasive regime competition and changes, this balance of power comes down to a new situation where the 'relationship of technical and political decisions' is 'one of the most crucial problems of public policy' (Bell, 1973: 364).

Under such conditions, the technocrat formally remains in a bureaucratic position of subordination to political leadership: 'it is not the technocratic who ultimately holds power, but the politician' (Bell, 1973: 360). On the other hand, the structure and dynamics of post-industrial society pose considerable management problems for the political system, which can only be resolved with the aid of the new 'technical and professional intelligentsia' and the 'members of the new technocratic elite, with their new techniques of decision-making', which 'have now become essential to the formulation and analysis of decisions on which political judgements have to be made, if not to the wielding of power' (Bell, 1973: 362). At the core of this new techniques of decision making we find a pervasive commitment to social engineering through *planning*: 'the rise of the new elites based on skill derives from simple fact that knowledge and planning – military planning, economic planning, social planning – have become the basic requisites for all organized action in modern society' (Bell, 1973: 362).

Bell's principal example of this development is the implementation of the Program Planning Budgeting System (PBBS) in the defence sector and elsewhere (with considerable involvement from RAND), labelled the McNamara 'revolution' and earning the then Secretary of Defense a place alongside Saint-Simon and Taylor as 'a hierophant in the pantheon of technocracy' (Bell, 1973: 357). More generally, however, planning represents an increasingly dominant mode and locus of decision making in the post-industrial society, understood as society that has become 'for the first time, a national society, in which crucial decisions affecting all parts of the society are simultaneously … are made by the government rather than through the market' (Bell, 1973: 364). This broader understanding of planning clearly invokes the image of a planned economy, or at least a mixed economy, based on extensive governmental involvement in all aspects of economic and social behaviour and development. In this respect, planning represents an ideal and material form of social engineering providing the new technocratic elite with extensive influence of public policy during the golden years of technocracy.

The extent of such influence has of course remained a matter of debate ever since. An examination of the *limits of technocratic politics* in the United States at the verge of the 1980s came to a more critical conclusion, based on a survey of the trend towards econometric accounting, the use of macroeconomic policy advice, the social indicators movement under the 'efficiency' doctrine and the use of futurology (Straussman, 1978). In contrast to Bell's sweeping statements, Straussman found only partial evidence for increased technocratic influence on public policy, and mostly limited to the econometric accounting and the social indicators movement. Bell may have been too focused on the avant-garde of this development, spearheaded by RAND, but the general commitment to planning and social engineering in public policy during the period does merit the suggestion that technocracy enjoyed a golden era during the post-war years, reaching a sort of pinnacle in the 1960s and 1970s. Moreover, this development not only includes the United States, but certainly also the post-industrial runners up on the Anglophone family tree, as well as in Western and Northern Europe. In order to complete this picture, however, it is necessary the look at economic knowledge as a source of technocratic influence on public policy during the golden years.

The birth of the econocracy

In stark contrast to the more reserved conclusions about the limits of technocratic politics, a contemporary analysis by Peter Self argued that 'econocrats' wielded significant and comprehensive influence on public policy in the United Kingdom (1975). The source of this difference in results is partly methodological: whereas Straussman relied primarily on headcounts of individual technocrats (an approach discussed in the next chapter), Self sought to trace the influence of the 'politics and philosophy of cost-benefit analysis' on public policy more broadly, thus arriving at the concept of 'econocracy', a form of rule based on the simple 'belief that there exist economic tests or yardsticks according to which policy decisions can and should be made' (Self, 1975: 5). Self contrasts this understanding of an econocracy with the more conventional understanding of technocracy as a form of policy making based on the advice of technical experts (essentially meaning engineers), arguing that the former 'is much more ambitious, and consequently more dangerous to the public, than *any* kind of technocracy' (Self, 1975: 5). This distinction between technocracy and econocracy is clearly drawn too rigidly, but it does lay out an important line of argument: the belated realization of technocracy was brought about, perhaps more than anything else, by the increasing influence of economic science, knowledge and methods on public policy.

The golden years of technocracy thus coincide with the construction of the 'the economy' as a distinct object of political concern and regulation in the second half of the 20th century. Early efforts notwithstanding (the first macroeconomic model was created in 1936 to assess the possible effects of policy responses to the Great Depression by Dutch economist Jan Tinbergen, recipient of the first Nobel prize in economics), the political creation of an economy in the current sense is largely a post-war affair. A simple but telling indicator: before 1950, references to the economy in the winning party manifesto in the United Kingdom was zero (with two exceptions), subsequently climbing to 59 mentions in 2015 (Earle et al, 2017: 16). Indeed, economic tools were used for a variety of purposes and so extensively during the Second World War that it 'raised the status of the discipline and cemented its central role in government', prompting one economist to dub it the 'economists' war' (Earle et al, 2017: 16). Based on this status, economists became the principal architects of information systems, statistics and institutional framework (Bretton Woods, IMF, the World Bank, OECD, GATT, WTO and so on) for management of the economy in the climate of post-war desire to engage in ambitious social engineering.

The new status and influence of the discipline was also the result of a concerted effort to make economics the 'hard' or 'technical' social science par excellence, based on the so-called neoclassical paradigm. Conceptually, neoclassical economics substitutes the traditional subject of political economy (the production and distribution of goods in relation to the satisfaction of human needs) for a narrower focus on exchange and the study of 'human behaviour as a relationship between ends and scarce means which have alternative uses' (Robbins, 1935: 16), thus shifting the focus of economics from a specific subject to a particular understanding of human behaviour as rational choice (Becker, 1976). From this definition, neoclassical economics has developed a more or less unified theoretical framework, based on the axioms of (aggregated) individual behaviour, rational means–ends calculation and equilibrium, as well as increasingly formal, technical and mathematical models of economic behaviour and the overall economy. In the process, the neoclassical paradigm has all but monopolized the economic discipline and provided economic experts with their powerful position in political life (Earle et al, 2017: 93). On a side note, a significant number of RAND affiliates have been involved in this development, including several Nobel laurates.

Economic knowledge informed by the neoclassical paradigm thus provides technocracy with a particular brand of scientism, based on the proposition that economics is essentially a form of hard or technical science, discovering and codifying the fundamental laws and forces of individual and aggregated economic behaviour. The flaws and political effects of such scientism have become a key component of more recent debate about the econocracy and the status of economic science (Chang, 2014; Earle et al, 2017). Viewed in the historical context of technocracy, it remains clear that the neoclassical paradigm is a prime example of the scientific codification and enrichment of theoretical knowledge for purposes of social engineering, described so aptly by Bell. Indeed, the neoclassical paradigm not only embodies the axial principle itself, but has also been practically involved in antecedent 'intellectual technologies' such as game theory (see also Chapter 7). As such, economics shaped by the neoclassical paradigm enables pervasive planning and social engineering at the root level of human behaviour and choice, regardless of whatever stance is taken in relation to debates over the 'planned' economy vis-à-vis the 'free' market economy.

For all its mathematical prowess, the neoclassical paradigm is still based on an essentially mechanical world-view based largely on analogy with Newtonian physics: the basic equilibrium model of the market treats individual and aggregated behaviour as knowable and predictable forces interacting according to 'fixed mechanical relationships' in 'stand-alone, abstract system that emerges naturally from the actions of individual agents', resulting in a 'detached, technocratic vision of the economy' (Earle et al, 2017: 39). The most basic form of this equilibrium model is supply and demand on the level of microeconomics, but the logic applies to variables such as unemployment and inflation, taxes and investment and informs a broad span of macroeconomic thinking and policy, up to an including the formal model that provides the argument for independent central banks (Earle et al, 2017: 39). As such, the new technocracy is in many ways still an econocracy, albeit with certain modifications. However, technocracy has also changed more substantially after the end of the golden years.

Fourth revolution: a quiet or not so quiet technocratic revolution?

Although the basic trends and principles observed by Bell have proven prescient and largely correct, it has also become clear that post-industrial society has moved beyond the parameters of his original forecasting. Bell himself seemed reluctant to acknowledge this: his reflection on the original forecasting a quarter of a century after its initial publication took note of new trajectories of technological development, but also reinforced the axial principle of post-industrial society (Bell, 1999). In a particularly telling confrontation, Bell defends his original decision to subsume the embryonic informational revolution under the axial principle of knowledge society, even in the face of the mounting number of contributions, spearheaded by Castells' comprehensive analysis of the network society and the information age, suggesting that post-industrial society had undergone an informational revolution (Bell, 1999: 24). At the same time, however, Bell did recognize the existence of a new informational 'infrastructure' of society (1999: 17) and the increasing dominance of informational and social networks (1999: 58).

In other words: even Bell was unwilling to pass the torch. It was clear by the turn of the millennium that the informational revolution, visible only in its most embryonic form in the immediate aftermath of the Second World War, had now become a full-blown industrial revolution in its own right, overruling, displacing and/or subsuming other dimensions highlighted by Bell. Simply put: Bell had not included the drastic increase in networking capacity prompted by the development of new information and communication technologies (ICTs) among the five dimensions of post-industrial society. A quarter of a century later, however, it was clear that technologically enhanced network capacity had become the new 'axial' principle of post-industrial society. Bell's analysis may have captured the type of techno-economic system and social structure operating at a moment of time when advanced industrialism was turning into post-industrialism, but it ultimately also remained on the side of the former. This has important implications for the belated realization thesis: if the conditions that made technocracy thrive in the golden years were actually a form of advanced industrialism, what then happens to technocracy with the transition to post-industrialism proper?

On the one hand, this has to do with the nature of the latest industrial revolution itself. Bell's reluctance to accept the impact of the informational revolution clearly hinges on the idea that it was already incorporated in the third industrial revolution, regardless of subsequent ICT innovations and their effect on other technologies. More fundamentally, this points to a possible shift from previous industrial revolutions to a new pattern of more frequent and overlapping revolutions eliding into each other. In this view, the third industrial revolution is a more or less continuous revolution from the Second World War to the present day (Rifkin, 2011). Although there is much to be said for the view that the very logic of industrial revolutions has changed, I shall nevertheless proceed from the idea that the informational revolution marks a rather clear dividing line in the transition from industrial to post-industrial society. Even Bell seems to have accepted as much, in spite of his general suspicion of fundamental revisions to his original forecasting. Indeed, the impact of the informational transition seems visible in all the major aspects of the transition from industrial to post-industrial society noted by Bell at the turn of the millennium: the shift from fabrication to information processing as the basic mode of production; from division of labour to networking as a new principle of economic organization; from dependence on energy resources (oil, gas, nuclear energy) to dependence on information, programming, algorithms and data transmission; from machine technology to intellectual technology; and from financial capital to human capital (1999: 84).

These are clearly the basic contours of the network society, which I shall discuss in more detail in Chapter 5. The network society is, however, only dimension of the fully developed post-industrial society. As I shall argue in Chapter 6, post-industrial society is also a risk society in the sense that that interconnectedness of network society has also resulted in a new preoccupation with risk management turned directly against the concepts of security, responsibility and compensation prevailing under advanced industrialism. Under these conditions, the function and content of the axial principle originally observed by Bell have also changed, even if current post-industrial society is still a knowledge society, as I shall discuss in Chapter 7. Taken together, all of these transformations mean that we have moved decisively beyond the advanced industrialism into post-industrialism proper. The decisive turning point in all three cases, moreover, occurs in 1980s, roughly, and thus at the end of the golden years. This would seem to suggest one explanation for the ensuing silence on the subject of technocracy. By the terms of the belated realization thesis, technocracy thrived under advanced industrialism and may have been assumed to wither away with these conditions as society became truly post-industrial.

A further factor here may be the rise of liberalism in the 1980s, following the various crises of the 1970s. The decade is more or less universally recognized as the beginning of the end for the kind of extensive social planning and engineering that advanced industrial technocracy excels in. Having finally achieved a form of belated realization of the visions prophesized by its early proponents, then, technocracy may have been assumed to wither away together with everything it has conventionally been associated with: liberalism triumphed over socialism and the end of history appeared on the horizon, welfare state expansion turned to welfare state retrenchment, Keynesian economic policy was replaced by monetarism (although it is now largely forgotten) and neoclassical economics, managerial capitalism was abandoned in favour of shareholder capitalism, planning and big government was met with a new rallying cry for minimal government. Taken together, all of these developments support the interpretation of the 1980s as the turning point towards a new neoliberal hegemony. In any event, the 1980s were not exactly conducive to an industrial technocracy wedded to bureaucracy, extensive planning and state regulation.

However, technocracy clearly did not wither away with the various events of the 1980s. The decade rather marks the decisive turning point from the original industrial version of technocracy to its post-industrial form. One of the few contributions that did take note of this development during the period of relative academic silence is Fischer's analysis of the 'quiet' technocratic revolution (Fischer, 1990: 19). The latest technocratic revolution, in this view, has meant a technocratic retreat into the background of policy processes, a complete abandonment of earlier utopian postures and the overt pursuit of political influence in more or less direct conflict with democratically elected leadership. This is not to say that technocrats exert less influence on public policy. Rather the opposite: technocrats have become even more influential due to 'an increasing reliance in the political system on technical expertise for the definition of, if not the actual resolution of, social and political problems … as a result, there will be more and more emphasis on the planning of political and social life' (Fischer, 1990: 102). In this way, the quiet technocratic revolution is essentially an extension of the belated realization thesis, suggesting a 'striking continuity of basic technocratic ideas' (Fischer, 1990: 109) and the persistence of an 'ever-recurring intellectual doctrine' of which Saint-Simon is one of the most 'original exponents' (Meynaud, 1968: 12).

Although the idea of quiet revolution indicates a shift in the technocratic modus operandi concomitant with the idea of a new type of technocracy, my view on the latest technocratic revolution differs in at least two important ways. First, the new technocracy does not simply display a striking continuity of basic technocratic ideas, but rather a significant degree of change and even opposition to earlier industrial forms of technocracy. There is of course a certain historical consistency to the key technocratic principles and ideas. However, network society, risk society and the most recent incarnation of the knowledge society are all, for various reasons, broadly incompatible with the original formula of industrial technocracy. Rather than yet another step in the belated realization of industrial technocracy, then, the latest technocratic revolution has meant a reversal from a compromise with bureaucracy against democracy to a compromise with democracy against bureaucracy. Second, this development has been far from quiet and faceless. Perhaps the new technocracy did operate somewhat silently, or at least undetected, for a certain amount of time. However, the new governance has also provided the new technocracy with a highly visible, assertive and constantly expanding policy programme of transformation from government to governance for decades.

Indeed, the new technocracy even has its own manifestos in the mould of Smyth's call for national industrial management a century ago, such as the ambitiously titled and self-published *Technocracy in America* (Khanna, 2017). Khanna is the author of best-sellers such as *Connectography: Mapping the Future of Global Civilization* (2016), a popularized analysis of the network society, and *The Future Is Asian* (2019), as well as a TED-talk speaker, recipient of various prizes and places on prominent lists of influential thinkers. His technocratic manifesto identifies so-called 'direct technocracy', meaning 'a blend of technocracy and democracy assisted by technology' as the 'superior model for 21st century governance' (Khanna, 2017: 120). Traditional democracy, by the same logic, has reached a cul-de-sac and 'has to be seen not as a universal solution but a principle to be observed in the quest towards the higher objective of good governance' (Khanna, 2017: 21). The realization of this higher purpose is seen to have been accomplished with great success by 'info-states', such as Singapore, which make the most of the informational revolution, define 'their geography by their connectivity rather than just their territory' and remain committed to 'problem-solving', 'getting the job done' and 'output legitimacy' (Khanna, 2017: 14). These attributes, in turn, suggests that 'today's technocratic regimes bear little resemblance to those associated with the term a generation or two ago ... they are civil rather than military, inclusive rather than clique, data-driven rather than dogmatic, and more transparent than opaque' (Khanna, 2017: 22). In the proud messianic style of its predecessors, this is indeed a worthy manifesto for the new technocracy.

Conclusion

There are of course more details in the history of technocracy than have been presented here. However, the overview of the four major technocratic revolutions should convey the essentials: the particular historical era in which technocracy has flourished, the intimate relationship with the various industrial revolutions that has shaped the technocratic idea of government as a form of (post-)industrial management, the logic of social engineering and its roots in the broader social epistemology of enlightenment engineering, the decreasing importance of the engineers themselves and the arrival of a new technocratic elite in possession of theoretical and scientifically codified knowledge, the belated realization and increased influence of technocracy under the conditions of advanced industrialism, and ultimately the point where industrial technocracy reaches its limits, roughly from the 1980s onwards. The crucial shift in the history of technocracy occurring in this latter stage has of course been sketched out in rather vague fashion. Before I develop the framework (Chapter 4) and analysis (Chapters 5–7) of this missing part of the story in more detail, the following chapter deals with another issue already hinted at: who are the technocrats and what kind of political power do they wield?

3

Who Are the Technocrats? From the Technocstructure to Technocratic Government

Macron is the ultimate technocrat.

(Poulain, 2019)

The face of technocracy

At the time of writing, in 2019, the opposition between technocracy and populism comes to a head with particular force in two conflicts: three years of increased political turmoil in the United Kingdom following the referendum on membership of the European Union in 2016 and widespread protests by the so-called *gilets jaunes* ('Yellow Vests') against reforms and taxes imposed by Emmanuel Macron. In the first case, technocracy appears in its ultimate faceless incarnation of the EU machinery and the distant power of Brussels, opposed by more or less populist politicians and crowds taking to the streets with signs saying 'No Deal, No Problem' and 'Let Our People Go'. In the second case, technocracy has a very recognizable face: since Macron's road to presidential office in 2017 began, he has been the consensus exemplar of a technocratic head of government, the ultimate technocrat and the leader of a 'technocratic revolution' (Stetler, 2016). Faced with the protests of the Yellow Vests and abysmal approval ratings, however, Macron declared his willingness to hear the voice of the people and initiated a 'grand national debate' in a direct letter to the citizenry of France early 2019. Since then, the Yellow Vest movement has dwindled, but the conflict remains essentially unsolved and public dissatisfaction with Macron largely unchanged.

But why and how exactly is Macron a technocrat? One of the more widely voiced reasons is that he is a product of the French system of Grands Écoles/Corps, having been educated at the ENA and subsequently becoming a member of the Inspection des Finances. In a somewhat curious turn of events, Macron's suggestions for reform after the grand national debate included a plan to shut down his alma mater, in effect closing the institution that allegedly made him a technocrat. Moreover, Macron seems to follow the career path of professional politician (although his turn as an investment banker is ambiguous in this respect), having served both as a bureaucrat and minister of economy and finance. In addition to his education and career, Macron is viewed as the ultimate technocratic because of his attitude to politics and his desire to rule France 'like Jupiter' free of dirty politics (Bengali, 2017) and substituting left and right for what works and getting things done (Goldhammer, 2018). Moreover, the majority of cross-partisan ministers in office under Macron's tenure have been considered technocrats for similar reasons (Stephens, 2019). In more formal terms, however, it is questionable whether Macron's government (technically the first and second Philippe governments so far) is actually technocratic. Before getting to the issue of how to qualify as a technocratic head of state and/or minister, however, more fundamental questions of how to identify technocrats and their potential means of political influence have to be resolved.

This chapter is dedicated to these questions and, more generally, the actor-centred approach to technocracy. Although I am primarily interested in individual technocrats as agents of change and carriers of a particular art of government, observed at a different level of analysis, the question of where and how to find the technocrats clearly merits some consideration. The answer to this question, however, is less straightforward than it might seem. In formal and institutional terms, technocrats are simply bureaucrats (both administrative and political), elected politicians, ministers or heads of state. Within these groups, the best available criteria in the search for technocrats are educational background, previous occupations, career tracks and the attitudinal lodestars of more or less coherent belief systems. In the end, however, there are no firm or universally agreed up criteria with which to identify the technocrats, and the best available headcounts remain rough estimates of their numbers within bureaucratic elites, legislative elites and/or executive elites.

This also to say that technocrats do not constitute an elite, a ruling class nor even a profession in their own right. Ever since Saint-Simon pointed to the need for a new elite of 'industrials', the search for the technocrats has been influenced by the idea of a distinct technocratic elite in the vein of a ruling class or a unified power elite as understood in classical elite theory. This view can, however, be brushed aside from the outset. However, current and more pluralist elite studies do offer a guideline for a search for the technocrat as members of 'strategic elites' (Keller, 1963) and political elites in a broader sense – 'persons who are able, by the virtue of their strategic positions in powerful organizations and movements, to affect political outcomes regularly and substantially' (Higley and Burton, 2006: 7). Following this line of argument, the question is not so much whether technocrats constitute a uniform class or elite consistently ruling over society (they do not), but whether technocrats take on positions outside and within the political system that make it possible to consistently affect political decisions and outcomes (they do). Before looking at these positions of political influence in more detail, however, we need first to establish some basic conditions of membership in the broader social and organizational group of technocrats.

The technostructure

Initially, the technocrats were simply the engineers. During the first and second technocratic revolution, government as social engineering should be understood rather literally as the actual or desired rule of engineers bringing the social epistemology of enlightenment engineering to bear on government. The belated realization of technocracy with the third technocratic revolution, however, coincided with the expansion of the list of potential members of the group well beyond the ranks of the engineers. The most comprehensive analysis of the logic behind this expansion is provided in Galbraith's discussion of the 'technostructure' as an 'association of men of diverse technical knowledge, experience and other talent which modern industrial technology and planning require. It extends from the leadership of the modern industrial enterprise down to just short of the labor force and embraces a large number of people and large variety of talent' (Galbraith, 1967: 74). The technological imperatives and demand for planning under advanced industrialism, in other words, makes the technostructure a 'new factor of production' and the 'new locus of power' in advanced industrial enterprises and society at large (Galbraith, 1967: 74).

The technostructure is thus defined essentially as a function within a large modern organization, more specifically the 'guiding intelligence' or 'the brain' the organization (Galbraith, 1967: 86). Who actually serves this function, however, remains less clear. As Galbraith states, the technostructure includes anyone who brings 'specialized knowledge, talent or expertise to group decision-making', since most decisions and '*all* that are important' depend in knowledge and information dispersed throughout the organization (Galbraith, 1967: 86, original emphasis). One of the few attempts to specify the actual members of the technostructure lists technicians, engineers and scientists alongside designers and sales executives, linking up at the margins with foremen and supervisory personal on the one side and the inner circle of executive management on the other (Galbraith, 1967: 161). The technostructure was given sharper contours as one of the five distinct groups in Mintzberg's widely used organization theory, the others being the strategic apex/top management, the middle and line managers, the operating core and the support staff. Here, the technostructure includes 'those analysts, out of the formal "line" structure, who apply analytic techniques to the design and maintenance of the structure and to the adaptation of the organization to its environment (eg accountants, work schedulers, long-range planners)' (1980: 323). The technostructure is furthermore defined by its preference for standardization of work processes and outputs as a mechanism of coordination, which in turn is seen as a part of a broader organizational struggle between the different groups within the organization.

In current usage, the technostructure is probably understood in terms closer to Mintzberg's. However, this approach is clearly more restrictive and disregards the open-ended and fluid nature of the technostructure as conceived by Galbraith. In the latter case, inclusion in the technostructure rests on the inclusive and flexible criteria of participation in group decision-making based on knowledge, expertise and skill, in conjunction with the assumption of a particular motivational structure of strong identification with organizational goals and the desire to impact these (Galbraith, 1967: 166). Galbraith's analysis of the technostructure also has a broader socio-economic outlook. Viewed in more macroscopic terms, the rise of the technostructure is clearly also a vital part of what is now referred to as managerial capitalism. In other words: under advanced industrialism, capitalism comes to be dominated by technological systems and vertically integrated bureaucracies, and the operation of these, in turn, depends on the technostructure.

In this way, Galbraith's analysis shares important features with Burnham's earlier claim about a 'managerial revolution' and the emergence of a managerial society (1941). Burnham's book has become famous in part because of some rather faulty predictions, but due to its analysis of the increasing power of managers with the progress of industrialization it also remains a foundational text for any discussion of managerialism. Although Burnham described this development somewhat problematically as the formation and dominance of a managerial class in strictly Marxist terms, he also defined the managerial revolution in more organizational terms as the increasing dominance of large-scale bureaucracies dependent on people with technical knowledge, expertise and skills. Burnham's outline of this group includes the highly skilled workers trained in engineering, physics and chemistry needed in practically every branch of industrial production, and managers in the 'purest sense': those specialized in 'technical direction and coordination of the process of production', including production managers, superintendents, administrative engineers, supervisory technicians and, in public organizations, 'administrators, commissioners, bureau heads and so on' (Burnham, 1941: 81).

Galbraith acknowledged the affinity with the idea of a managerial revolution, but also emphasized that subsequent developments had passed power 'further down into the organization', making management less important than the guiding intelligence of the technostructure (1967: 128). However, the underlying focus on a group defined by their possession of the scientific and technical knowledge critical to operation of modern large-scale organizations remains much the same. With the technostructure, we thus arrive at an expanded and open-ended list of potential technocrats. Engineers are still members of the group, followed closely by others schooled in more or less hard sciences, but also a host of other organizational jobs, roles and functions, including managerial functions short of top-level or executive management. It is this idea of the technostructure that provides the answer to Fischer's particular search for the technocrats in his analysis of the quiet technocratic revolution: from this 'vantage point, the technostructure – policy planners, economists, engineers, management specialists, computer analysts, social scientists and technologists – process the critical information essential to the stable and efficient operation of our contemporary institutions' (Fischer, 1990: 110).

A current version of the list may include stakeholder managers, communication experts risk analysts, auditors, inspectors, comptrollers and so forth. In the end, however, the technostructure remains fluid and open-ended group based on a combination of membership criteria such as organizational functions and job descriptions, educational background, beliefs and motives. A broad outline of the technostructure thus provides us with an initial and inclusive answer to the question of who the technocrats are. However, it does not address the pivotal question of political influence directly. The influence of the technostructure on overall strategy, direction and success of private companies remain a contested issue in itself, in particular with the assumed transition from managerial capitalism to stakeholder/ financial capitalism during the 1980s, but even if the technostructure is still the brain and guiding intelligence of business, this does not translate into political influence. Indeed, it can be rather safely assumed that the average member of the technostructure in a private company has no particular political influence in that capacity (save for certain exceptional acts such as whistleblowing, sabotage and so on). Political influence of private companies remains in the hands of a rather short list of owners and top-level managers of large corporations – people specifically excluded from the technostructure.

However, the technostructure may gain political influence in another way: through membership of the scientific elite. As Galbraith made clear, the rise of the technostructure as the guiding intelligence of the individual organization is intimately related to the new dominance of scientific research and educational institutions on the societal level: the engineers and scientists within the technostructure thus connects 'at the edges' with a growing body of educators and research scientists within the 'educational and scientific estate', that is, the universities and other knowledge-producing and/or educational institutions that provide the industrial system with its most critical factor of production (1967: 283). In other words: the technostructure is an organizational expression of the axial principle of knowledge society, and it is connected to the 'axial structure' of this society, including educational institutions, universities and think tanks. The technostructure thus constitutes an ecology of elite circulation and recruitment, and it is through positions in the upper echelons of knowledge institutions, in effect membership of the scientific elite, that its members may reach a position of political influence. That is, however, so long as we focus on political influence attained from a position outside the political system. Inside the political system, the technostructure is also an endemic feature of the public bureaucracy.

The bureaucratic elite: the techno-bureaucrats

Although the rise of managers and the technostructure was extrapolated primarily from the realm of private enterprise, Burnham and Galbraith both extended their claims to government and the public domain, based on the idea that the proliferation and dominance of large-scale bureaucracies are equally visible in state and market. The influence of the technostructure in the two domains, correspondingly, remains much the same: in the domain of the state activities, this suggests that the extensive management of the economy, improvement of education, technical and scientific progress, and national defence initiatives can all be seen as 'goals with which the technostructure can identify itself', or, 'plausibly, these goals reflect the adaptation of public goals to the goals of the technostructure' (Galbraith, 1967: 309). More broadly, members of the technostructure 'wield great public influence as, in effect, an extended arm of the bureaucracy' (Galbraith, 1967: 295). In this capacity members of the technostructure function as *techno-bureaucrats*. The techno-bureaucrats, however, do not constitute a distinct bureaucratic branch in any sense of the word, but retain the overall function of a guiding intelligence and hence the fluid and open-ended composition of the technostructure. The issue, then, is how to single out the techno-bureaucrats within the ranks of the bureaucrats more generally and the bureaucratic elite in particular.

I owe the term 'techno-bureaucrats' to Meynaud's landmark analysis of technocracy, published almost simultaneously with Galbraith's. Meynaud starts from a definition of 'technologists' broadly resembling the technostructure. The status of a fully fledged technocrat, in turn, is reserved for instances where 'the technologist himself acquires the capacity for making decisions, or carries the most weight in determining the choices of the person officially responsible for them' within the political system (Meynaud, 1968: 30). In principle, this ascension of technologists to a position of political power could include the realization of a pure technocracy, open dispossession of power and a complete regime change. The reality, however, is rather a 'slipping sideways of power' where technologists acquire the ability to influence the official holder of political power, thus resulting in an 'effective shift of power' where the 'politician retains the appearance of power but loses, to some degree, the substance of it' (Meynaud, 1968: 30). This is of course the kind of influence traditionally associated with the rule of officials and the political power of bureaucracy, and the bureaucratic elite in particular, in a democratic polity, subject to ongoing controversy.

More generally, Meynaud identifies three channels of technocratic influence in the political system: higher civil service, high military personnel and the scientific elite (1968: 32). The latter channel has already been discussed as the main source of influence from a position outside the political system. The second channel builds on other observations of the military–industrial complex as a sphere of technocratic influence and breeding ground for national industrial management since the first industrial revolution, but really coming into its own with the third technocratic revolution. However, the higher civil service takes precedence as the most important channel for technocratic influence. It is here that Meynaud introduces the pivotal idea of a techno-bureaucracy, meaning a form of bureaucracy where technocrats have come to occupy a position of significant influence on the operations of the public bureaucracy and hence on public policy (see also Chapter 4). This, in turn, means that the search for technocrats becomes a matter of identifying the techno-bureaucrats among the upper echelons of state bureaucracy.

Writing from a French perspective, it comes as no surprise that Meynaud's first impulse is to look for the techno-bureaucrats among the cadres of the Grand Corps and the former pupils of Grands Écoles, albeit concluding that this is ultimately a flawed method of elite identification (Meynaud, 1968: 21). Even within the prestigious Grand Corps, rank-and-file staff are not likely to exercise significant political influence, and would thus have to be considered ordinary members of the technostructure. Conversely, senior civil servants from regular ministries, departments, agencies and so forth may well qualify as technocrats. The broader problem Meynaud encounters here is that there are no clear-cut institutional or positional criteria circumscribing the ranks of the techno-bureaucrats. We do have established institutional and positional criteria delimiting public bureaucrats and the bureaucratic elite, but how do we single out the technocrats within these broader groups? Technocratic institutions (the Grand Corps being the emblematic example) or positions (such as independent experts and policy advisers) may provide a useful lead, but ultimately the search has to adopt different criteria to locate technocrats with the bureaucracy and the bureaucratic elite in particular.

One rather widely used solution is to rely on educational background, a method of identification well known in elite studies. Having first identified elite groups by institutional and positional criteria, cohort studies of national elites will typically include educational background as an individual-level background variable. Used in a search for technocrats in bureaucratic elites, this approach follows the basic idea that 'while it should not be assumed that changes in decision rules [or policy formulation, implementation and evaluation more generally] follow changes in recruitment patterns, the latter are at least one indicator of technocratization' that 'brings some evidence to bear on whether a change in the structure of power has taken place' (Straussman, 1978: 25). Again, the French case illustrates the point in the extreme since the rigid system of recruitment from the Grands Écoles almost ensures promotion to top-level positions in public service (and beyond). Short of such a system, however, the identification of the techno-bureaucrats comes down to a more open-ended choice of education and careers profiles used to distinguish the techno-bureaucrats from other (senior) civil servants in the analysis of recruitment patterns.

A related question here is, of course, whom to consider a non-technocratic and conventional bureaucrat. Although there is no universal agreement on the answer, the lawyer appear the most apparent candidate. Since Weber, university-trained lawyers have stood out as embodiment of bureaucracy and the underlying rational-legal authority. As Weber was the first to acknowledge, however, there is also a rather German or at least continental flavour to the idea that the quintessential bureaucrat is a lawyer (1921). In the British case, a background in humanities and classical studies has historically been far from uncommon among bureaucrats in general and the bureaucratic elite in particular (Page & Wright, 1999). Even if we include higher civil servants trained in the humanities, however, the lawyer still carries particular weight as the historical exemplar of the traditional type of bureaucrat that we would expect to be more or less displaced by technocrats in a techno-bureaucracy.

The particular strength of the lawyer, and a key reason for their indispensability to bureaucracy according to Weber, is that their knowledge, although technical, is general and flexible, enabling them to serve a wide variety of purposes and masters. A background in the humanities suggests an even more general, and in this case rather non-technical, form of knowledge and skill set. Both lawyers and humanists are in this sense members of a generalist administrative class with no formal training or education related to their particular policy field. Correspondingly, the difference between the techno-bureaucrats and traditional bureaucrats is sometimes portrayed as a contrast or even 'cold war' between technical specialists and bureaucratic generalists, illustrated somewhat satirically in the image of a Ministry of Civil Aviation staffed by three thousand technical specialists and led by 'former students of Greek and Latin' (Meynaud, 1968: 36).

However, the simplified contrast between specialists and generalists also overlooks the fact that the techno-bureaucrats are not simply highly promoted specialists, but members of the bureaucratic elite in possession of both specialized *and* generalist skills. This point is not only relevant to the more apparently generalist disciplines of management and administration, but has bearing on supposedly specialist disciplines such as material engineering, economic analysis and accounting as well.

Indeed, an important feature of the Grand Corps and Grands Écoles system has always been to produce an elite possessing both specialized skills and the 'organizational dexterity' associated with generalized skills (Suleiman, 1978: 158). Although the balance between specialized and generalist skills is of course variable, the French system is rooted in the idea of 'technocratic generalists' (Genieys, 2010: 10). This is not a logic limited to the French case, particular as it may be. Although their educational backgrounds differ, techno-bureaucrats should still be seen as a type of generalist trained differently from their lawyer and humanist counterparts.

In addition to educational background and recruitment patterns, elite research offers an additional road to the identification of techno-bureaucrats: the study of elite culture and belief systems. In elite studies, such belief systems will typically be viewed as a more or less direct product of educational background and professional career, but they nevertheless remain a distinct variable and object of research in their own right. In Bell's outline, the 'mind-view' of technocrats revolves around the 'emphasis on the logical, practical, problem-solving, instrumental, and disciplined approach to objectives' and its 'reliance on a calculus, on precision and measurement and a concept of a system' (Bell, 1973: 349). The defining analysis of the technocratic belief system, however, is Putnam's simultaneous test of elite transformation in advanced industrial societies and the theory of technocracy (1977). Synthesizing the technocratic literature of the preceding decades, Putnam (1977) sums up the 'technocratic mentality' in six 'lodestars':

- an apolitical role based on the replacement of politics with technics;
- scepticism and even hostility towards politicians and political institutions;
- disregard for the openness and equality of political democracy tending towards authoritarianism and absolutism;
- the belief that social and political conflict is misguided or even contrived;
- policy as a question of pragmatics, not ideology or morality; and
- technological progress is good and questions of social justice are unimportant.

Drawing on his broader comparative study of political elites (1976), Putnam goes on to combine data on the educational background of top-levels bureaucrats in Britain, Germany and Italy with attitudinal stances on issues such as political neutrality, tolerance of party politics and democracy. The educational data from Italy shows a rough 50/

50 split between traditional bureaucrats trained in law and humanities vis-à-vis those with a background in natural sciences, engineering or social science, with the balance tipping somewhat towards the former in Germany and towards the latter in Great Britain. Matching this background to attitudinal items reveals a strong commitment to the technocratic lodestars among senior civil servants trained in hard science and technology, whereas those trained in social science (almost exclusively economics and political science) display much less animosity towards politics (Putnam, 1977: 403). This distinction seems to match what Meynaud had identified years earlier as possible split between an 'unpolished' and even 'brutal' type of technocrat trained in hard science and thus uninclined towards a compromise with politics vis-à-vis a more compromising type typically trained in economics, administration and social sciences (1968: 65).

Putnam's study is remarkable as one of the few attempts to identify the technocratic mindset as a distinct culture and belief system within the bureaucratic elite. In particular, the six lodestars still stand out as the definitive outline of this belief system. However, the study is also exemplary in a less fortunate way: it is secondary analysis of data compiled without any initial relation to the question of technocracy. Studies designed specifically to identify the technocrats within the broader bureaucratic elite are, generally speaking, few to none. This is particularly the case with studies of elite culture and belief systems, which are already fewer in numbers due to the more resource intensive nature of the research. The use of education and recruitment patterns as a method of identification is somewhat better helped by the more or less systematic inclusion of such variables in most mappings of national bureaucratic elites. However, a specific search for techno-bureaucrats is still faced with the problem of extrapolating conclusions from standard background variables. The point comes across clearly if we turn to the most well-known output of the wider elite study that Putnam drew on his one attempt to eke out the technocratic belief system: the 'APR' study of bureaucratic and political elites in the 'Western democracies' of Germany, Italy, the Netherlands, Great Britain and the United States (Aberbach et al, 1981).

Based on the criterion of a background in technical and natural sciences, we could thus conclude that share of techno-bureaucrats in national bureaucratic elites at the far end of the golden years varies between 10 per cent (Italy) and 42 per cent (United States) (Aberbach et al, 1981: 52). If we include a background in social science, Germany has the lowest share at 31 per cent, whereas the United States would claim the top spot with 71 per cent of its national bureaucratic elite matching the educational background of a techno-bureaucrat. The German slant of Weber's reflections also shine through rather clearly: 66 per cent of German civil servants were lawyers at the time, as opposed to 3 per cent in Great Britain and 18 per cent in the United States. Turning to attitudinal indicators, 69 per cent of bureaucratic elite members across countries identified with the role of a technician applying specialized knowledge to solve technical policy problems, which is only surpassed by the role of policy maker at 74 per cent (Aberbach et al, 1981: 89). By contrast, only 36 per cent identify with the role of a legalist, focusing on legal responsibilities and procedure. A more recent scoping review on subsequent research along similar lines reports that an educational background in law has become even less prominent among civil servants, whereas social sciences has been on the rise (Lee & Raadschelders, 2008: 423). Case-based approaches have show similar tendencies (Page & Wright, 1999).

So how many techno-bureaucrats are there? Citing contemporary French and British studies, Meynaud attempted a basic headcount of people capable of 'wielding true technocratic influence in the political field' from one of the three basic spheres of technocratic influence, which puts 'the number of men who, by virtue of their position, are able to influence and sometimes decide on the line of action taken by politicians' somewhere between 100 and 300, and in any event 'no more than a few hundreds' (Meynaud, 1968: 54). In a similar type of exercise, technocratic members of the bureaucratic elite in a position to wield significant influence over public policy is estimated to included a 'few hundred' (Etzioni-Halevy, 1983: 57). Even such numbers, however, amount to a significant proportion of the bureaucratic elite. As demonstrated by comparative studies, moreover, the proportion of technocrats is subject to significant national variation, approaching as much three quarters in the case of the United States. By the established measures, then, technocrats have certainly made their way into the ranks of the bureaucratic elite and can thus be assumed to exercise significant political influence from this position. This is not to say that technocrats found among rank-and-file bureaucrats are automatically precluded from political influence, depending on their role in policy development and implementation, but the higher civil service remains the operational criterion within the parameters of elite research.

An importation addition here is, of course, that the higher civil service does not exclusively mean the *national* civil service. Although a matter of ongoing debate, it is largely uncontroversial to state that institutions such as the European Central Bank, IMF, World Bank, OECD, WTO and WHO exercise substantial influence on national politics through a combination of direct control over decisions, funding and loans, standard-setting, accumulation and diffusion of knowledge, and so on. These tools effectively open up an additional channel of technocratic influence on political decisions, even to the extent that the political influence of international and transnational institutions is sometimes taken *in toto* as evidence of increasingly technocratic politics. This is not entirely unfounded, as the mandate and function of many of the relevant institutions is indeed particularly conducive to the technocratic belief system and career path. In keeping with the approach of the chapter, however, international organizations still have to be seen as institutional platforms for bureaucratic elites that can be populated more or less extensively by techno-bureaucrats. A particularly crucial case is the EU, which I shall discuss in more detail later (Chapter 5). For now, suffice to say that the administrative apparatus of the General Directorates is clearly one of the more important places to look for the techno-bureaucrats in the international sphere. However, we also need to extend our search for the technocrats to a different brand of bureaucrat altogether.

Political bureaucrats: technocrats as political advisers and party professionals

The question of the distinction between the purely administrative bureaucracy and the overtly political bureaucracy is essentially unresolved. In Weber's original analysis of the issue, however, the distinction is seen as the result of modern party politics, which introduces a pervasive split between two categories that are 'by no means rigidly but nevertheless distinctly separated': 'the "administrative" official on the one hand, and the "political" official on the other' (Weber, 1921: 9). This distinction, equally constitutive and fuzzy today, is resolved differently in various political systems from the spoils system to smaller cabinets or just a few advisers serving as political officials. Across these various systems, however, the political bureaucrat embodies the intrusion of party politics into the realm of public bureaucracy, and a type of bureaucrat formally located in the upper tiers of the public administration, albeit temporarily, with the purpose of conducting party politics. In current terminology, this group is composed of political and ministerial advisers taking care of functions such as policy research, analysis and evaluation, negotiation and networking, speech-writing, communication and working with the media (Blick, 2004; Eichbaum & Shaw, 2007; Hustedt & Salomonsen, 2017).

Whether such political officials should be included in the ranks of the bureaucratic elite, or whether the latter should be reserved solely for administrative officials, depends on the theoretical starting point and the particulars of national political systems. In terms of formal position, many high-level advisers clearly qualify as members of the bureaucratic elite. On the other hand, their functions, obligations and ethos differ from their purely administrative counterparts. Either way, political bureaucrats are rarely singled out in elite studies, making it difficult to gauge the average number of technocrats found among them. The APR study did in fact single out the political officials in the case of the United States because of the spoils system, thus making it possible to observe that only 10 per cent in this group had a background in engineering or natural science, whereas 38 per cent had a background in social sciences (compared to 42 and 29 per cent, respectively, for administrative officials). This prominence of a background in social science, together with a background in communication, seem to hold more generally for political and ministerial advisers, as do certain motives and beliefs separating political from administrative officials (Blick, 2004; Connaughton, 2010; Askim et al, 2017).

Going back to Weber, the root of this motivational structure and belief system has to do with fact that the political official is ultimately a professional politician. The professional politician, using Weber's deceptively simple baseline criterion, lives 'off' politics, as opposed to politicians living 'for' politics (1921). Historically, the role of the professional politician has been taken on by politic advisers and expert officials in the service of monarchs and princes. In the era of modern mass democracy and party politics, however, the role is taken up by the political officials in strict opposition to the purely administrative official. Indeed, the political official is, in spite of the formal position within the public bureaucracy, much more closely associated – in terms of function, motives and career path – with the other major incarnation of the professional politician: the party bureaucrat. The professional politician, as originally defined by Weber, is thus a type of political bureaucrat found in national public administrations and the 'machinery' of party bureaucracies dominating modern mass democracy.

The latter comes in two variations in Weber's analysis. In the continental tradition, the university-trained lawyer is the quintessential party bureaucrat. In addition to serving as administrative officials, lawyers are seen to have been instrumental to 'modern democracy' and the 'management of politics through parties' since the French Revolution (Weber, 1921: 11). A second type of party bureaucrat is the entrepreneur, represented by the party 'boss' in the United States and the election agent in the United Kingdom, running party machineries organized more as capitalist enterprises hoarding and trading votes (Weber, 1921: 19). Either way, the party bureaucrat is operating a party machine born 'of mass franchise, of the necessity to woo and organize the masses, and develop the utmost unity of direction and the strictest discipline' (Weber, 1921: 15). Modern democracy thus implies extensive bureaucratization of politics, making the 'instincts of officialdom' and ultimately the 'rule of officials' general formula for party politics and parliamentary democracy (Weber, 1921: 20).

In this sense, Weber's discussion and critique of professional politicians is deeply embedded in the era of the mass party (1880–1960); a type of party geared towards political battles for and against pervasive social reform and under conditions of mass suffrage and enfranchisement, as well as the political cleavages associated with industrial class society (Katz & Mair, 1995). The mass party, thus understood, represents the high point of party machineries run on purely bureaucratic principles. Much as the technocrats made their way into the bureaucratic elites of public bureaucracies, however, party bureaucracies where also gradually 'taken over' by technocrats during the golden years of technocracy: political control by rationalized party machines, or 'partocracy', increasingly 'stems from technocratic or, more exactly, techno-bureaucratic operation or skills', and the result 'seems already underway: the beginning of technical parties, which base their strategy on psychological methods, using public opinion poll techniques and surveys' (Meynaud, 1968: 67). We thus encounter a particular type of techno-bureaucrat operating as 'professional party leaders' and 'political technicians', manipulating the internal principles of party bureaucracy in order to gain power at the cost of formal political power (Meynaud, 1968: 67).

Whereas Weber observed party secretaries, whips and bosses operating the bureaucratic machines of the mass party, Meynaud observed a new group of political professionals running a new type of techno-bureaucratic machinery in the emerging technical parties. These parties, more generally, bear a striking resemblance to the so-called cartel party. The mass party was supplemented by the catch-all party, attempting to attract a larger share of the voter base through dealignment and focus on social amelioration, roughly from 1945 onwards. The cartel party model emerges during the 1970s, providing the first type of political party designed to enable politics as a profession (Katz & Mair, 1995: 18). Indeed, as a later reflection on the failings of party democracy brings more to light, the cartel party can be seen as the first type of party designed primarily for the exercise of technocratic politics (Mair, 2013). During the golden years of technocracy, in other words, the party machinery increasingly became a techno-bureaucracy and the party bureaucrat increasingly a techno-bureaucrat. In the course of this development, the technocrat also becomes increasingly associated with the functions, motives and career path of the professional politician bridging between the formal positions of the political official and the party bureaucrat.

In general, these two positions are largely interchangeable and closely connected in the running of party politics and the career path of the professional politician. As suggested already by Weber, the job of the political official and the party bureaucrat were merely anchor points in a wider set of career options for the professional politician, also including jobs in interest organizations and pressure groups formally located outside the political system. Today, this list has been expanded to positions in the political and bureaucratic consultancy business, various forms of lobbying and other job options in the broader career arc of what is sometimes referred to as policy experts or policy professionals (Svallfors, 2016). Notably, Weber also included journalism in this career path. In the current climate of mediatized politics, experts in political communication, public relations and marketing, have of course become even more pronounced figureheads among political advisers, party professionals and policy experts. Although members of this group may on occasion take on a (temporary) position as adviser in the higher echelons of the public administration, they largely fall outside the ranks of the bureaucratic elite. In sum, however, the professionalization of politics opens up an important channel of technocratic influence based on a position in the machinery of party politics. This, however, also brings the technocrat closer to the heart of politics.

Parliamentary elites: the technopols

Although Galbraith found private corporations and public administrations alike to be increasingly dependent on the technostructure, he was also adamant that any member of the technostructure 'is strongly inhibited in his political role. He cannot divest himself of the organization which gives him being. And he cannot carry it with him into political life' (Galbraith, 1967: 295). Similarly, Meynaud quickly excluded the possibility of technocrats in elected office from the possible channels of technocratic influence. For some undisclosed reason, Putnam limited his search for the technocratic mentality to the bureaucratic elite and excluded the elected political elite. In his claim about the limits of technocratic politics (1978), Straussman settled as a matter of principle that technocrats serve only as 'counsel' and not as 'princes', and Bell stated that technocrats could either compete or corporate with politicians, but did not include the option of *becoming* politicians (1973). In all of these cases, then, the option of technocrats taking up elected office is simply ruled out without much consideration. In addition to Putnam's claim that technocrats can only thrive in a surrounding bureaucratic structure, the assumed absence of technocrats from elected office may be due to the technocratic animosity towards ideology and factional politics. In any event, the assumption clearly belies empirical reality.

Although animosity towards traditional politics is indeed an integral part of technocracy, technocratic politicians, or *technopols*, are nevertheless an apparent part of political life. Technocratic politicians are inherently defined by a dual mindset and skill set that incorporates both the technocratic approach to politics and the willingness and ability to operate within the political institutions of party politics and parliamentary democracy. Although this mindset and skill set is internally incongruent and potentially unstable in principle, it can nevertheless be said to constitute a particular competence or habitus, which is far from peripheral in electoral politics. Indeed, technocratic politicians have been able to enjoy considerable success and influence in the game of party politics and parliamentary democracy. The importance of technopols vis-à-vis the traditional emphasis on the higher civil service as a source of technocratic influence gains further importance from the fact that technocracy increasingly works by weakening bureaucracy, at least in its purely administrative dimension.

The concept of technopols was originally coined in relation to economic reforms in South America, supposedly to dissociate it from the 'authoritarian' connotations of technocrats pure and simple, and became particularly popular when a 'Manual for Technopols' was added to the Washington Consensus on economic reform packages (Williamson, 1994). In this context, 'technopols' refers almost exclusively to the members of particular reform governments carrying out economic reforms, historically of the more liberal persuasion, guided by the motif that implementation of necessary policies requires solutions and reforms that are not just 'technically correct, but also politically enduring' (Domínguez, 1997: 7). Used in this way to delimit a rather particular group of high-level government reformers, the technopols include only a small clique assumed to possess a certain *esprit de corps*, developed through university training and long-standing party membership, leading to a combination of economic credentials and a certain ideological and party-political *savoir faire* (Domínguez, 1997).

More generally, the technopol is seen here to embody a combination, or even 'convergence', of technical *and* political resources and skills, which gives the technopol a distinct type of political competence, habitus and 'ability to exercise a collective influence on the policy-making process as well the management of government and the political party – or coalition – to which they belong' (Joignant, 2011: 522). By the same token, technopols have political career options and incentives that do not apply to technocrats keeping their distance to politics (Alexiadou, 2018).

Using the habitus of the technopol in a more general search for technocratic politicians, however, requires a few qualifications. First of all, the use of the concept in the Southern American context focused almost exclusively on executive elites, that is, the technocratic government. We shall return to this issue in the next section, but a more inclusive and comprehensive search for the technopols must begin with legislative and parliamentary elites. Second, the more or less pronounced assumption that technopols only take up elected office temporarily and more or less unwillingly to put themselves in the service of necessary reforms have to be completely abandoned. Nothing in the habitus of the technopol suggests a predisposition towards short visits in politics. Indeed, it could be said that the particular mindset and skill set of the technopol is well suited to sustain a long career in politics. Third, the ranks of technopols must be expanded to make room for members that have acquired their political skills as party bureaucrats rather than through the electoral machinery of political parties. As originally conceived, the technopol is assumed to have harnessed skills such as deliberation, ideological manoeuvring, network building and involvement in programmatic politics through ordinary party membership and leadership, whereas experience from party bureaucracy has merely been seen as the rare exception to this rule (Joignant, 2011: 532), keeping the technopol a safe distance from the popular discourse on professional politicians (Joignant, 2011: 536). However, the technopol may well be a political bureaucrat switching sides to elected office for shorter or longer periods of time, thus including elected office in the broader career part of the professional politician. Indeed, the road of the professional politician may offer a path of least resistance to political influence with fewer demands on participation in traditional party politics.

Within the parameters of elite research, the search for technopols in parliamentary and legislative elites is faced with the same opportunities and problems as in the case the bureaucratic elite. In institutional and positional terms, the parliamentary elite can be defined rather straightforwardly by parliamentary membership or by a more restrictive criterion of decision-making power used to distinguish high-ranking or leading parliamentarians (such as senior members, speakers, members of key committees and group chairpersons) from the backbenchers (newcomers, rank-and-file members of the party groups and so on). Key variables used in mappings of these elites typically revolve around gender, race, religion and so forth, often with a view to normative discussions of bias and representation (Mellors, 1978; Norris & Lovenduski, 1995; Müller & Saalfeld, 1997; Norris, 1997; Best & Cotta, 2000; Best et al, 2001; Jun, 2003). The search for the technopols are, however, once again restricted largely to a secondary interpretation of variables such as educational background, attitudinal stances and professional experience.

Indeed, the APR study directly compared bureaucratic elites and parliamentary elites in this respect and found the proportion of parliamentarians with a background in engineering/natural sciences (8 per cent) and social sciences (10 per cent) across countries to be significantly lower than in the bureaucratic elite (23 and 24 per cent, respectively), and the commitment to the role of technician (29 per cent) vis-à-vis the role of political advocate (64 per cent) to be practically inverse of the pattern found in the bureaucratic elite (69 and 24 per cent, respectively) (Aberbach et al, 1981: 52). Moreover, the APR study also gave rise to a more general discussion of technocratic politicians (Lee & Raadschelders, 2008). In general, the share of parliamentarians with a university degree has always been considerably lower than in the bureaucratic elite, significant variations notwithstanding. A marked trend in European parliaments, however, is that representatives with a background in law have increasingly been substituted by representatives with a background in social science. The latter group presently makes up between 40 and 60 per cent in a study of ten Western democracies (Gaxie & Godmer, 2007: 122). The proportion of parliamentarians with a background in engineering and natural sciences has, according to the same study, been moderately declining since its last peak at the end of the 1970s. As with the bureaucratic elites, such numbers do not make it possible to provide a conclusive headcount of technopols in national parliaments, but nevertheless indicate that their numbers are significant by conventional measures.

The search for technopols can be further aided by a branch of parliamentary and legislative studies focused on the professional background and career paths of national parliamentarians. While there is no standard taxonomy on the matter, we can distinguish broadly between three types of profession (Cairney, 2007): non-facilitating professions (blue- and white-collar workers in private businesses), so-called brokerage professions that have historically proved conducive, although technically unrelated to politics (lawyers, teachers, lecturers, academic professionals and the civil service in some systems) and instrumental professions with a direct link to politics (party or parliamentary staff, journalism, public relations, union work, interest groups and think tanks). The latter group of instrumental professions are largely identical to the career path associated with professional politicians, reflecting both Weber's original outline of this career path and more recent observations about the 'increasing professionalization of party staff, not just in the sense of employing pollsters rather than ward-heelers to keep abreast of public opinion, but particularly the increasing specialization of the party-political career path and its increasing separation from other occupational career tracks' (Katz & Mair, 2009: 761).

Used in a search for the technopols, the first group of non-facilitating positions could include any number of ordinary members of the technostructure of private corporations pursuing elected office through ordinary party membership. However, the group may be defined as much by their business outlook as by a particularly technocratic outlook on politics. The second group of brokerage occupations is where we would the more scientifically trained technopols – academic professionals pursuing office through party membership. This group would also include the economic reformers of South America, even if they typically only became a subject of interest once in government. In this group, potential technopols can then be separated from the decisively non-technocratic brokerage professions of lawyers and teachers. The last group, by contrast, is made up more or less entirely of technopols in the sense of professional politicians and political technicians who have harnessed their political skills by living off politics.

Whereas the non-facilitating and, in particular, the brokerage professions constitute the traditional route to parliament, the route of the professional politician has become a more 'instrumental' and potentially direct route to parliament in the current state of affairs (Allen, 2013). In general, the instrumental path of the professional politician has become more prominent among parliamentarians (Cairney, 2007; Gaxie & Godmer, 2007) and shown to get people elected to parliament at younger age and reach higher office at a faster pace, at least in the United Kingdom (Allen, 2013). Moreover, this dynamic appears to be particularly pronounced for ministerial advisers, who are on a 'supercharged' version of the instrumental pathway to parliament: advisers that choose to pursue a seat in parliament enjoy exceptional electoral success and even faster rise to high-level positions than other members of parliament with instrumental experience (Goplerud, 2013).

The importance of such observations for an attempt to track down the technopols is this: the instrumental and direct route to elected office solves the potential dilemma inherent to the habitus of the technopol. The route to parliament based on participation in traditional party politics still requires a marriage of opposites for the technocrat, that is, the technocratic mentality and the ideological, tactical and personal squabbles of party politics. By contrast, the instrumental route largely makes it possible to develop a skill set that still marries technocratic skills to party-political skills, or political skills more generally, with a much higher degree of integration and, at the same time, bypass the long and tedious road through party politics to parliament. More than a pathway to a stable income and a generous pension, as suggested by popular and populist critiques of professional politicians, the career arch of the professional politician thus represents a path of least political resistance to the implementation of technically correct policy solutions for the technopol. By the same token, the technopol is also less likely to consider elected office the crowning achievement of their political career: the positions on the professional career path are not only a direct stepping stone to parliament, but also a likely exit strategy from parliament. In the meantime, however, technopols may of course end up in government.

Executive elites: technocratic government

Technocratic power and influence in the political system reaches its pinnacle with the formation of a technocratic government. In practical terms, this narrows down to a search for technocrats to heads of state (prime ministers, presidents, premiers and the like) and the executive leaders within specific policy domains of the state apparatus (ministers, secretaries, deputies and similar). In most countries, this executive elite would include 20–40 individuals, and the search for technocrats in government comes down to what appears a manageable profiling of its individual members. However, the search for technocrats in the governmental elite is not just a matter of a simple headcount, but also raises the more fundamental issue of a fully or partially realized technocratic regime. The issue of technocracy vis-à-vis other political regimes is dealt with more in the ensuing chapter, but we also encounter the issue here since the appearance of technocrats in government is always indicative of a more or less complete installation of a technocratic regime.

In the context of established democracies, this is also to say that a technocratic government inherently suggests a potential suspension of democracy. Indeed, this suspension of normal democratic procedure is the essential idea of the most widely used definition of technocratic government as the opposite of party government, meaning that major political decisions are not made by elected officials and policy is neither decided nor enacted by political parties (McDonnell & Valbruzzi, 2014; Pastorella, 2015; Pinto et al, 2018). Following this definition, based on suspension of the particular procedures of *party* democracy, technocratic governments are found by looking for non-partisan and unelected members of the executive, usually with particular attention to the head of state and the minister of finance (Best & Cotta, 2000; Alexiadou, 2018). In addition to non-partisanship, a secondary criterion of expertise is used more or less systematically. In sum, this means that technocratic ministers are defined by the absence of a 'party stigma' and their specialist or general expertise, based on which they are assigned control over 'ministerial portfolios that correspond to their specialized skills and professional training', or are 'chosen for their technical and managerial capacities, regardless of the specific policy areas of government' (Pinto et al, 2018: 22). Furthermore, a tendency for technocratic government to act as reform or crisis government is often highlighted, albeit not as a strict criterion.

This is the line of argument that has made Mario Monti's cabinet, composed entirely of unelected professionals and battling the Italian debt crisis from 2011 to 2013, the poster child of technocratic government: short-lived governments (usually one to two years and sometimes as little as two weeks), suspending leadership by party representatives in order to manage economic crises, major transitions between economic systems and/or radical reforms of the labour market, taxes, pensions or public expenditure. However, the regime change to technocratic government, even in the Monti case is still based on temporary delegation within the parameters of a formally democratic system. More generally, Monti's cabinet represents the rare example of 'fully technocratic governments' where the prime minister is a technocrat; the majority of ministers are technocrats; and the government in question is a reform government, or at least has a mandate to change the status quo. Based on such criteria, there have only been six fully technocratic governments (Monti's cabinet being the latest) among the current EU countries (McDonnell &

Valbruzzi, 2014: 665). The other five instances have been decisively less high-profile.

Below the threshold of fully technocratic government, we find an array of quasi-technocratic government populated less extensively by technocratic ministers. Based on the criterion of a technocratic prime minister, there have been 24 technocratic governments among post-war European democracies, limited to just eight countries: Bulgaria, Czechia, Hungary, Romania, Italy, Portugal, Finland and Greece. In all cases, the governments in question were led by prime ministers without any party affiliation, neither at the time of appointment nor in their previous career. In lieu of party politics, the rationale behind their appointment is defined as non-party-political 'expertise' (usually in economics). In 16 of the cases, the minister of the economy is also classified as a technocrat according to these criteria. The overall proportion of technocratic ministers in each government ranges from 5 to 100 per cent (McDonnell & Valbruzzi, 2014: 659). A more expansive study of 13 European countries (Czechia, Estonia, France, Hungary, Italy, Latvia, Lithuania, Poland, Portugal, Romania, Slovakia, Spain, Sweden) over time finds appointment of non-partisan ministers to be a completely standard practice, the lowest average of such ministers being 16 per cent (in France) and the highest being 52 per cent (in Lithuania), which reflect a more general tendency for the proportion of non-partisan ministers to be somewhat higher in democracies with a more recent history of transition from non-democratic rule (Cotta, 2018: 273). However, the detailed case studies behind these number show considerable national variation in the practices and causes of appointing non-partisan ministers (Pinto et al, 2018).

The identification of technocratic governments in this way is based on the research agenda of comparative politics. If, as stated in an exemplary rendition of this agenda, 'the presence of non-political ministers' is becoming the rule more than the exception, 'what can explain it?' (Pinto et al, 2018: 7). The answer, following this line of argument, are the standard list of political system variables (including overall form of government, strength of the executive, cabinet status and electoral system) in combination with external factors such as economic crisis and European integration (Pinto et al, 2018: 16). Within this overall agenda, particular attention has been given to the general weakening of party democracy and the institutional diffusion of presidential and semi-presidential systems outside of the established family tree of presidential systems, which are seen to increase the likelihood of non-partisan ministers in government due to executive powers of appointment. The short list of fully technocratic governments and long list of governments populated by non-partisan ministers based on this agenda is certainly consistent and informative. However, it is also based on an essentially negative definition of technocratic government that tends conflate individual attributes and institutional procedures of appointment.

More to the point: defining technocratic government as the opposite of party government completely excludes the technopols from consideration. Techno-bureaucrats are not excluded since work as a purely administrative official does not clash with non-partisanship, but the skills and resources of technopols, whether drawn from party membership or work as a party bureaucrat, are in violation of this criterion. The criterion of non-partisanship restricts eligible members of government to pure 'outsiders', recruited directly to a position as minister or head of state from leading positions in organizations outside of the party-political apparatus. As acknowledged even by proponents of the non-partisanship criterion, however, the strict distinction between 'politicians' and 'experts', or 'insiders' and 'outsiders', cannot be 'applied as a rigid dichotomy, since these categories are not always mutually exclusive. Indeed, a significant number of ministers do combine both skills' (Pinto et al, 2018: 6). Indeed they do. This is the combination of skills that the technopol possesses.

Methodologically, the issue here is that the absence of party stigma is an individual attribute derived from the assumed institutional conflict between technocracy and party democracy, whereas technopols are identified simply by individual-level variables such as educational background, attitudes and career paths that do not preclude a marriage of technocracy and party politics. Pragmatically, the issue can be resolved if we consider a government composed of technopols an expert or diploma government rather than a fully technocratic government: in the former, the majority of ministers are in possession of specialized or general expertise and knowledge relative to their field, but also elected members of parliament or at least members of political parties (Bovens & Wille, 2017; Alexiadou, 2018). Although there may be reasons to uphold a distinction between fully technocratic governments such as the Monti government and the expert government of Macron in this way, the latter should certainly be included in a sufficiently comprehensive search for technocratic governments. The Monti government may be more fully technocratic in institutional terms, but the Macron government is in many ways considerably more important. In order to fully appreciate the actual scope and problematic of technocratic governments (and populist reactions to these), it is necessary to include governments populated more or less extensively by technopols.

Going by a criterion of non-partisanship and suspension of party politics, Macron cannot be considered 'the ultimate technocrat', nor even a technocratic head of state. Although Macron only founded *La République En Marche!* to run his bid for election, it must still be considered a party-political platform, and his government is cross-partisan rather than non-partisan. Moreover, Macron carries a historical party stigma since he was a member of the Socialist Party from 2006 to 2009. The exclusion of the Macron government from the list of technocratic governments can of course be considered a necessary victim of a more rigorous definition, but here it looks more like making one of the most important examples of the current conflict between technocracy and populism disappear with a sleight of hand. The same point can be extended to Obama's presidency, which has also been consistently interpreted as technocratic. Obama's background as a lawyer does not qualify him as a technopol, but judged by other criteria Obama's insistence on a reasoned and fact-based approach to policy is routinely taken as evidence for a technocratic mindset, even to the extent that it has been identified as the second 'pillar' of his presidency, on par with his ability to revitalize and embody the American Dream under the motto 'Yes we can' (Purdy, 2016). Hillary Clinton, by way of the same argument, lost to Trump's populist agenda primarily because she offered only a technocratic pillar (Stabe, 2016).

Looking further into the past, it has also been argued that Macron's template for government is found in the 'technocratic centrist ... tradition of Bill Clinton, Tony Blair and Gerhard Schröder' (Elliott, 2018). The current occupant of the latter's chair, Angela Merkel (a former scientist in the field of quantum chemistry), has become infamous for her Politics Without Alternatives (*Politik der Alternativlosigkeit*) and use of so-called TINA rhetoric (There Is No Alternative) in her implementation of austerity measures during the euro crisis. This has earned Merkel a reputation for being a technocratic head of state, and the politics without alternatives has been seen as immediate the cause of the populist counter-reaction that is now headed by the party Alternative für Deutchland (AfD). But again, Merkel's government is clearly not fully technocratic by the criterion of non-partisanship, nor even necessarily an expert government. The same point will of course apply to the executive elites originally identified as technopols in the Southern American context. Insisting on a formal opposition to party government, however, would render such arguments null and void and exclude Macron, Merkel, Obama, (Bill) Clinton, Schröder and Blair from the list of technocratic heads of state. However, they have all, in various ways, carried the technocratic approach to politics with them to the highest seats of power.

Conclusion

Beyond the members of the precious few non-party governments in party democracies, technocrats remain an elusive bunch. There is no universal agreement on the criteria used to single out technocrats, and the best available headcounts remain very rough estimates. On top of this comes the problem of political influence. We can of course safely assume that technocrats in government exercise political power and influence, but the issue gets increasingly tricky beyond that. A seat in parliament obviously grants a certain amount of formal power, but whether technocrats feature more prominently in core parliamentary elites or reside among the backbenchers is an open question, although some indication of the former can be found. The biggest problem, however, concerns the techno-bureaucrats. Here, the problem of technocratic influence essentially reiterates the eternal and never settled debate about the rule of officials: how much de facto power does the bureaucracy wield vis-à-vis political leadership?

My approach to these issues is, however, rather pragmatic: what the chapter has also shown is that there are reasons to claim that we find technocrats in all positions of political influence in the political system. Beyond that, my primary concern in the remainder of the book is with technocracy as a general type of governmental rationality and practice, which can be exercised by any number of bureaucrats, parliamentarians, ministers and heads of state in ways that would be exceedingly difficult to track down through elite studies or other actor-centred approaches. This is of course a matter of a difference in approach to the study of political power as much as it is a difference between levels and objects of analysis. This is not to say that better headcounts of technocrats would not help advance the analysis of technocracy – they most certainly would – but for the remainder of the book, the outline of techno-bureaucrats and the technopols in this chapter mainly serves to identify potential carriers of a distinct art of government. The logic behind this approach is outlined in more detail in the ensuing chapter.

4

4

The Technocratic Regime: Technocracy, Bureaucracy and Democracy

> Having a technocratically empowered cabinet is particularly important to overcome the nearly perpetual reality of divided government.
>
> (Khanna, 2017: 61)

The art of government

The institutionalization of technocratic rule has always been associated with the creation of governing bodies such as councils, committees, directorates and cabinets bestowing supreme power on scientists, engineers and other experts appointed on the basis of strict meritocracy rather than popular election. In this respect, there is a direct line from the proposed substitution of the American presidential system with government by executive cabinet or committee, as proposed in Khanna's manifesto for the new technocracy, to Smyth's National Council of Managing Scientists, Veblen's Soviet of Technicians and Saint-Simon's model of government. These visions of technocratic rule are, of course, mostly utopian: the complete transferral of executive power to technocratic bodies of government remains a largely unrealized blueprint. Fully technocratic governments may approximate the blueprint, but so far they remain short-lived exceptions within polities that do not otherwise conform to technocratic visions. The expert councils and committees that have become an integral part of government practically all over the globe may function as platforms for scientific and technical influence on public policy, at least part of the time, but they are not supreme bodies wielding executive power in the manner proposed by grander technocratic utopias.

Nevertheless, technocratic institutions do exist, sometimes extensively so, in modern government. More importantly, however, the preoccupation with councils, committees and cabinets also narrows down the search for technocratic regimes to a form of government in the institutional or even constitutional sense of the term, focused on the formal distribution and exercise of power, the role and nature of the executive, the number of decision-making bodies, checks and balances, delegation to subordinate institutions, oversight, transparency and so on. These are, of course, important dimensions of a political regime, but they are also limited to the domain of formal and quasi-formal political institutions. In a broader sense, a political regime can interpreted as distinct form of governmental rationality and practice, or an 'art of government' embodying a more general 'principle and method for the rationalization of the exercise of government' (Foucault, 2008: 318). Thus understood, different regimes may be more or less dependent on the apparatus of formal and quasi-formal political institutions and procedures.

Broadening the view on political regimes in this way is important due to the high degree of technocratic flexibility in relation to the formal design of the polity and the underlying question of the balance between democracy and autocracy. Simply put, technocracy is neither inherently autocratic nor democratic. Although technocracy has historically been associated with autocracy because of its opposition to factional politics and popular participation, technocracy is capable of working in lockstep with anything from complete autocracy to complete democracy. In this respect, technocracy is much like bureaucracy. Indeed, technocracy has more often than not been confused with bureaucracy by proponents and critics of technocratic rule alike, chiefly because industrial technocracy developed largely through a technocratic 'takeover' of bureaucratic institutions. Important as this historical development is, however, it also tends to cloud the fact that bureaucracy and technocracy are, on a deeper level, opposed political regimes competing for representation of non-political *rationality* in the political system. This competition, notably, takes place along a different axis from the opposition between democracy and autocracy, which is based on opposing, mutually incompatible, representations of *sovereignty*. The chapter works out the details of this argument and concludes with a corresponding outline of the general framework followed in the ensuing analysis of the new technocracy.

Political regimes and the political system

The interpretation of political regimes as arts of government is based on Foucault's later lectures (2007) and the entire tradition of 'governmentality studies' that they spawned (Burchell et al, 1991; Rose, 1996; Dean, 2010; Dardot & Laval, 2013). Understood in this way, political regimes are expressions of broader and historically developed configurations of power, applied specifically as principles and methods for rationalization of the exercise of government and political authority. The majority of Foucault's work traced such power configurations, in particular so-called disciplinary power, outside of the political realm, in what effectively amounts to a form of historical sociology defined by its focus on the mechanisms of power throughout the social fabric (Behrent, 2010). Foucault's later lectures, however, turned more directly to the problem of government and political authority. The agenda arising from this endeavour is summarized in the very last words of the lecture series:

> What is politics, in the end, if not both the interplay of these different arts of government, with their different reference points, and the debate to which these different arts of government give rise? It seems to me that it is here that politics is born. Good, well that's it. Thank you. (Foucault, 2008: 313)

I have discussed the implications of this approach to government elsewhere (2018). The argument can, however, also be laid out in the more conventional terms of Easton's systems analysis of political life. Although it may initially seem a strange partnership, Easton's model of the political system provides a more established framework for understanding the role of competing arts of government in political life. On the one hand, Easton's model is universally known to the point of being the foundational language of politics. On the other hand, political systems theory is also much (and unfairly) derided for its supposed formalism and association with functionalist system theory in the vein of Talcott Parsons (Bang, 1998). In general, the principal advantage of Easton's model it that it enables a view of concrete historical political regimes as competing configurations of the political system and decision-making procedures, based on different solutions to the general problem of binding decisions and underlying logics of political authority. Thus understood, the political system is fundamentally programmed by different regimes based on different codes and representations of political authority, in a process that bears more than a passing resemblance to the interplay of competing arts of government and their different reference points.

In general, Easton defines a regime as 'the general matrix of regularized expectations within the limits of which political actions are usually considered authoritative, regardless of how or where these expectations may be expressed' (Easton, 1965: 193–4). Regimes consist of values (goals and principles), norms and resources of authority, indicative of the processes of signification, legitimization and power inside the political system (the following outline of Easton's framework draws on Bang & Esmark (2009) and should be accredited principally to the former). The values serve as broad limits with regard to what can be taken for granted in the guidance of day-to-day policy without violating deep feelings or important segments of the political community. The norms specify the kinds of procedures that are expected and acceptable in the processing and implementing of demands. The resources, which may be material as well as symbolic, and formal as well as informal, embody the way in which power is distributed and organized with regard to the authoritative making and implementing of decisions (Easton, 1965: 193). A specific regime at any moment in time will be the product of the accommodation among the pressures for new goals, rules or structures stimulated by social change and the limits imposed by existing conventions and practices. Thus understood, particular regimes structure the interaction between political authorities and laypeople in a particular way, as well as the relation between the input side and the output side of the political system.

Political authorities can be occupants of highly specialized roles as politicians, ministers, judges, administrators and so on, but they can also be journalists, opinion leaders or scientists who do not perform a formal political role at all. Either way, they must engage in the daily affairs of a political system; they must be recognized by most members of society as having the responsibility for these matters; and their actions must be accepted as binding most of the time by at least most of the relevant members, as long as they act within the limits their role (Easton, 1965: 212). Laypeople, for their part, include groups of individuals who are drawn together by the fact that they participate in a common political structure and set of processes, however tight or loose their ties may be. It does not matter whether people form a group in the sense of a community with common traditions and culture, as traditionally highlighted in political sociology. A political community may well have different — even antagonistic and actively struggling — cultures and traditions or they may be entirely separate nationalities

(Easton, 1965: 177). But as long as they do not opt out or exit from this community, they cannot escape being linked by a common division of political labour, however low their level of cohesion may be. In this dimension, technocracy is defined by its emphasis on technical and scientific experts as ultimate political authorities and the image of the broader political community of citizens and laypeople as being largely ignorant, irrational or even flat-out dangerous.

Next, the regime also mediates the relation between input and output. The input side of the political system, in Easton's near-universal terminology, includes the demands, issues and support that stimulate activity, conflict and competition in the political system, whereas the output side refers to actions and ultimately outcome and effects. The input side can be broadly equated with 'politics' in the sense of the more or less systemic organization of political demands, issue, support or pressures, political mobilization around political interests, ideologies and/or identities, movements, parties and so forth. Correspondingly, the output side can be equated with 'policy' in the sense of the concrete actions that have to be carried out for decisions to be made felt as binding in the production of intermediate political outcomes (Bang & Esmark, 2009). The relation between politics and policy is entirely circular and arbitrary, but always mediated by the regime. In this dimension, technocracy operates through what has been called 'policy-politics', which is to say a form of decision making where politics are wholly subordinate to and encapsulated in the pursuit of specific political outcomes deemed necessary for the political system purely in terms of their effect rather than their congruence with specific or generalized demands and support on the input side of the political system. This logic of policy-politics stands in contrast to the democratic and bureaucratic logic of politics-policy, according to which policy is a neutral implementation of politics (Bang & Esmark, 2009).

This is also to say that the regime is located in the domain of 'polity', albeit in the particular sense of a broad matrix of values, norms and principles, resources of authority and process of signification and legitimization of power. In other words, the regime is not a polity in the sense of a formal constitutional arrangement, a particular form of state or even a form of political organization more broadly. The regime is rather what opens up the so-called 'black box' of the political system. Properly understood, the black box in Easton's model contains the different ways that the relationship between political leaders and laypeople, as well as the link between input and output, can be programmed based on different codes and representations of political authority. Correspondingly, historically specific regimes can be understood as historically contingent but relatively stable programmes linked to the overall problem of producing authoritatively binding decisions within the political system. The question is, then, how technocracy fits into the broader history and analysis of political regimes from this perspective.

Regime types: looking for technocracy

Regime typologies rarely assign a prominent place to technocracy. The hierarchy of polities outlined in book VIII of Plato's *Republic*, the mother of all regime typologies, does not include technocracy for obvious reasons. It does, however, start with something approaching a meritocracy: the aristocratic rule of Philosopher Kings and a caste system based on the 'tripartite theory of the soul'. In Plato's view, aristocracy is supposedly a rule of wisdom and virtue. The Philosopher King is not ruler by might or name, but by the virtue of a 'soul of gold', harnessed through rigorous training and education in metaphysics and the idea of the absolute good, which puts his exercise of power beyond personal interests and pursuit of fame, wealth or power for the sake of power. From there, things can only get worse: aristocracy degenerate into timocracy when those more predisposed towards pecuniary matters, social status and honour than virtue are included in the ruling circles. Timocracies becomes oligarchies when hoarding of wealth completely overrules virtue. The resulting social tensions between rich and poor may then result in the revolutionary overturn of oligarchy and establishment of the even less virtuous democracy, which ultimately degrades into tyranny as counteraction to the unrestricted freedom and chaos of democracy.

For those inclined to see political regimes as the eternal recurrence of ancient polities, technocracy is clearly most akin to the proto-meritocracy found in Plato's idea of the aristocracy as the rule of virtue, wisdom and Philosopher Kings. In more current terminology, this would suggest that technocracy can largely be equated with a 'noocracy' (the rule of mind or intellect). However, this affinity across millennia also stretches the value of anachronistic reinterpretation. Although meritocratic recruitment is indeed a constitutive principle of technocracy, the world of (post-) industrial management has little to do with the world of virtuous Philosopher Kings schooled in metaphysics. Based on Aristotle's reworked typology of true and defective forms of government by the one, the few or the many, technocracy can be understood simply as a form of rule by the few, either in the true form of the aristocracy or the degenerated form of the oligarchy. Here, technocracy amounts to an oligarchy of scientists and/or technicians (as opposed to an oligarchy based on wealth), which may be technically correct but also largely uninformative.

More generally, the problem with the various interpretations of technocracy as a synonym for meritocracy, intellectual aristocracy or oligarchy is that they do not really define or capture technocracy as a distinct form of rule. This is not merely a problem in relation to ancient regime typologies. Indeed, it could be argued that the problem is even exacerbated by most current typologies structured around a basic distinction between democratic and authoritarian forms of rule. This distinction can be said to have consolidated itself as the organizing perspective of comparative politics, studies of democratization and political science more generally (Burnell & Schlumberger, 2012). The polity data series, for example, classifies countries according to this distinction, based on a score from −10 (full autocracy) to +10 (full democracy). The intermediate position is then defined as 'anocracy' (regimes that display autocratic and democratic elements at the same time). The 'freedom score' calculated by Freedom House does not use regime classifications, but de facto operates along a scale (0–100) from full autocracy to full democracy (the scales are discussed at the Polity Project section of http://systemicpeace.org and at http://freedomhouse.org).

Such numerical and continuous scales are of course just one way to measure regime types. The majority of conceptual and analytical regime typologies are categorical: more or less detailed classifications and taxonomies of variation and subtypes based on a founding distinction between democracy and autocracy. Moreover, regime typologies vary with respect to their underlying research focus and measures, which can broadly be divided into the horizontal division of power (separation of powers, checks and balances), the vertical division of power (civil liberties and rights), procedures of appointment and selection to political office (who rules) and the degree of formalized rules identifying power holders and their competences (Skaaning, 2006; Boix et al, 2013). Although additional aspects such as socio-geographical organization (such as nation-states vs empires), publicity (monarchy vs republics) and religious influence (theocracy vs secular rule) can be included, the overarching issue remains democracy vis-à-vis autocracy.

Within this framework, there has been a steady proliferation of more refined typologies of democratic regimes (Lijphart, 1999), authoritarian regimes (Linz, 2000) and anocracies (Regan & Bell, 2010) or hybrid regimes more generally (Levitsky & Way, 2002). The merits of such typologies are obvious: they are formal and largely rigorous frameworks essential to the explanatory potential of comparative politics as well as the ever-important analysis of democratization and democratic progress.

For the matters at hand, however, available regime typologies are also remarkably inept insofar as they have little or nothing to say about technocracy. Technocracy will appear on occasion as a peripheral regime type either in the intermediate range between democracy or autocracy or as a variation on the latter. The solution to this issue, however, is not to incorporate technocracy better in existing regime typologies based on the opposition between democracy and autocracy. Rather, what we need is a revised regime classification that situates technocracy entirely outside of the axis between democracy and autocracy, but in a distinct relationship of opposition to the bureaucratic regime that technocracy has competed directly with throughout its existence. The underlying logic behind this approach is that we are ultimately dealing with two different forms of political authority. Whereas the oppositional relationship between democracy and autocracy is founded on a codification of political authority as sovereignty, the technocratic regime is based on codification of political authority as rationality, in direct competition with the historically dominant alternative based on this form of authority: the bureaucratic regime.

Alternatives to technocracy: a revised regime typology

This distinction between two essentially different codes and representations of political authority is based on a historical bifurcation between sovereignty and an entirely different logic to the extent that in the end 'we have two completely different systems of power' (Foucault, 2007: 66). It should be noted up front that Foucault refers to this new type of political authority as *security* rather than rationality, or more specifically as a new configuration of power called an 'apparatus (*dispositif*) of security' (Foucault, 2007: 66). In contrast to arts of government premised on sovereignty, arts of government based on the logic of security are concerned with the active management of the population intended to ensure the 'security (*sécurité*) of the population and, consequently, of those who govern it' (Foucault, 2007: 66). Although this historical bifurcation opens up the series of lectures that constitute the founding text of governmentality studies, it also gradually fades into the background as Foucault becomes increasingly interested in alternative concepts such as biopolitics and liberal governmentality.

However, the new political rationality of security is nevertheless the operative logic behind the development of *raison d'état* as a distinct art of government. In contrast to the more conventional understanding of *raison d'état* as a new programme of state sovereignty, opposed to the logic of imperialism, Foucault ascribes a more vital and fundamental role to *raison d'état* as the point of bifurcation between sovereignty and security. Thus understood, *raison d'état* constitutes an art of government concerned with the management of the population as a system of forces, including everything considered relevant to the overall well-being of the population such as size, health, longevity, productivity and happiness, in order to ensure the safety of the population and those who govern it. All of these forces must be developed to the point of their maximum capacity without disrupting the overall balance of forces. Seen in the light of Foucault's earlier work on disciplinary power, *raison d'état* can thus be understood as a disciplinary art of government, i.e. a form of government based on the exercise of the type of disciplinary power Foucault had already analysed extensively in penal practies, education, medicine and so forth (Esmark, 2018).

This interpretation of *raison d'état*, in turn, provides an alternative entry point to the analysis of bureaucracy and the modern state administration. According to this line of argument, the modern bureaucratic administration was born as a *police* function 'installed in order to make *raison d'état* function … It is the intervention of this field of practices called police that brings to light this new subject [the population] in this, if you like, general absolutist theory of *raison d'état*' (Foucault, 2007: 286). Police, thus understood, is clearly not limited to police force in its current form, nor specifically attached to the connotations of the police state. Disciplinary police is rather the basic formula for bureaucratic administration or simply 'administrative modernity par excellence' (Foucault, 2007: 321). Except for the old dynastic branches of the monarchical court administrations (the army, the treasury and perhaps justice), all the basic policies and branches of the modern administration owe their existence to the disciplinary police. The modern bureaucracy can thus be seen as the material expression of a disciplinary art of government viewing 'a generalized discipline as the essential form in which one conceived of the possibility and necessity of police intervention' (Foucault, 2007: 343).

Going back to a number of key texts from the era of French bureau development, Foucault thus reminds us that the majority of bureaus were developed as necessary domains of good police required to ensure the overall welfare or well-being of the population: 'the objective of police is everything from the being to well-being, everything that may produce this well-being beyond being, and in such a way that the well-being of individuals is the state's strength' (Foucault, 2007: 328). Necessary bureaus include, on average, those for literacy, health, charity, religion, morals, theatre and games, property and production (Foucault, 2007: 334). Taken to its full conclusion, this line of argument traces the entire array of modern welfare state policies and its corresponding bureaucracy back to *raison d'état* and the idea of managing the population as a system of forces. Clearly, *raison d'état* did not immediately give birth to a fully fledged welfare state. Nevertheless, the current notion of welfare is intimately related to the embryonic idea of the welfare or well-being of the population as the basic source of state strength in *raison d'état*.

This historical development from early expansion of state bureaucracies to the fully developed administration of the welfare state is ultimately premised on the historical schism between sovereignty and security. Although operating in the service of different political rulers and masters laying claims to various forms of political sovereignty, the bureaucratic regime and its exercise of 'police force' is not ultimately premised on claims to sovereignty, but rather in its ability to provide security for the population and those who govern it. Notably, this implies that the bureaucratic regime is ultimately completely indifferent to the question of sovereignty, which is to say whether political leaders lay claim to supreme power based on divine mandate, hereditary prerogatives, military might or popular election. Indeed, the bureaucratic regime and its underlying logic of security stands in an orthogonal relationship with political authority based on sovereignty: it is indifferent towards the autocracy/democracy distinction and historically capable of positioning itself anywhere along the axis between them. This indifference to the problem of sovereignty is also an important attribute of bureaucracy as understood in Weber's foundational work, of course.

Weber infamously abstracted three forms of authority from historical experience that, in one way or another, provide viable solutions to the problem of arriving at binding and legitimate decisions for a specific group or community: traditional authority, charismatic authority and rational-legal authority. Traditional authority is premodern in origin and autocratic in nature by current standards. Charismatic authority is also premodern in origin, but spans the entire spectrum from autocracy to democracy. Rational-legal authority, by contrast, is the prevailing authority in the modern era and shifts the entire logic of political authority away from the traditional right and might or charismatic glory of the ruler to impersonal rule. In other words: whereas traditional and charismatic authority belongs decisively in the realm of sovereignty in its various feudal and modern incarnations, rational–legal authority is rather the result of the core dynamic of modernity, that is, the process of 'rationalization' Weber saw expressed in capitalist production as well as the centralization of legislation, jurisdiction and use of force in the modern state and its 'quantitative extension of administrative tasks' (Weber, 1978: 969).

The spread and consolidation of rational–legal authority with the forces of rationalization, in turn, leads to the bold historical claim that 'the development of modern forms of organization in all fields is nothing less than identical with the development and continual spread of bureaucratic administration' (Weber, 1978: 223). Weber's basic outline of bureaucratic principles, such as functionally and legally separated spheres of competence and jurisdiction, hierarchy, impersonality, obligations, procedural compliance, meritocratic recruitment and promotions, salaried professionals and so on, is derived directly from the fundamental categories of rational–legal authority and the claim that the 'purest type of exercise of legal authority is that which employs a bureaucratic administrative staff' (Weber, 1978: 220). It is the intrinsic relation between rational–legal authority and bureaucratic principles of organization that makes bureaucracy the 'most rational known means of exercising authority over human beings ... superior to any other form in precision, in stability, in the stringency of its discipline, and in its reliability' (Weber, 1978: 223).

Thus, with Weber we arrive of the idea of rationality as a form of political authority underpinning a bureaucratic regime operating outside the logic of sovereignty. Indeed, it is rational–legal authority that makes bureaucracy indispensable but completely indifferent to political leadership (or leadership as such) at one and the same time. Bureaucracy is in this sense neither inherently democratic, nor autocratic. That bureaucracy is not inherently democratic is clear from Weber's own argument that the 'direct rule of the *demos*' and broad public influence 'inevitably comes into conflict with bureaucratic tendencies' (1978: 985). On the other hand, it is equally clear that bureaucracy and rational–legal authority also accompany the process of 'passive democratization', 'the leveling of social differences' and ultimately 'modern mass democracy' (Weber, 1978: 983). This co-evolution of modern democracy and bureaucracy has made bureaucracy 'part of society's long-term commitment to a *Rechtsstaat* and procedural rationality for coping with conflicts and power differentials' (Olsen, 2006: 3). Indeed, there is an intrinsic relation with 'constitutional democracy and the separation of powers' (Olsen, 2006: 9).

In various ways, Foucault and Weber thus point to a decisive schism in political authority behind the emergence of the modern bureaucratic regime. Whereas Foucault describes this development in terms of contrast between security and sovereignty, Weber's tripartite distinction between forms of authority identifies bureaucracy with rational-legal authority. The resulting images of a bureaucracy as disciplinary police and a form of organization representing precision, stability, reliability and stringency of discipline are, however, much the same, as is the emphasis on the indifference of bureaucracy to the political authority of sovereignty. Equipped with this understanding of bureaucracy and its relation to the battle of democracy and autocracy, we are now in a position to discuss technocracy more systematically in relation to these historical alternatives. The basic framework for this is outlined in Figure 1.

Figure 1 illustrates two points. First, technocracy is positioned opposite to bureaucracy. The preceding chapter has already introduced the idea of the 'techno-bureaucrats' and the wider issue of the intimate relationship between bureaucracy and technocracy. Understood more generally, this relationship is a matter of two regimes vying for the same role: ensuring purely rational and non-political decisions within the political system. The back-and-forth between bureaucracy and

Figure 1: Four basic regimes

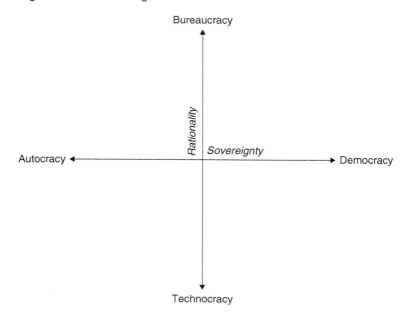

technocracy is thus played out on an axis defined by the political authority of rationality, historically dominated by the bureaucratic regime. Second, the orthogonal relation between this axis and the interplay between autocracy and democracy indicates that bureaucracy and technocracy are logically and substantially indistinct in relation to different regimes premised on the political authority of sovereignty. In historical terms, this means that the full range of possible alliances with democracy, autocracy and anything in between is and has been available to bureaucracy and technocracy. Both points are developed more fully in the ensuing sections.

Technocracy vs bureaucracy

The idea of bureaucratic regime, and its grip on the modern political system, is aptly summarized with the rhetorical question: 'can there really be much doubt who governs our complex societies? Public bureaucracies, staffed largely by permanent civil servants, are responsible for the vast majority of policy initiatives taken by governments … In a literal sense, the modern political system is essentially "bureaucratic" – characterized by the "rule of officials"' (Putnam, 1973: 257). One of the central problems in coming to terms with the technocratic regime is that it can be rather difficult to distinguish between technocracy and this rule of officials, in particular since a large proportion of technocrats will indeed be bureaucratic officials in the formal sense, as discussed in Chapter 3. This issue of separation between bureaucracy and technocracy has been a persistent problem up to and including current more or less interchangeable use of the two terms today, in particular in the broader and more pejorative sense.

If we look to the founding text on bureaucracy, this should probably not surprise us. Although he did not use the term 'technocracy', Weber viewed reliance on technical expertise as integral to bureaucracy. The broader trends of industrialization and technological progress, moreover, can be seen as more less endemic to the process of rationalization. On a more anecdotal level, Weber toured the United States and its capitalist enterprises extensively at a time when the second industrial revolution was in full bloom. Weber's definitive analysis of bureaucracy arrived (posthumously) with *Economy and Society*, a few years after Smyth had brought the concept of technocracy to the world in his obscure manifest. In other words, Weber was fully aware of and even immersed in the events of the second technocratic revolution. There is little doubt then, that bureaucracy and technocracy are essentially identical phenomena from Weber's perspective: the technocratic mindset can be seen simply an expression of modern rationalization, and its concrete organization simply a matter of bureaucratic administration.

The term 'bureaucracy' itself had, of course, been introduced earlier in the extended history of the French Revolution that also gave birth to technocracy as form of governmental rationality and practice, if not yet a concept. From this perspective, the history of the French Revolution culminating in the creation of the 'Napoleonic' administration is, at one and the same time, the birth of bureaucracy and technocracy. The Napoleonic tradition is both a central template for bureaucracy as administrative modernity par excellence and the universally recognized exemplar of institutionalized technocratic influence: the Grand Corps l'État and their highly formalized system of recruitment from the Grands Écoles. From this perspective, it could be argued that technocracy emerged simply as a French variation of bureaucracy, embodied in the Napoleonic administrative tradition and its diffusion to other European countries. By the same logic, the later addition of technocracy in the United States can be conceived as an additional variation of the basic bureaucratic regime embodied in the American administrative tradition, or the post-imperial and post-war Anglo-American tradition in a broader sense.

In his analysis of the 'bureaucratic phenomenon' in France, Crozier interpreted technocracy as a potential variant of bureaucratic organization 'where technical experts, or managers, through their role as technicians of organizational life, are coming to hold more and more power' (1964: 165). However, Crozier also largely dismissed the idea of the increasing power of technical experts and managers on the grounds that the process of rationalization actually works against such tendencies: although their critical role in innovation gives technical experts a certain degree of power, rationalization also means that innovations can be swiftly transformed to standardized production and routines carried out by non-experts, leaving experts with a 'shifting and fragile power' anywhere but at the very 'frontline of progress' (1964: 165). The point here is not so much that Crozier was wrong, chiefly because technical experts are understood in much too narrow terms as material engineers, but rather that his in-depth analysis treats technocracy as a marginal aspect of the French model of bureaucracy and its role in the overall development of industrial society (1964: 294).

In spite of this more or less dominant tendency to interpret technocracy as a part, branch or variation of bureaucracy, I take technocracy to constitute a regime in its own right, logically and ideationally opposed to bureaucracy. Historically, this argument builds on the idea of 'a new or second stage in that "rationalization" which Max Weber had already comprehended as the basis for the development of bureaucratic domination' (Habermas, 1971: 62). Weber's understanding of bureaucratic domination is, according to this line of argument, based more or less exclusively on the idea of bureaucratic organizations as a pure expression of legal-procedural authority, populated by officials trained in law and the management and operated with discipline and efficiency akin to military organizations. However, this form of bureaucratic domination is also based on a *decisionistic* model of political authority where bureaucracy and its legal-procedural authority are still submitted to a form of political leadership based on non-rational authority. Correspondingly, the arrival of a second stage in bureaucratic domination and rationalization, not entirely foreseen by Weber, occurs the moment the decisionistic model 'is being abandoned by many in favour of a *technocratic model*', which effectively 'reverses' the relation between scientific expertise and political leadership, thus submitting the latter to the former (Habermas, 1971: 63, original emphasis).

I shall return to the implications of the decisionistic model in more detail in Chapter 9, based on the proposition that a reversal back to the principles of the decisionistic model may be one way to rein technocracy back in. Since the transition from this model to a technocratic model effectively marks the point where technocracy start to take over the political system more fundamentally, a return to the former may be worth considering. For now, however, the key point about the two models is the underlying idea of a fundamental shift in political authority and rationalization of bureaucratic domination from legal-procedural authority to technologic-scientific authority, caused by the extensive 'scientization of politics' since the Second World War. This is not to say that bureaucracy disappears as a form of organization. Formally, the political system may retain its basic blueprint, but materially political leadership is reduced to a 'stopgap in a still imperfect rationalization of power, in which the initiative has in any event passed to scientific analysis and technical planning' (Habermas, 1971: 64). Indeed, politics potentially becomes even more pervasively bureaucratic in the second stage or phase of bureaucratic domination based on the technocratic model. The space for political decisions based on competing interests, ideologies, goals and needs, which in Weber's terminology comes down to a matter of charismatic authority, is effectively minimized as the state increasingly becomes an 'organ of a thoroughly rational administration' (Habermas, 1971: 64), that is, 'an "administrative" state designed for technocratic governance' (Fischer, 1990: 25).

In general, I shall refer to this second stage in bureaucratic domination as the technocratic 'takeover' of bureaucracy – the technocratic appropriation of bureaucracy for purposes of extensive social planning and engineering. In addition to Habermas' broader discussion of changes in political authority and the logic of domination, the dynamics of this takeover is extensively explored in Meynaud's discussion of 'techno-bureaucracy', meaning a development and expansion of bureaucracy driven by technocrats 'in a position to gain support from a bureaucratic machine or manipulate its fundamental principles' (Meynaud, 1968: 65). Techno-bureaucracy, with a more recent formulation, thus means fitting 'the bureaucratic organization to the technological mission of society' (Fischer, 1990: 64). Although techno-bureaucracy implies that technocrats seek influence *through* bureaucratic institutions and centres, thus making it difficult to maintain the distinction in practice, the technocratic orientation towards technological innovation and scientific expertise is distinct from, or even opposed to, adherence to legal-procedural authority. Technocrats are more inclined to pursue control of political decisions and: 'in practice, bureaucracy obeys other impulses and uses other instruments, for example, by force of inertia or simply by stifling any wayward measure, it effectively protects routine' (Meynaud, 1968: 63).

However, the technocratic appropriation of bureaucracy should not necessarily be viewed as a hostile takeover. The tendency of 'old-established bureaucracies' to turn to the authority of technical competence and scientific expertise may be seen as a way to add a factor of power and prestige to bureaucracy that was not necessarily there in the first place: 'technocracy may be thought of in one sense as a means of promoting and extending bureaucracy, or, to put it another way, as the fusion between technology and bureaucracy with the first adding an element of dynamism to the second' (Meynaud, 1968: 64). Making a similar observation about the technocratic 'culture of objectivity' and infatuation with quantification, Porter states that 'the appeal of numbers is especially compelling to bureaucratic officials who lack the mandate of popular election, or divine right ... objectivity lends authority to officials who have very little of their own' (1995: 28). In other words, the creation of a techno-bureaucracy can also be thought of as a way to increase bureaucratic power and ultimately the rule of officials.

However: whereas the technocratic takeover of bureaucracy and the creation of techno-bureaucracies is an integral part of the third technocratic revolution and the golden years of technocracy, a distinctive feature of the new technocracy is also its deeply anti-bureaucratic stance. This is the first part of what I described as the changing regime relations that occur with the transition from industrial to post-industrial technocracy: from a compromise or even alliance with bureaucracy, captured in the formula of the techno-bureaucracy, to a pervasive rejection of bureaucracy as viable solution to the challenges of post-industrial society. This development means that the technocratic appropriation of bureaucracy has shifted considerably towards an outright attack on bureaucracy. Correspondingly, techno-bureaucracies, insofar as this is still the right term to use, have tipped decisively in favour of technocracy. We have in this sense moved beyond the limits of what can reasonably be called bureaucratic domination or rationalization.

The ensuing chapters will analyse this development in more detail, but the main point is this: the inherent opposition between the legal-procedural rationality and technological-scientific rationality has become more adversarial, and the technocratic belief in and need for bureaucratic organization has drastically decreased. The old problem of distinguishing technocracy formally from bureaucracy and the rule of officials obviously still persists since bureaucratic principles of organization are still in operation everywhere. However, the new technocracy also seeks to supplant bureaucratic organization with alternative forms of organization; bureaucratic order-and-command with alternative forms of steering, control and regulation, and planning and programming with experimentation and innovation. With the new technocracy, the original rejection of the decisionistic model, or simply traditional politics, has become more radical: 'it lacks the technical proficiency and specialist knowledge required to select the optimal policy choice; it is costly, inefficient, bureaucratic and self-referential to the point of being tiresome' (Hay, 2007: 93).

Technocracy vs democracy

Whereas the separation of technocracy from bureaucracy has always presented a problem, technocracy is usually drawn in sharp contrast to democracy (Fischer, 1990; Martin, 2005), or even seen to harbour an inherent preference for authoritarian rule (Meynaud, 1968; Putnam, 1977). Although basically confirming this point, Figure 1 also highlights that the matter is not one of direct regime competition, but rather indifference and an orthogonal relationship between regime types and their underlying forms of political authority. Just as with bureaucracy, technocracy is capable, in principle at least, of operating in conjunction with both democratic and autocratic forms of rule. This is not meant to downplay the sometimes radical anti-democratic sentiments of technocrats. It is, however, necessary to emphasize that the assumption of an inherent gravitation towards authoritarian rule is misconstrued and, more importantly in relation the new technocracy, that the technocratic approximation to democratic rule may present an equally important but different set of problems. Nevertheless, the conflict between technocracy and democracy is a reasonable place to start.

Technocratic decision-making can of course assume the form of more or less wholesale abandonment of representative democracy and its key institutions. However, this is clearly not the modus operandi of technocracy in most advanced democracies. Under these conditions, the problem is rather that technocracy seeks to short-circuit *deliberative* democracy through a mode of communication that 'severs the criteria for justifying the organization of social life from any normative regulation of interaction, thus depoliticizing them' (Habermas, 1971: 112). This conflict can be seen, first, as a contrast between the technocratic model and a pragmatic model of reciprocal communication and critical interaction between politics and expertise (Habermas, 1971: 67). Second, it appears as a conflict between instrumental/purposive-rational action ('system') and symbolic interaction, intersubjectively shared ordinary language, emancipation and the extension of communication free of domination ('lifeworld') (Habermas, 1971: 93). Technocratic depoliticization thus works against the grain of deliberative democracy by blocking the public exercise of reciprocal communication and the necessary test of technical solutions against practical experience, values and needs of ordinary citizens – and vice versa – in the public sphere. Technocrats exert 'minimal efforts to reveal details of measures taken to those concerned and obtain their consent' (Meynaud, 1968: 59).

The conflict between depoliticization and deliberative democracy can also assume a more direct form in the shape of technocratic preference for exclusion of the public, discretionary power and outright secrecy. In short: 'convinced of his infallibility, the technocrat is a skilled hand at closed politics' (Meynaud, 1968: 59). This may of course be a bit of stereotype, but even if technocrats may not always be entirely convinced of their infallibility, the aversion towards public deliberation and inclusion of the public are rather consistent features. The institutionalized technocracy of the French Grand Corps once again provides the basic template for this line of argument: the Corps are institutional forums for reasoned exchange between professionals enjoying extensive insulation from public and political interference: the system relies on measurement and quantification in order to provide an administrative elite with the numbers necessary to exercise 'expert judgement and general managerial skills' with a significant degree of discretion and even secrecy (Porter, 1995: 146). A similar reasoning lies behind the interpretation of committee systems as an institutional expression of technocracy and the extensive reliance on 'comitology' in the EU as one its technocratic pillars (Wallace & Smith, 1995; Martin, 2005). In a techno-bureaucracy, decision-making is still submitted to basic bureaucratic standards of documentation, some degree of transparency and conditional access, but this should not cloud the fact that technocracy resides in basic conflict with a strong democratic principle of publicity.

The second source of conflict between technocracy and democracy is elitism. The relationship between democracy and elitism is of course essentially contested in its own right. Although classical elite theory can largely be seen as an argument about the reality of oligarchy vs the utopia of democracy, democratic elite theory holds that elitism and democracy are not in conflict or that they may even be mutually constitutive. The primary function of elections and public assemblies, from this perspective, is to identify and appoint the most talented leaders. In other words, democratic elections are simply a form of meritocratic appointment, which means that any perceived conflict between democratically elected technocrats and standards of broader popular representation vanish. In a more expanded version of the argument, democracy is seen as means to achieve a balanced alternative to consolidated oligarchies through elite autonomy and elite circulation (Etzioni-Halevy, 1993). However, it is also largely undisputed that democratic elitism views democracy in rather minimalist representative and electoral terms, making few or no claims about the value of extended inclusion, participation and self-government.

In this respect, the technocratic preference for meritocracy and some measure of oligarchy is a source of conflict with democracy. Technocracy generally favours meritocratic appointment over popular representation and the rule of the few over inclusive participation. Indeed, Young's satirical analysis *The Rise of the Meritocracy* (1958) can be read as a critique on a society and educational system adapted to technocratic principles in this respect. Straightforward displacement of popular representation by meritocratic appointment is, of course, one of the most clear-cut examples of substitution of democracy for technocratic rule. The problem is further exacerbated if meritocratic appointment hardens into a consolidated oligarchy: a fully fledged and enduring oligarchy of scientific experts is no less undemocratic than an oligarchy of military leaders or business tycoons (both of which are certainly more common than technocratic oligarchies). In this way, the councils, committees and cabinets found in the various utopian blueprints for technocratic government bear a strong resemblance to institutionalized oligarchy.

Even if the preference for meritocracy and some measure of oligarchy is not fully implemented, it remains incompatible with *participatory* and direct democracy. Whereas elitism and representative democracy can be mediated in various ways, elitism and participatory democracy remain in fundamental conflict since the latter is rooted in the particular and more demanding ideal of self-government. Elitism, however defined and practised, involves a fundamental distinction between governing elites and the broader public, which cannot be reconciled with a standard of self-government. This conflict is especially central in populist counter-reactions to technocracy. In academic terms, analyses of populism often emphasize its foundations in ideals of broad popular engagement in politics and a communitarian vision of democracy (Goodwyn, 1978). This is clearly not to say that populist rhetoric should be confused with democratic theory, but beyond the highly questionable political tactics based on the elite/people distinction, a material conflict remains between technocratic elitism and extensive popular participation in politics.

The relationship between technocracy and democracy is historically variable, but the transition from industrial to post-industrial technocracy nevertheless involves a rather distinct trend: in the place of earlier staunch rejections of technocracy, the new technocracy more or less consistently declares its full support of democracy and even its ambition to further and strengthen democracy through increased stakeholder involvement, reflexivity and accountability. Indeed, these bids for democratic legitimacy directly challenge the idea of an inherent conflict with the standards of public deliberation and participation. Rather than overt anti-politics, secrecy and discretion, the new technocracy purports to increase transparency, accountability and the public exercise of reflexivity. In parallel fashion, the blatant rejection of public participation is replaced by increased stakeholder involvement and inclusion of non-state actors in the policy process. The democratic value of stakeholder involvement, reflexivity or accountability are, however, questionable at best.

Rather than strong democratic standards, they represent an attempt to move the yardsticks of technocracy and democracy closer together in a new claim to the 'output' legitimacy of technocratic rule. Through this development, strong democratic standards are effectively dissolved in broader concepts of legitimacy through the formulation and implementation of necessary and efficient policies. Indeed, this development has been helped along by staunch critics of old technocracy situated within or at the margins of the new governance, who in turn have become supporters of the new technocracy. The point is not that the technocratic embrace of technocracy is merely a matter of strategic lip service and strategic communication. The new technocracy *is*, by and large, more open, inclusive, reflexive and accountable than earlier technocracy. However, this should not cloud the fact that this still falls well short of democracy. Claims about democratic technocracy remain inherently problematic and should be treated with caution and a critical attitude accordingly.

In conjunction with the relationship to bureaucracy, we thus have a simultaneous change in regime relations: from pro-bureaucracy and anti-democracy to anti-bureaucracy and pro-democracy. This has, in turn, given rise to the line of argument found everywhere in the new technocracy: less bureaucracy means more democracy and vice versa. This is certainly not just a technocratic invention, but resonates all the way back to Weber's own reservations about the non-democratic nature of bureaucracy. However, this logic also dispenses with the long co-evolution of bureaucracy and democracy and the important working relationship and division of labour between embodied by the *Rechtsstaat* and the decisionistic model. Moreover, the inverse relationship between bureaucracy and democracy also rests on the idea that technocracy can be taken out of the equation. Once alerted to the presence of technocracy in the equation, however, it also becomes apparent that less bureaucracy, at least when it comes to most of the new governance, simply means more technocracy. Before this argument can be developed in more detail, we need briefly to consider the relation between the technocratic regime and political ideology.

Regime and ideology: technocracy and the Third Way

The relation between political regimes and political ideologies is, of course, a subject of considerable debate. One view is that political ideologies can be viewed as regimes in their own right, or at least as the principal source of regime classification (see, for example, Esping-Andersen, 1990; Jessop, 2002; Geddes, 2005). None of the four regimes already discussed, however, are direct expressions of political ideology in this way. However, the relationship between ideology and the four regimes is an intimate and dynamic one, as evidenced by the long tradition of research in the role of political ideologies and movements in the historical back-and-forth between democracy and autocracy. Along similar lines, both bureaucracy and technocracy have been seen to express specific ideological predispositions, or at least to thrive better under some ideological configurations than others. In other words: does technocracy display a particular ideological orientation or bias?

In general, my answer is no. Rather the opposite: technocracy thrives beyond ideology. As such, the anti-ideological stance of technocracy should, broadly speaking, be taken at face value rather as a cover-up for a particular ideological orientation. The optimal technocratic position is always 'beyond' political ideology, as defined by the 'apolitical ideology' of technical and scientific expertise (Fischer, 1990: 21). The technocratic project is strongly opposed to the established ideologies of parliamentary and party politics, attempting instead to substitute traditional politics with the 'politics of expertise' and depoliticized decisions presented as necessary interventions above political contestation and debate (Fischer, 1990: 26). In Habermas' original outline of this argument: technocracy may be less apparently 'repressive' and less relevant for a critique of ideology than the conventional list of grand ideologies, but the abstraction from questions of practical experience and social forces also make the technocratic 'fetish of science' functionally equivalent to an ideology insofar as it even more efficiently impedes broad political thought, reflection and debate about the foundations of society (1971: 111).

In the real world of party politics and parliamentary democracy, however, this position beyond ideology is always subject to compromises with political ideology. In this way, it is of course possible to look for a particular ideological imprint on technocratic decisions. Moreover, the technocratic preference for comprehensive management and social engineering can be seen to come with a certain ideological gravitation in itself. In general, however, there is a more apparent and important result of the technocratic attempt to establish a position a beyond ideology: the natural affinity between this position and Third Way politics. Due to its inherent scientism and progressivism, technocracy is, more or less by definition, opposed to conservatism. However, technocrats have historically not only been able to migrate between socialism and liberalism, but also to take an active role in engineering the great compromise between the two main ideologies of the modern era (I am setting aside the question of the relation between socialism and communism here for pragmatic reasons.). For all their apparent differences, socialism and liberalism are both deeply modern ideologies with affinities for scientific rationalism and progressivism, rooted in the problems and potentials of industrial society.

The idea that industrial technocracy is broadly aligned with socialism is rather widespread – for good reason. The most prominent technocrats of the French Revolution were 'Techno-Jacobins'. Saint-Simon's vision of a society based on the principles of industry is considered a monument in technocratic as well as utopian socialist thought. More generally, the particular institutionalization of technocracy in France seems difficult to disengage from the history of French socialism. The second technocratic revolution in the United States coincided with the progressive era and Veblen's technocratic bible is certainly a critique of capitalism on the broader family tree of socialist thought (Akin, 1977; Segal, 1985; Tilman, 2014). Scientific management also played a significant role in Lenin's thought and Soviet socialism in general, although not without controversy (Sochor, 1981), and Bell characterized Marxism as a great source of technocratic thought (1973: 354). Post-war technocracy has, for its part, has been associated with 'advanced' or 'developed' Soviet socialism (Hoffmann & Laird, 1985; Kelley, 1986), and even the cultural revolution in China (Andreas, 2009). Although each of these cases present their own particularities and context, they seem also suggest a particular affinity between socialism/communism and the inherent emphasis on social planning and engineering in industrial technocracy. In the case of the Soviet Union and China, this argument clearly overlaps with the assumption of an inherent gravitation towards authoritarian rule, but the logic also extends to welfare state expansion in social democracies.

It is equally possible, however, to make a case for an association between industrial technocracy and liberalism, as evidenced in particular by the history of American technocracy. Technocratic thinking may have overlapped with various spurts of socialism in the United States, particularly during the second technocratic revolution, but it seems a far stretch to suggest that technocratic influence is or has been dependent more generally on an alliance with socialism. American technocracy does not work against but with the grain of liberalism. In a wider sense, this argument rests on an understanding of liberalism as being equally invested in the governmental exercise of (post-)industrial management in accordance with the demands of (post-)industrial society, production and innovation. Liberalism is, as stated by Walter Lippmann in *The Good Society*, 'the philosophy of the industrial revolution, and its objective is to adapt the social order to the new mode of production' (1937: 238). As Lippmann goes on to say, however, liberalism is also only a partially developed philosophy in this respect, beset with errors. Lippmann's attempt to correct these errors and set the agenda for a more active and intervening form of liberalism can be considered a founding moment in the development of *neoliberalism*.

Neoliberalism, thus understood, begins with the fundamental 'social problem' of the 'maladjustment' of the social order to the 'inexorable law of the industrial revolution', the industrial mode of production and its division of labour (Lippmann, 1937: 209). The proposition that this problem had to be given the same central position in liberalism that it already enjoyed in socialism is what forced liberalism into a development towards *neo*liberalism. On the one hand, this exercise clearly involves a staunch rejection of the answers provided by socialism, communism or any other form of 'collectivism', up to and including the New Deal, relying on extensive social planning and control of the economy. On the other hand, however, a new liberal agenda would also have to abandon traditional laissez-faire liberalism. Faced with the 'inexorable law' of the industrial revolution, laissez-faire amounts to little more than an 'obscurantist' and 'pedantic principle of public policy' and an 'imaginary' market system of classical economics, which have 'sterilized liberalism and turned it into a defense of the status quo' (Lippmann, 1937: 204). An adequate liberal agenda, by contrast, would involve considerable governmental activity, intervention and extensive reforms in areas such as education, social insurance, public investments and service, improvements of markets and so on that are 'radical in relation to the social order and conservative in relation to the economy and division of labor' (Lippmann, 1937: 232).

The Good Society is crucial not only because of its content, but also because it was the immediate occasion for the so-called 'Walter Lippmann colloquium' held in Paris in 1938, which gathered a number of distinguished thinkers for a discussion of Lippmann's call for a new liberal agenda (Reinhoudt & Audier, 2018). As proposed by Lippmann, the starting point for the colloquium was the question of how to develop an alternative to the socialist idea of the planned economy, seen as the common root of an authoritarian tendency in Nazi Germany, the Soviet Union, New Deal America and United Kingdom at the time of the Beveridge Plan (Foucault, 2008: 111). However, opinions were divided on the proper liberal alternative to socialist industrialism. On the one hand, colloquium participants such as Raymond Aron and the Germans Wilhelm Röpke and Alexander Rüstow (the latter being the alleged author of the concept of neoliberalism) sided with Lippmann's agenda. On the other hand, participants such as Friedrich Hayek and Ludwig von Mises rather saw a form of purified or radicalized laissez-faire as the key to a renewal of liberalism, rescuing classical liberalism from the practical politics that had supposedly deformed it (Dardot & Laval, 2013).

The later formation of the Mount Pèlerin Society in 1947 provided a more institutionalized forum for expansion of the agenda originally coined in the Lippmann colloquium (Mirowski & Plehwe, 2009). For a time, the two camps can even be said to rally under the same banner and maintain a degree of theoretical and practical proximity (Dardot & Laval, 2013: 73). However, the two camps have also given rise to rather different trajectories. The laissez-faire camp of Mises and Hayek came to exercise great influence on the type of anarcho-liberalism that is more commonly associated with Anglo-American neoliberalism and Chicago school economics today. With Rüstow and Röpke as central figures, the more intervening and social liberalism came to play a significant role in post-war German 'ordoliberalism' and 'the social market economy', and by extension also in the blueprint for what was to become the EU (Bulmer & Paterson, 2013; Siems & Schnyder, 2014). While the former represents a form of market fundamentalism associated with highly ideological neoliberalism, the latter is essentially a form of Third Way politics. Indeed, the social market economy and German ordoliberalism constitute a pervasive compromise between socialism and liberalism both in the abstract and in the practical sense.

In the same manner that later variations of the Third Way politics have been accused of being highly skewed towards the liberal side, the social market economy clearly also rests on a fundamental acceptance of what the ordoliberals (inspired by legal theory) call the 'economic constitution' of the market economy vis-à-vis the planned economy. However, Third Way liberalism also remains decisively different from laissez-faire liberalism. This point has been developed in particular detail by Foucault in his analysis of neoliberalism as a form of governmental rationality and practice derived from the 'positive' and 'social' liberalism of German ordoliberalism, which is 'active, vigilant and intervening in a way that neither the classical liberalism of the nineteenth century or the contemporary American anarcho-capitalism could accept' (Foucault, 2008: 133). This difference, in turn, leads Foucault to conclude that: 'we should not be under any illusion that today's neo-liberalism is, as is too often said, the resurgence or recurrence of old forms of liberal economics … now being reactivated by capitalism for a variety of reasons to do with its omnipotence and crisis' (Foucault, 2008: 117).

Neoliberalism, rather, is shaped by the agenda found in Lippmann's original draft, German ordoliberalism and ultimately Third Way politics in the modern centrist tradition of Schröder, Clinton and Blair. This is clearly a contested viewpoint. In his examination of the 'strange non-death' of neoliberalism, Colin Crouch states that ordoliberalism can largely be dismissed since it does 'not realistically describe today's economy. Chicago, for all its defects, does do that' (Crouch, 2011: 165). Nevertheless, Foucault makes a convincing case for the ideological compromise of the Third Way as a historical condition for the emergence of a type of 'omnipresent' government that, reflecting Lippmann's agenda more or less to the letter, combines the principles of a 'light' intervention in the market and 'heavy' intervention in civil society, national society and the 'social factors which now increasingly become the object of governmental intervention' (Foucault, 2008: 141). The 'anti-government' sentiments of market fundamentalism and laissez-faire clearly also influence politics and policy, but 'omnipresent' government may well be more important. In any event, we are left with two forms of liberalism, neither of which are opposed to technocracy. Rather the opposite.

The liberal opposition to planning should not be confused for an opposition towards technocracy in the sense of (post-)industrial management, social engineering, scientism and so forth. Both liberal camps declare their opposition to planning readily and repeatedly, but planning here simply means the planned economy in a narrow sense. Both anarcho-liberalism and ordoliberalism are clearly 'constitutionally' opposed to the planned economy. However, their respective alternatives provide ample space for technocratic management and influence. The principal difference between the two forms of liberalism in this respect is that anarcho-liberalism rests more or less exclusively on the market, which in effect may mean transferral of power to big corporations (Crouch, 2011), whereas social liberalism can be seen to involve a more expansive and intervening art of omnipresent government. While the former largely corresponds to a restricted form of economic technocracy (econocracy), which relies almost exclusively on economic scientism and sides more or less directly with traditional liberal ideology and economics, the latter involves a more expansive and omnipresent form of technocratic management defined by the fundamental problem of adjusting the social order to the iron law of industrial revolutions.

The latter form of omnipresent government is, as I have elaborated elsewhere, the fundamental logic behind the transition from government to governance (Esmark, 2018). Omnipresent government, in the terms of the more popular credo, means 'minimum government, maximum governance'. This is an art of government that is particularly conducive to technocratic principles. Indeed, omnipresent government rests on a deep and pervasive opposition to the type of 'disciplinary government' found in *raison d'état* and its bureaucratic 'police' administration 'almost term by term' (Foucault, 2007: 347). Disciplinary government ultimately rests on a fundamental opposition between security and freedom, leading to a detailed regulation of the nation and individual citizens in order to carefully develop and balance the population as a system of forces. Omnipresent government, by contrast, is structured around a basic 'game' of freedom and security where freedom is governmentally increased, managed and guided as a 'correlative of the deployment of apparatuses or security' (Foucault, 2007: 48). This game of freedom and security is, at one and the same time, opposed to bureaucracy (at least as an instrument of disciplinary government) and aligned with democracy (at least as doctrine of freedom).

From regime to public policy: a model of the new technocracy

The basic dimensions of technocracy are governmental managerialism, technological progressivism, social engineering, scientism and depoliticization of political decisions. These attributes imply an opposition to bureaucracy when technocracy lays claim to a position of pure rationality within the political system. Moreover, they provide technocracy with a basic indifference to the choice between democracy and autocracy, making technocracy capable of working in lockstep with both. Finally, technocracy is ideologically flexible, at least when it comes to the issue of socialism versus liberalism, but always strives for a position beyond ideology and flourishes under the conditions of this position represented by the Third Way and neoliberalism (as defined in the preceding section). Within these 'constants', however, the technocratic regime has also changed significantly from industrial techno-bureaucracy to a new compromise with democracy against bureaucracy. This development does not fundamentally challenge the constitutive dimensions of the technocratic regime, but it does make the opposition to bureaucracy and new claims to legitimacy a part of the technocratic art of government and its matrix of generalized and regular expectations about the authority of collectively binding decisions.

This reversal of the original technocratic formula is the decisive difference between industrial technocracy and a post-industrial technocracy immersed in the structures and dynamics of network society, risk society and the (somewhat transformed) knowledge society.

This analysis is developed in full in the next three chapters. In general, the argument follows Bell's original proposition that the political system becomes increasingly technocratic with the advance of post-industrial society. However, the analysis also breaks away from the idea that the effect of post-industrial development is a belated realization of technocracy much as it was conceived in its original industrial incarnation. This has to do with the fact that Bell's analysis sought to grasp the basic structures and dynamics of post-industrial society in the midst of what was effectively advanced industrialism. Correspondingly, we have to revise the analysis in light of the emergence of network society, risk society and the transformation of knowledge society, which in turn gives rise to a more decisively post-industrial version of the technocratic regime. This development has taken place since the 1980s, and it is most pronounced in countries that have proceeded furthest along the curve of post-industrial development.

This revised version of Bell's original hypothesis gives priority to technological development and innovation, in particular ICT and informational networks, as a source of increased regime competition and change in the political system. Even if the development of ICT and proliferation of informational networks have been rather rapid judged by the standards of technological innovation, the informational revolution is still a slow and fundamental structural trend that can only be viewed appropriately in a prolonged historical perspective. By comparison, even deep and long-lasting trends such as global economic forces are more cyclical and short term. Even though socio-economic forces and events such as fiscal crises do have significant effects on public policy, they also take place *within* the more fundamental advance of network society, risk society and knowledge society. These three societal configurations comprise a set of global forces that are more directly related to technological development, more fundamental and more one-directional than other forces such as market integration, trade liberalization, increased global competition and so on.

As Bell emphasizes, however, the focus on technology is not meant to suggest technological determinism. Rather, technology enters into a dynamic relation with social behaviours, patterns and institutions. Technocratic reform and influence tend to increase during periods of rapid technological progress, but technological innovation and change is merely a window of opportunity that does not predetermine a specific outcome. Out of this broader socio-technological approach, the ensuing analysis rests on an abstraction of three key relationships between technology and, respectively, *organization*, *regulation* and *calculation*. Each of these relationships constitutes a particular dimension of interplay between technological change and social and political transformation. On the societal level, this is encapsulated in distinct structures and dynamics of network society, risk society and knowledge society. On the political level, the three dimensions capture distinct processes of transformation of state, government and the political system. States are clearly not helpless victims of the challenges of network society, risk society and knowledge society, but also active co-sponsors and co-developers of post-industrial society. Or, put differently: technocratic 'regimes also support the further development of the conditions that created them' (Centeno, 1993: 316).

The principal architect of this development has been the new governance. Following the trajectories from technology to organization, regulation and calculation, the new governance has provided the current configuration of the technocratic regime with three intersecting policy paradigms:

- In the domain of organization, the new technocracy pursues *an imperative but difficult transition to the network state* and the exercise of *network management* linking interests, identities, forms of knowledge and resources in the face of changes brought about by new ICTs, digitalization and the proliferation of informational networks in the network society.
- In the domain of regulation, the new technocracy is defined by the *internalization of risk and the impossibility of insurance against harm and uncertainty* and the exercise of *risk management* ensuring constant organizational change, adaptation and flexibility in the face of increasing complexity, uncertainty and wicked problems in risk society.
- As for the practices of *calculation*, measurement and provision of scientific knowledge, the new technocracy is defined by the paradigm of *learning from evidence and the continuous improvement of policy* and the exercise of *performance management* ensuring evidence, learning, accountability and experimentation in knowledge society.

Taken together, this amounts to the overview of the current technocratic regime seen in Figure 2.

If the hallmarks of early technocracy were appropriation of large-scale bureaucracies, safety through prudent foresight and rules, and the creation of extensive planning systems, the hallmarks of the new technocracy are connective governance, risk management and performance management. Each of these paradigms have, in their

Figure 2: The policy paradigms of the New Technocracy

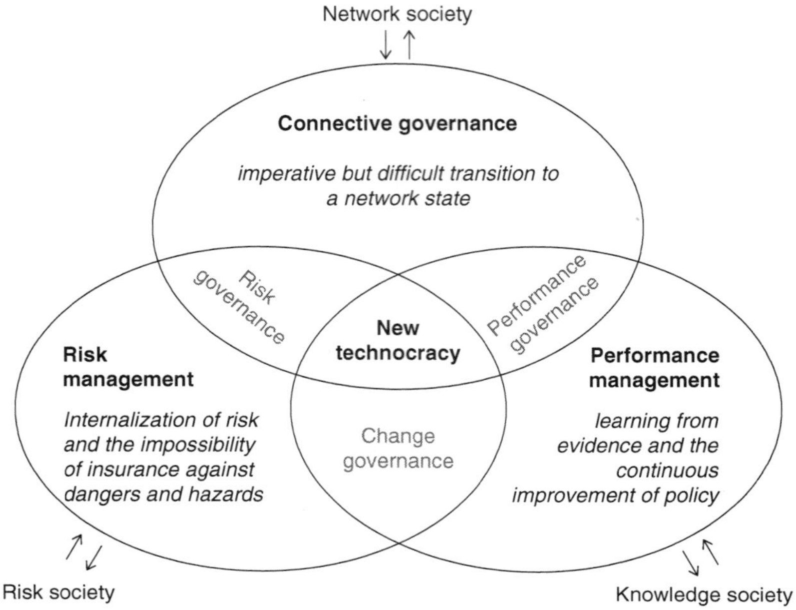

Network society
↓ ↑

Connective governance

*imperative but difficult transition to
a network state*

Risk governance

**New
technocracy**

Performance governance

**Risk
management**

*Internalization of risk
and the impossibility
of insurance against
dangers and hazards*

Change
governance

**Performance
management**

*learning from
evidence and the
continuous
improvement of policy*

↗↙
Risk society

↙↗
Knowledge society

distinct ways, contributed to the overall reversal from a technocratic compromise with bureaucracy against democracy to a compromise with democracy against bureaucracy: the new technocracy is more connective, informational, open and accountable in the domain of organization,; more adaptive, reflexive and even 'ironic' in the domain of regulation; and more innovative, learning and experimental in the domain of calculation. In this way, the intersecting principles of network, risk and performance management provide the new technocracy with an alternative to industrial technocracy. This is not to say, however, that the new technocracy has abandoned managerialism, technological progressivism, social engineering, scientism or depoliticization. All of these technocratic principles are, however, brought to bear on government and public policy in a rather different way by the new technocracy.

Conclusion

In a critical analysis of industrial technocracy during its golden years, the following guideline is proposed: 'if a political system is becoming increasingly technocratic, the change should occur in the decision rules which apply to the formulation, implementation and evaluation of policy' (Straussman, 1978: 25). In this way, the broader issue of regime competition and change within the parameters already outlined can be observed more specifically as a matter of the relative weight given to technocratic vis-à-vis bureaucratic and/or democratic decision rules in the development and implementation of public policy. Whereas Straussman only found partial evidence of a more technocratic political system, my argument in the ensuing chapters is that the current political system is indeed highly technocratic. There is, of course, also a methodological difference here: while Straussman looked for formal institutional changes and the numbers of technocrats found in the public bureaucracy, I look for broader policy paradigms as an operational expression of highly general art of government. My slightly revised guideline of analysis is thus that the degree to which the political system is becoming more technocratic can be observed in the constitutive principles and forms of legitimization that drive the formulation, implementation and evaluation of public policy, across and above specific policy sectors. This is what the next three chapters are about.

5

Technocratic Organization:
The Power of Networks

From Brussels to Silicon Valley, coping with the failures of
technocratic rule.

(Shahbaz, 2018)

What really happened in the 1980s?

The fourth and latest technocratic revolution begins in the 1980s,
a decade usually recognized as a watershed in political history for
reasons such as Thatcher, Reagan, the end of Keynesian economic
policy and the mixed economy, welfare state retrenchment, the fall
of the Berlin Wall, the end of history and so forth. In one way or
another, the common narrative of the key events in the 1980s is the
rise of liberalism, less state and more market, or at least the acceptance
of free market capitalism as the limit of the state. The most decisive
technocratic event of the 1980s, however, had little to do with changes
in the balance of power in a zero–sum game between state and market,
but rather with a third form of organization: the network. Recalling
the general observation that technocratic revolutions occur during
times of rapid technological innovation and progress, the importance
of the 1980s lies rather in the onset of the information age and the
emergence of network society. Of course, no type of society or
social order arrives fully packaged within the span of a decade, but in
hindsight it is reasonable to view the 1980s as the decisive step towards
a situation where:

> the network society is not the future that we must reach
> as the next stage of human progress by embracing the

new technological paradigm. It is our society, in different degrees, and under different forms depending on countries and cultures. Any policy, any strategy, any human project, has to start from this basic fact. It is not our destination, but our point of departure to wherever 'we' want to go, be it heaven, hell, or just a refurbished home. (Castells, 2005: 12)

Many of the key technological innovations were of course in place much earlier, and the embryonic informational revolution was, as noted by Bell and many others, already under way in the immediate aftermath of the Second World War. It is only 'since the mid-1980s', however, that 'microcomputers cannot be conceived of in isolation: they perform in networks, with increasing mobility' (Castells, 2010a: 43). Innovations in digital ICT leads to a fundamental transformation of the 'world of media' and proliferation of interactive networks (Castells, 2010a: 365), which in turn leads to a 'substantial process of economic and organizational restructuring' in the 'major corporations and governments' in the leading countries of the world, also during the 1980s (Castells, 2010a: 60). At the most fundamental level, the drastically increased network capacity produced by the informational revolutions start to change the very spatio-temporal fabric of society during the 1980s creating a new 'space of flows' defined by the connectivity of global networks, as opposed to the 'space of places' defined by geographical locality (Castells, 2010a: 407) and a new temporality of 'timeless time', immediacy and simultaneity (Castells, 2010a: 460).

What does all of this mean for technocracy? Bell offered no reflections on his original hypothesis about the rise of technocracy in post-industrial society in his (partial and reserved) acceptance of the changes brought about by the informational revolution since his original forecasting. Castells, for his part, has not made any distinct claims about this logic. However, his extensive analysis of the constitutive technologies behind the informational revolution does suggest that its key innovations and entrepreneurs embody a combination of countercultural values and an element of 'technocratic culture' (Castells, 2010a: 387). This is, of course, where Silicon Valley comes into the picture: it was and still is the most important hub for technological innovation in the network society, and it has shaped the technological progressivism of the informational revolution more than any other entrepreneurial milieu (Morozov, 2013). Just as the mechanical engineers placed themselves as the spearhead of earlier industrial revolutions, the information engineers of Silicon Valley now represent the avant-garde of post-industrial innovation, organization and techno-utopianism. Indeed, a conservative critic of the 'folly of the technocratic elite' has referred to the entrepreneurs of Silicon Valley simply as 'Bacon's Bastards', wrongly believing that their 'algorithms will save the world' (Beran, 2017).

In the end, however, the entrepreneurs and information engineers of Silicon Valley and elsewhere are simply an addition to the technostructure. The informational revolution has not brought about the rule of technical engineers any more than previous revolutions. The particular nature of the new informational infrastructure of society may place technical engineers in more vital positions of control and/or disruption of the techno-economic system (hacking and shutting down), but this does not translate into political influence per se and certainly not a new age of technocratic rule. The political influence of Zuckerberg, Bezos, Page, Brin and other tech chief executive officers, for their part, is not substantially different from that of Vanderbilt. Their business model and the nature of the critical infrastructure they control may be different, and their immediate impact on everyday lives may well be more pervasive, but they are nevertheless members of the economic elite interacting with politics and state in the usual manner of business tycoons. The informational revolution may have its own ranks of progressive engineers shaped by countercultural values, entrepreneurial capitalism and high-tech progressivism, but political influence from within the political system is still restricted to techno-bureaucrats and technopols.

This is then what takes us from Silicon Valley to Brussels, as suggested by the research director of Freedom House at the opening of this chapter. For all their apparent differences, Facebook and the EU are both technocratic network organizations placing 'enormous confidence on top-down technocratic governance' (Shahbaz, 2018). Half a century apart, both organizations where founded on the idea of creating technological infrastructures linking productive forces across borders, and today the original network logic of the EU and the logic of informational networks incarnated by Facebook have to a large degree become part of the same overall policy paradigm of network organization. With a formulation coined by Castells, the core of this paradigm can be summed in the principle of an *imperative but difficult transition to a network state*. This is then where we find the more general implication for the original correlation between post-industrial society and technocracy suggested by Bell. As post-industrial society becomes a fully fledged network society, technocracy becomes increasingly invested in network management and ultimately the creation of a network state, resulting in the first and fundamental trajectory from government to governance.

In essence, the imperative but difficult transition to a network state suggests a necessary transformation from the nation-state to a new form of state and statehood in accordance with the new challenges and potentials of network society. As such, it does not imply the complete abandonment of the state, but rather a type of state fundamentally embedded in and permeated by networks. Political decision-making and authority in the network state, correspondingly, depends on the extensive creation, utilization and management of flexible networks, opening up the state to informational flows and cooperation with multiple stakeholders. For the same reason, the creation of a network state inevitably comes into conflict with bureaucratic organization, now seen as a quintessentially industrial and outdated form of organization. Indeed, network organization is essential to the new technocratic partnership with democracy against bureaucracy.

The end of hierarchy? Technology and social organization

Although industrial revolutions are ultimately created by technological innovations, they also take place in an interplay between technology and social organization: the first industrial revolution linked the creation of steam power energy with factories as a basic form of social organization (Bell, 1999: 33). The same logic can be applied to subsequent industrial revolutions up to and including the emergence of post-industrial society. The interplay between technology and social organization constitutes a basic matrix of social actions and decisions that reverberate throughout society. Proceeding from this starting point (and indeed the specific example mentioned by Bell), the network society can be understood as the result of 'the interaction between the new technological paradigm and social organization at large' (Castells, 2005: 3). This is essentially the relationship between the informational revolution and the network society: ICT innovations reshape society according to the organizational morphology of networks.

The new technological paradigm thus arrives with the digital 'transformation of communication technology', which 'extends the reach of communication media to all domains of social life in a network that is at the same time global and local, generic and customized in an ever-changing pattern' (Castells, 2007: 239). On one level, the arrival of digital ICTs simply marks the beginning of another phase in the well-established history of innovations in media technology: the printing press, the telegraph, telephone, radio and TV (van Dijk, 2006). However, the arrival of digital ICTs also means that media technology, for the first time, becomes something else and more important than machine technology. Whereas 'old' media were essentially extensions of mechanical machine technology, the digital nature of 'new' media constitutes a different order of technology that overtakes and incorporates mechanical machine technology as the lead technology of society. Digital media not only involves a leap in the capacity for communication and exchange of information: they create a new technological infrastructure on which everything else increasingly depends in network society.

Media and communication systems thus become the primary infrastructure of society: 'digital communication networks are the backbone of the network society, just as power networks (meaning energy networks) were the infrastructure on which industrial society was built' (Castells, 2005: 4). Whereas industrial society was primarily defined by technological revolutions in the realm of transportation and energy systems, the informational revolution means that communication now becomes the 'major mode of connection between people' and the basic 'mode of transaction' (Bell, 1999: 46). The implications of this technological revolution extends to major societal domains: 'wealth, power, and knowledge generation are largely dependent on the ability to reap the benefits of the new technological system, rooted in microelectronics, computing and digital communication, with its growing connection to the biological revolution and its derivative, genetic engineering' (Castells, 2005: 3).

The new informational infrastructure of network society is not only materially different from energy and/or transportation infrastructures: it also involves a drastic increase in network capacity that reorients society increasingly towards the social morphology of networks. Networks are, of course, an old and even primary form of social organization. However, the informational revolution provides network organization with new capabilities. While networks may always have been a highly adaptable and flexible form of organization, their major weakness has been the inability to scale up and coordinate resources beyond a certain point of size and complexity. Hence, the world of production, power and war came to be dominated by large, vertically integrated bureaucratic organizations with the advance of industrialization, whereas networks were largely relegated to the smaller communities of the private domain. The energy and transportation networks of industrial society, simply put, did not function as social form of organization in the basic sense, but rather as a correlate to bureaucratic organization. With the informational revolution, however, networks start to overcome their capacity problems, thus combining flexibility, adaptation and decentralized performance with a capacity for coordinated action and shared decision-making.

The development and spread of digital communication technology have drastically enhanced network building and network performance to the point where 'key social structures and activities are organized around electronically processed information networks' (Castells, 2001). This ability of the informational revolution to overcome earlier deficiencies of network organization makes the drastic increase in the connective capacity of networks the core socio-technological dynamic of network society. The key dimensions of network capacity include, inter alia, globalization (networks have the potential for global reach and reduce the importance of space and territory), openness (the organization of networks in nodes and hubs ensures multiple points of entry and continuous extension), flexibility (networks can be build and modified faster than other forms of organization), scalability (networks can be formed and reformed to suit any level of action or governance), complexity (networks represent a form of 'ordered complexity', making disordered complexity manageable), self-organization (networks can form and function without central or hierarchical guidance) and recursion (networks process information in a non-linear and modulating way) (Lash, 2002; Castells, 2005; Crozier, 2007; Chadwick, 2013).

These are not exactly attributes associated with bureaucracy. Indeed, bureaucratic organization is more or less a point-by-point contradiction of the capacities associated with network organization after the informational revolution. Bureaucracy is bound to a national/ local heritage and cannot be rescaled quickly or easily. Bureaucracy may be constitutionally bound by rules of publicity, but it also remains inherently committed to secrecy and non-disclosure. Bureaucratic procedures and hierarchical order-and-command stand in the way of flexibility and flow. Bureaucratic demands for centralization, oversight and control contradict self-governance. Bureaucracy has limited capacity to organize complexity and remains committed to a linear logic of information processing. Taken to its radical conclusion, this contrast between network organization and bureaucratic organization suggests that 'the rational bureaucratic model of the state is in complete contradiction to the demands and process of the network society' (Castells, 2005: 17). The solution to this problem is clear: an imperative but difficult transition from the rational bureaucratic model of the industrial state to a network state.

In a broader sense, the conflict between bureaucracy and network society reflects what has been called the 'end of power' and the rise of 'micropowers' (Naím, 2013). The core idea behind this view is that bureaucratic organization has lost its essential function for the consolidation and exercise of power in business, politics and war. The traditional mega-players of big business and global superpowers are being challenged by new micropowers that 'wear down, impede, undermine, sabotage, and outflank the mega-players in ways that the latter, for all their vast resources, find themselves ill-equipped and ill-prepared to resist' (Naím, 2013: 52). From guerrillas and insurgents to fringe political parties, innovative start-ups, hackers and loosely organized activists and upstart alternative media, the logic remains the same: the old advantages associated with integrated large-scale bureaucratic organization is giving way to the advantages of speed, flexibility, self-organization and so on. This change in the organizational basis of power: 'signals the exhaustion of the Weberian bureaucracy, the system of organization that delivered the benefits and also the tragedies of the twentieth century. *The decoupling of power from size, and thus the decoupling of the capacity to use power effectively from the control of a large Weberian bureaucracy, is changing the world*' (Naím, 2013: 52, original emphasis).

The formulation may be a bit on the nose, but it also captures the idea of a fundamental conflict between bureaucracy and network society with considerable clarity. Although Naím's claim does not explicate this link, his conceptualization of key social transformations in the terms of a 'more revolution', a 'mobility revolution' and a 'mentality revolution' bears considerable resemblance to the emancipatory effects often attached to the informational revolution (2013: 72). Similarly, the micropowers and their organizational alternative to the large and supposedly defunct Weberian bureaucracy clearly seem to embody what has elsewhere been called 'network power' (Grewal, 2008). However, the 'end-of-power' thesis also paints a somewhat one-sided picture of state and government as a failing 'macropower' challenged from below. This is a narrative that is often heard more generally in popular discourse, and it is particularly pronounced in the techno-optimism of Silicon Valley technocrats and their proselytes: network society challenges the old order of macropowers and strengthens new and progressive micropowers. However, the decoupling of power from bureaucratic organization is not only taking place bottom-up or outside of the political system, but also top-down and inside the political system. The imperative but difficult transition to a network state is an expression of this, and it constitutes the core of the network paradigm of the new technocracy. However, this paradigm has to be seen in the wider context of the relationship between the economy, civil society and the state in network society.

From network society to the network state

As noted, Bell proved unwilling to concede that the informational revolution had fundamentally moved beyond the parameters of his original forecasting. Castells, not surprisingly, begs to differ: 'I propose to shift the analytical emphasis from *post-industrialism* (a relevant question of social forecasting, still without an answer at the moment of its formulation), to *informationalism*' (Castells, 2010a: 219, original emphasis). The broader argument here is that the network society is not simply a continuation of the patterns and trends observed by Bell, but a society defined through and through by the informational revolution and its diffusion in all spheres of economic and social activity. In what effectively amounts to a substitution of Bell's axial principle with a new post-industrial principle of informationalism, Castells thus holds that network society is fundamentally shaped by the proliferation of informational networks, enabled by the development and diffusion of information technologies. However, the contrast should not be overstated: the network society is indeed based on a new axial principle of informationalism, but in other respects it still displays similarities with the era of advanced industrialism, particularly in the economic system.

The economy

The first and most fundamental level of transformation in the network society is what Bell refers to as the techno-economic system. Reflecting the dimensions of analysis originally outlined by Bell, more or less to the letter, Castells maps out the contours of the new global economy, changes in business and enterprise models and the cluster of occupational, professional and educational patterns involved in the pervasive 'transformation of work' (Castells, 2010a: 216). In this domain, the principal contrast with advanced industrialism comes down to the fact that techno-economic system of network society no longer operates on the codification and proliferation of theoretical knowledge per se, but rather on the organization of the 'production system around the principles of maximizing knowledge-based productivity through the development and diffusion of information technologies, and by fulfilling the prerequisites for their utilization (primarily human resources and communication infrastructure)' (Castells, 2010a: 219–20). In other words, the old axial principle of knowledge-based productivity and growth is now being subsumed under and made dependent on the new axial principle of informationalism. By the same token, however, it also remains clear that the networked economy is still a knowledge economy.

The principal effect of the informational revolution on the techno-economic system is the emergence of global network economy. The global economy rests on certain macro-principles such as the free movement of goods, capital, people and services, but it is also realized on the national and regional level through particular strategies and policies of economic growth based on a commitment to: innovation based on generation and diffusion of new microelectronic/digital ICTs; scientific research, technological innovation and the transformation of organized labour into self-programmable human resources that can adapt constructively and creatively to a constantly changing global and local economy; and diffusion of a new form of management and organization around networking. It is only by fulfilling these conditions that a business, sector, region or country can generate continuous growth, innovation, productivity and 'sustain competitiveness in the long run' (Castells, 2005: 8). These are the essential features of what has become known in popular and policy discourse as the global economy, the new economy and the knowledge economy.

Taking issue both with the popular version of such concepts and Bell's more comprehensive discussion, however, Castells emphasizes that the decisive feature of the new economy is the proliferation of informational networks, prompting changes in the organizational and managerial principles of the business enterprise and systems of production. Surges in productivity and competitiveness depends not on knowledge per se, but through and through on network organization, which is 'as critical today as was the process of vertical integration of production in the large-scale organizations of the industrial era' (Castells, 2005: 8). Capital accumulation is still at the centre of network society alongside the development of ICT, but economic activity is increasingly performed by networks built around specific business projects. The firm continues to be the legal unit and the centre for accumulation of capital. Yet, the network is the operative unit. The firm is simply the connecting node between networks of production and networks of accumulation. In sum, the new network economy implies that: productivity and competitiveness are increasingly becoming a function of information processing in networks; firms and territories are organized in networks of production and communication; and core economic activities are basically global (Castells, 2010b: 77).

The new economy is thus defined by the arrival of networked production and innovation supplanting the industrial machinery of large-scale bureaucracies and accumulation of human resources that reached its peak under advanced industrialism. In the terms of the end-of-power thesis, this development is reflected in the declining macropowers of old industrial giants such as the Seven Sisters of the oil industry, the Big Four accounting firms (there were five before Arthur Andersen was implicated in the Enron scandal), the Big Three in the car industry and in television broadcasting, and even the two dominant computer companies at the dawn of the informational revolution (Naím, 2013: 159). While some firms with roots in the industrial economy are still going strong, tech giant and financial businesses have taken the lead in the global economy. However, the decreasing importance of big organization also means that the new giants as well as old ones are subject to a higher rate of turnover in business dominance and challenges to monopolization, albeit subject to important sectoral differences. Moreover, firms hailing from all over the world compete with each other and entrenched business regions and clusters. Although large or even giant multinationals are an apparent feature of the global economy, the constant challenge to established mega-players posed by micropowers puts corporate dominance under siege and accelerates the rise *and* fall of big businesses.

The new economy also fundamentally reshapes the opposition between capital and labour, perhaps the core principle of social organization in industrial society (Castells, 2005: 9). In the network economy, the opposition between capital and labour is, strictly speaking, dysfunctional because competitiveness and success rely on the ability of both parties to situate the interests they defend in the new forms of production and innovation. In the networked economy based on the primacy of creativity, flexibility and technological *savoir faire*, the workplace is no longer a site for organized conflict and punctuated equilibriums between wage and work, but a site nurtured and created by capital as an environment for the mutually beneficial self-development and self-fulfilment of the most desirable parts of the globally mobile workforce. The 'creative class' of global knowledge workers may be the vanguard of this new workforce, but the gradual erosion of the opposition between labour and capital also includes the more mundane part of the workforce willing 'to use their autonomy to be more productive if they have a vested interest in the competitiveness of the firm' (Castells, 2005: 11).

Civil society and social identity

If Bell's focus was on the techno-economic system (although he did rehearse the issue of 'culture' and his own growing conservatism more broadly in *The Cultural Contradictions of Capitalism* in 1978), the focus of Alain Touraine's contemporary analysis of post-industrialism was rather civil society, social movements and identity. Bridging between these two aspects of post-industrial society, Castells' analysis moves from the techno-economic system to the radical claim that the onset and consolidation of the information age are 'tantamount to the dissolution of [civil] society as a meaningful social system' (Castells, 2010b: 420). This claim is part of a broader argument about the transformation of social identity in network society, distinguishing three distinct types of identity and their corresponding forms of socialization, mobilization and political participation: legitimizing identities, resistance identities and project identities. From the vantage point of the political system, such identities are equivalent to different configurations of the public, citizens, laypeople and the political community interacting with political authorities through the political regime.

Legitimizing identities can generally be understood as mechanisms that link social actors to the institutionalized programmes and purposes of social institutions such as churches, parties, unions, civic associations and so on. On the one hand, legitimizing identities is thus an extension of institutional control and domination, instrumentalizing social actors in relation to institutional purpose. However, legitimizing identities are also the central component of social capital, trust and thick communities traditionally ascribed significant importance in democratic theory as a source of civic engagement and participation (Putnam, 2000). As such, legitimizing identities are what constitute civil society, understood both in its democratic meaning and as a rationalization of institutional and structural domination. The dissolution of civil society in the information age is, correspondingly, synonymous with the general erosion of legitimizing identities and their corresponding institutions. The traditional institutions and organizations of civil society that were built around the democratic state and around the social contract of labour and capital have become 'large empty shells', increasingly unable able to provide meaning to people's lives and so distant to the network processes and structures that really matter that they appear 'to most people as a sarcastic grimace on the new face of history' (Castells, 2010b: 420).

The dissolution of the legitimizing identities constructed around the democratic state and the industrial contract between capital and labour amounts to a pervasive loss of identity and belonging in the process of globalization. These dynamics are readily available in explanations of populism as a form of anti-globalism, fuelled not only by the detrimental effects of the new global economy but also by the decay of traditional civil society institutions. Continuing this line of argument, populism can be seen as a form of resistance identity. In the network society, such identities are founded on communal resistance rather than the reconstruction of the institutions of civil society, because 'the crisis of these institutions, and the emergence of resistance identities, originate precisely from the new characteristics of network society that undermine the former and induce the latter' (Castells, 2010b: 423). The structures and dynamics of the globally networked economy comes into conflict with the institutions and identities of a civil society deeply rooted in the industrial era. Following 'an old law of social evolution', however, 'resistance confronts domination' and 'alternative projects challenge the logic embedded in the new global order' (Castells, 2010b: 72).

In stark contrast to legitimizing identities and the institutional framework of civil society, resistance identities are networked and loosely organized social movements built on unequivocal commitment to the communal logic and sharp distinctions between in and out, us and them, which ultimately amounts to a form of identity politics (Castells, 2010b: 8). As a result, movements founded on a resistance identity 'barely communicate', neither with the state nor with each other, as it would potentially defy the strong oppositional logic and the sharp distinction between friends and enemies. On the one hand, such resistance identities include Alt-Right, PEGIDA and other movements founded a reassertion of traditional values of God, nation and the family, which are supposedly being flushed away by globalization, the dissolution of civil society and individualism. While this position is typically associated with the Right, resistance identities are equally found in the traditionally Left position of more or less radical anarchism, associated for example with Anonymous and the Occupy movement (Trottier & Fuchs, 2015).

The rise of resistance identities in the vacuum left by the dissolution of civil society and legitimizing identities is, broadly speaking, more a problem than a solution in network society. Although resistance identities follow a general and even necessary 'social law' of power and counter-power, they also tend to form isolated and antagonistic identities that do not glue together or offer much hope of reconstructing some measure of the cohesion delivered by the institutions and identities of civil society. The potential solution rests with project identities – identities created by social actors that seek to build a new identity that redefines their subjectivity or life in general, and by doing so seek to transform the overall social structure. The building of project identities creates subjects in the sense of collective actors through which individuals reach holistic meaning in their experience (Castells, 2010b: 8). Although such identities do not emerge from the former institutions of the civil society, but rather from the stratum of resistance identities, they offer the only form of identity capable of reconstructing 'a new civil society of sorts' (Castells, 2010b: 422). The trick is to turn the purely defensive and reactive struggle of resistance identities into a proactive of identities and movements invested in broader projects of social transformation to the benefit of inclusive subjects. The list of such identities and productive 'subjects of the information age' is open-ended, but includes, 'for the time being, ecologists, feminists, religious fundamentalists, nationalists, localists and the vast democratic movement that emerges as the coalition for global justice against capitalist globalization' (Castells, 2010b: 425).

Politics and the state

On the one hand, Bell's forecasting explicitly avoided deeper analysis of the political system and the state. On the other hand, however, it remained clear from the outset that post-industrial society would pose significant control and management problems for the political 'order' and the state (Bell, 1999). Indeed, this asymmetry between the dynamics of post-industrialism and the capacity of the political system is the underlying logic behind the belated realization hypothesis: faced with increasing control problems, the political system would have no choice but to rely increasingly on technocrats. This asymmetry is only exacerbated in network society: the globalization of the economy and what used to be civil society vis-à-vis the institutions and action horizon of the nation-state. It is this deepening asymmetry between network society and the nation-state that leads to the imperative but difficult transition to a network state: 'the actual operating unit of political management in a globalized world is a network state formed by nation-states, international institutions, associations of network states, regional and local governments, and non-governmental organization' (Castells, 2010b: 364).

This is not to say that the network state is the inevitable result of technological changes. The matrix of technology and social organization in network society has indeed shifted in a way that drives a transformation of the state and statehood, but the imperative and difficult creation of a network state is a process of transformation from government to governance that is equally shaped by the objectives, strategies, motives and decisions of state actors. The relation between network state and network society is a two-way street. In creating the network state, states are also creating and recreating network society. This is not to say that networks are under the full control of states. However, the image of a helpless state submitted to the forces of historical change is equally misguided. States are not victims adapting reactively to technological, economic and social changes outside their control. Indeed, the development of network society and the imperative but difficult transition to a network state is to a certain extent one and the same thing: 'reform of the public sector commands everything else in the process of productive shaping of the network society' (Castells, 2005: 17).

Technological innovation, economic and social change are taking network society to a certain point, but it is the actions and strategies of states, more or less controlling, more or less proactive and more or less expansive, that determine the course of development beyond this point. While different strategies will certainly mean different trajectories for the imperative but difficult transition to a network state from one case to the next, they do not detract from the overall point that the state is most decisive actor developing and shaping network society. Even if the network society poses control and management problems for the nation-state, the creation of a network state means that nation-states are increasingly embedded in and permeated by networks and decisively *not* that nation-states are simply withering away (Castells, 2010b: 365). The shaping and guiding of network society is, 'as has always been the case in other societies, in the hands of the public sector', regardless of the 'ideological discourses hiding this reality' and the fact that the public sector is where the 'organizational obstacles to innovation and networking are the most pronounced' due to the traditional allegiance to bureaucratic organization (Castells, 2005: 16).

What amounts to a conflict with bureaucracy, however, means new opportunities and potentials for technocracy. Whereas industrial technocracy, in particular during its golden years, remained part and parcel of the development of the nation-state and the welfare state defined by industrial interplay of technology and social organization, the new technocracy is deeply invested in an entirely different form of state: that of the network state. This transformation prompts a new conflict with bureaucracy challenging the original logic of the techno-bureaucracy and leads to a new partnership with democracy. Although the creation of a network state is a matter of organizational reform before anything else, it is in this sense also the process that involves a transformation from government to governance in a broader sense: 'the transition from nation-state to the network state is an organizational and political process prompted by the transformation of political management, representation and domination under the conditions of network society' (Castells, 2005: 16).

The new technocracy and connective governance

The main policy paradigm responsible for this process of organizational and political transformation under the conditions of network society is network or connective governance. The core logic of this paradigm is a transformation from government to governance based on the pervasive 'diffusion of interactive, multilayered networking as the organizational form of the public sector', effectively substituting the bureaucratic model of organization (Castells, 2005: 17). While Castells, and many with him, have been focused on the role of e-governance in this process, the diffusion and management of interactive and multilayered networking is a much broader agenda completely essential to the new governance. In general, the new governance has included two broad reform waves: the market-oriented reforms associated with NPM and the network-oriented reforms associated with network governance and later NPG (see Chapter 1). Together, these reform waves have made markets and networks establish organizational alternatives to bureaucracy (Christensen & Lægreid, 2007; Lodge & Gill, 2011; Christensen, 2014). Hence, it is now the mix of bureaucracy, markets and networks that matters, and political-administrative authorities must develop roles and capacities suited to the meta-governance of this mix (Keast et al, 2006; see also Considine & Lewis, 2003; Klijn & Edelenbos, 2007; Meuleman, 2008; Jessop, 2011).

Governance as meta-governance centres on the ability of public actors to select, calibrate and combine bureaucracy, markets and networks in relation to the specific policy problem at hand, based on the 'recognition that complexity excludes simple governance solutions and that effective governance often requires a combination of mechanisms oriented to different scales, different temporal horizons etc., that are appropriate to the object to be governed' (Jessop, 2011: 117). The underlying idea here is that every aspect of public policy, from indirect administrative policy and public sector reform to the direct interventions adopted across substantive policy sectors, are faced with a choice between three basic forms of organization and corresponding modes of governance: (1) bureaucratic organization, associated with hierarchy, the rule and command and the administrative state; (2) market organization, associated with anarchy, independence, competition, contracts and the historical experience of NPM reforms; and (3) network organization, associated with interdependence, reflexivity, negotiation, communication and dialogue and the historical experience of NPG reforms (Olsen, 2006; Esmark, 2008; Jessop, 2011). Indeed, the distinction between the three forms of organization and their corresponding modes of governance is the common denominator between the otherwise disparate variations constantly added to the new governance.

The choice of organizational form and the corresponding mode of governance is, in principle, left open. However, the new governance has from the outset gravitated towards networks as a necessary, and in most cases superior, form of organization. In earlier formulations, network organization was viewed as an attempt to repair the (intended or unintended) dysfunctional effects of NPM. However, this line of argument quickly gave way to a more or less explicit assumption about congruence between network organization and the imperatives of the surrounding society, including globalization, growing interdependence and connectivity, proliferation of wicked problems, the accumulation and dispersion of knowledge and resources beyond the state and so forth. Moreover, the challenges and potentials of digital ICTs and the informational revolution, beginning with the first steps towards digitalization of the public sector in the 1980s, have taken on an increasingly prominent role in the governance paradigm. In other words: whatever importance the historical context of NPM had for the emergence of the connective governance, subsequent development has made it clear that the deeper logic at stake is the creation of a network state in response to the demands of network society. For all efforts vested in sorting out the logic and effects of NPM, it was in a sense merely a brief historical intermission and a stepping stone towards the bigger issue of the imperative but difficult transition to a network state.

The conflict between NPG and NPM, correspondingly, is less immanent than the conflict between bureaucracy and network organization. The radical interpretation of the latter conflict, as represented by the idea of a complete contradiction between network society and the rational bureaucratic model, as well as the uncoupling of power from large-scale Weberian bureaucracies, certainly has its advocates among the proponents of the new governance. However, the logic of the mixed public sector also suggests a potential for a more amiable compromise between bureaucracy and networks. The emblematic expression of this compromise is the image of networks operating 'in the shadow of hierarchy' (Héritier & Lehmkuhl, 2008). While the continued existence of bureaucratic organizations is an obvious fact of (political) life, the image of a mixed public sector, the long shadow of hierarchy and a more or less amiable compromise also tend to misconstrue and underestimate the stakes of conflict. The conflict between bureaucracy and networks as a form of organization and mode of governance is essential to a new technocracy invested in the imperative but difficult transition to a network state. The corresponding diffusion of networks as the organizational form of the public sector follows three relatively distinct trajectories within the new governance: communicative governance, collaborative governance and MLG.

State and media: communicative governance

The first line of transition towards the network state concerns the relation between state and media. Of course, the state has always made use of the media for purposes of political communication, either through direct control or cooperation with the gatekeepers of private media outlets. Due to the proliferation of informational networks, however, new problems, strategies and practices of political communication now pervades all aspects of the state and has become an essential dimension of governance (Hajer, 2009). Whereas political communication in the industrial era was largely a question of controlling information in the relatively stable environment of conventional mass media, it is now faced with the proliferation of informational networks and flows (Crozier, 2007). Under these conditions, communication and management elide into each other in a new governance rationality of organization, managerial efficiency and state capacity, contrasting the 'old hierarchical organization adage of information control' with a network paradigm of communications management, integration of internal and external communication activities and an all-pervasive informational logic (Crozier, 2007: 7).

The most basic expression of this development is *e-governance*, which is concerned directly with the implementation of ICTs and their immediate effects on public sector performance. Indeed, the transition to a network state requires 'the diffusion of e-governance (a broader concept than e-government because it includes citizen participation and political decision-making); e-health; e-learning; e-security; and a system of dynamic regulation of the communication industry, adapting it to the values and needs of society' (Castells, 2005: 17). However, the list does not stop at health, learning and security. In the broader lingo of e-governance reforms, ICT affects all areas, domains and relations of the public sector: government-to-employee (G2E), government-to-government (G2G), government-to-business (G2B) and government-to-citizen (G2C). Implementation of ICTs along one or more of these dimensions is a global phenomenon, albeit with significant national variation. Frontrunners in the development include the usual suspects of advanced economies from Europe (the Nordic countries in particular), Asia (South Korea, Singapore) and the Anglophone family tree (Australia, United Kingdom, United States).

Historically, e-governance has developed from earlier concepts such as e-government and digital government, which were introduced in the early 1990s in the United States in conjunction with the arrival of NPG, thus linking the 'the creative use of information technologies' to the reinvention of government and the radical change from bureaucratic government to a more entrepreneurial, performance- and service-oriented public sector: 'online instead of in line', as one the central policy documents of the time put it (Dawes, 2008). Throughout this development, the field of application and possible effects of ICTs have steadily expanded. Whereas earlier concerns with digital government and e-government were to some degree focused on technical challenges and organizational adaptation, e-governance covers a broader spectrum. E-governance includes a wider set of policies and government actions pursuing economic and social change on the basis of ICTs and the tools to exploit them, including the regulative framework surrounding ICTs, improved service delivery, cost-effectiveness, citizen engagement and participation in democratic deliberation, and administrative and institutional reform (Dawes, 2008).

In spite of the expanding field of application, the basic dynamic of e-governance remains implementation of digital ICTs and digitalization. On the one hand, this gives e-governance a very clear role in the imperative but difficult transition to a network state: implementation of the hardware and technical engineering necessary to develop the internal and external information networks of the state. On the other hand, the focus on ICTs and digitalization has also limited the impact of e-governance on policy in a broader sense. Even if e-governance clearly extends beyond purely technical implementation, the scope of reform is still limited to the immediate effects of such implementation. Hence, it has been a persistent problem for e-governance to move beyond technical implementation and related changes in service delivery and administrative rationalization (Dawes, 2008). Discussions of public sector reform have, correspondingly, compartmentalized e-governance to some degree (Hood & Margetts, 2014). ICTs are often seen as a limited or even absent driver of public sector reform relative to other factors such as the unintended side effects of NPM, socio-economic forces, crisis and elite discretion (Pollitt & Bouckaert, 2011: 33).

An important exception to this rule is the hugely influential concept of *digital era governance* (DEG) (Dunleavy et al, 2006). Aiming explicitly to link the compartmentalized and technical focus of e-governance with the wider debate on public governance and management reform, the concept of DEG was introduced specifically to highlight 'that the advent of the digital era is now the most general, pervasive, and structurally distinctive influence on how governance arrangements are changing in advanced industrial states' (Dunleavy et al, 2006: 478). Infamously stating that 'NPM is dead', Dunleavy and colleagues point to a pervasive regime change from NPM to a public governance and management regime defined through and through by digitalization and the information-handling potentials of new ICTs. As such, DEG represents an image of the fully developed network state, or at least a significant move in that direction in leading-edge countries, embracing ICTs as the core principle of public sector reform. However, DEG and e-governance still converge in their focus on implementation of ICTs, digitalization and immediate effects in the domain of public service delivery and back-office processes.

The particular dynamics of the transition to a network state embodied by the rationality and practice of communicative governance are, however, more inclusive, open-ended and diverse than suggested by the focus on digitalization shared by e-governance and DEG. Rather than implementation and immediate effects of digital ICTs, even in the wider sense of these terms, the transition to a network state involves both reactive and proactive management of communication in context of 'hybrid' media systems where power is 'exercised by those who are successfully able to create, tap or steer information flows in ways that suit their goals and in ways that modify, enable, or disable the agency of others, across a range of older and newer media settings' (Chadwick, 2013: 285). The media system of network society is, the importance of digital ICTs notwithstanding, deeply hybrid, which has to do with the distinction between 'old' and 'new' media as well as the idea of 'media logic' vis-à-vis media technology.

Old and new media

Although new social media and digital ICTs are indeed the lead technology of the information age, the older technologies of the industrial age are meshed into the informational networks and flows of society, thus gaining rather than losing importance in the information age (Castells, 2007). In this dimension, hybridity simply means a combination of old and new media in the ongoing development of the media system. This is not something particular to the arrival of digital ICTs. The historical development of the media system has always been a process of hybridization between old and new media rather than a straightforward displacement of the old by the new (Chadwick, 2013: 32). In this respect, the current media system is as much a hybrid of the newer digital media and the older media technologies of the print press, visual media such as film and cinema and even radar (the first 'real-time' screen display of data), as it is a result of these new technologies in themselves (Chadwick, 2013: 45). The development hybrid media system is an ongoing process of cross-fertilization of old and new media, recycling of content and integration of media platforms.

What makes the most recent disruption of the media system particular, however, is that computerization, digitalization, the internet, wireless technology and mobile devices have allowed for a hitherto unseen degree of integration of the media technologies, platforms and genres accumulated thus far. This hitherto unseen degree of integration, in turn, provides the hybrid media system with two overarching and somewhat contrasting attributes. On the one hand, the current media system allows the speed and transience of real-time communication flows and multitasking facilitated by interfaces of computerized media devices (broadly akin to what Castells refers to as virtual and 'timeless time'). On the other hand, it provides an 'immense archival permanence', based on time-stamps, marking, tagging, global standards of metadata, databases and search engines making the internet the 'archive par excellence' (Chadwick, 2013: 48). In other words, the particular hybridity of the current media system enables immediate and potentially global multidirectional communication, as well as Big Data, machine learning and analytics.

Media technology and media logic

Hybridity is, however, not only a matter of media technology, but rather of hybrid media logics. Whereas media technology, in the simple and straightforward sense, refers to the physical attributes of each medium and its particular capacity for retrieving, storing and transmitting information, media logic refers to the standardized formats for 'selection, organization and presentation' of information, based on the 'distinctive features' of each medium (Altheide, 2013: 225). Using a slightly different terminology, media logic can be described as the more or less expansive protocols of action forming a nebula around the nucleus of media technology, that is, a 'vast clutter of normative rules and default conditions' surrounding the hardware of media technology itself (Gitelman, 2006: 66). On one level, media logic describes a relation between the media system and individual actors where media technologies both enable and constrain agency in hybrid networks and sociotechnical systems. On the macro level, however, media logic is intrinsically related to the socio-technological dynamics of mediatization: the increased impact of media logic throughout society due to the 'pervasive spread of media contents and platforms through all types of context and practice' (Couldry & Hepp, 2013: 191).

Traditionally, the process of mediatization has been associated with an overarching media logic in the singular, shaped by and associated with the journalistic news criteria, production values and genres of industrial-age mass media. This dynamic has been studied with particular intensity in the field of political campaigning, party politics and elections under the label of mediatized politics and democracy (Bennet & Entmann, 2001). Hybridity, by contrast suggests a fundamental 'disaggregation into different competing yet interdependent media *logics*' in the media system (Chadwick, 2013: 24, original emphasis). The diverse and polycentric media environment of network society cannot be subsumed under a single media logic. Hence, the ability to mobilize, traverse and integrate different media logics becomes imperative to communications management and the exercise of political power more generally. Electoral campaigning and informational politics is in this sense not about adaptation to a singular media logic but about the creative use of the new patterns of empowerment and disempowerment created by the complex and variegated patterns of interaction between older and newer media logics (Castells, 2007; Chadwick, 2013: 286).

In the context of the hybrid media system, then, the policies and reforms associated with e-governance and DEG are merely part of the equation that is communicative governance. The overriding project of communicative governance, including all the efforts related to the e-governance and DEG, is the development and utilization of a comprehensive and integrated communication infrastructure in the public sector, operating on an 'intersectoral plane as a central referent through which an array of policy sectors can be organized' and political communication 'oriented both internally and externally' (Crozier, 2007: 7). The creation of such an infrastructure represents a mediatization of public policy, parallel to the mediatization of politics.

In contrast to political communication campaigns aimed at electoral success, persuasion and generalized consent, however, mediatized policy revolves around interactive communication about policy problems and adequate solutions. Even if the two forms of communicative rationality and their respect infrastructures may intersect, the former involves strategic political communication geared towards the input side of the political system, the latter is rather a form of tactical communication oriented towards the output side of the political process (Bang, 2003: 241).

State and stakeholders: collaborative governance

The second line of transition towards the network state concerns the relation between state and private actors, or more generally connectivity across the public–private divide. Although communicative governance and cooperation with external stakeholders have to some degree always been linked, as suggested by the now universal inclusion of participatory governance under the umbrella of e-governance and adherence to 'smart governance', they are still distinct objectives. In the interplay between technology and social organization, communicative governance is concerned primarily with the former and its immediate effects, whereas collaborative governance is primarily concerned with the latter, that is, networks as a means to involve stakeholders in the development and implementation of public policy. Media technology may or may not be considered an instrument of facilitation and support in this endeavour, but the key issue is collaboration between multiple stakeholders in order to generate the information, knowledge and implementation capacities needed to match the technological and socio-economic problems of network society.

The introduction of this logic against the background of NPM-style reforms pointed to networks as a means to increase the connectivity of the state, both internally between sectors, branches and agencies, and externally in relation to non-state actors. The latter dimension is, however, by far the most important: the core of network governance, as originally conceived, is cooperation between state and external stakeholders in the development and implementation of public policy (Bovaird, 2005; Sørensen & Torfing, 2007; Klijn & Koppenjan, 2015). The original focus of network governance has since generated new permutations and variations within the governance paradigm, including co-governance (Kooiman, 2003: 96), interactive governance (Torfing et al, 2012) and NPG (Osborne, 2010). The core idea, however, is captured most straightforwardly by the concept of collaborative governance, meaning negotiation of policy solutions between public and private stakeholders under the auspices of public agencies, used extensively in planning, regulation, policy making, and public management (Sullivan & Skelcher, 2002; Ansell & Gash, 2008; O'Flynn & Wanna, 2008).

As such, collaborative governance is an exemplary expression of the broader mode of governance associated with the use of network organization across the public/private divide: integration of private stakeholders in the policy process through more or less formalized arenas based on dialogue, exchange of information, mutual adjustment of objectives and negotiated outcomes. While NPM reforms also involved some degree of cooperation with market actors through contract management and purchaser/provider relations, often in conjunction with privatization, the extensive use of policy networks involves a break with NPM logic, recognition of a more fundamental interdependence between the public and private sectors and a need for the state to reach out to non-state actors with valuable information, knowledge and an interests in shared outcomes, making 'collaboration a necessary imperative of modern management' (O'Flynn & Wanna, 2008: 88). This imperative is caused by external demands on the public sector that mirror the basic structures and process of network society (Klijn & Koppenjan, 2000; Yang & Bergrud, 2008).

Collaborative governance is thus widely understood as a necessary response to one or more of the following dimensions: technological developments (digital ICTs and increased technological sophistication), economic changes (development of world markets, global trade, international investment patterns, business aggregations and demand for uniform regulation and competitive neutrality) and social changes (greater international connectedness and travel, knowledge of other cultures, community demands and forms of mobilization). How and to what extent states have embraced the rationality and practice of collaborative governance is, however, subject to national institutions and traditions to an even greater degree than communicative governance (at least in the case of e-governance and DEG). Nevertheless the same groups emerge as the frontrunners, albeit for different reasons and with important variations: collaborative governance has thus been facilitated and shaped by the intrinsic features of the Westminster system in the Anglo-Saxon countries (O'Flynn & Wanna, 2008), by the consensus-oriented political culture in continental and Northern European countries (Sørensen & Torfing, 2007) and by the founding idea of social harmony in a number of Asian countries (Tao et al, 2010).

National variations notwithstanding, the rationality and practice of collaborative governance revolves around the development and management of a flexible and cross-sectoral infrastructure for coordination and involvement of stakeholders in the public sector. The basic organizational form of this infrastructure is that of multiple and overlapping networks within and across policy sectors. As with communicative governance, this infrastructure does not have a centre, a head or a central point of strategic control. Nevertheless, the multiplicity of networks used in relation to specific policy problems on different levels and stages of decision making amounts to a pervasive system of channels granting stakeholder access at various points of intersection throughout the public sector. At each of these points of intersection, involvement of external stakeholders is essentially about network management, not in the sense of a technological network or a media system, but as a form of public/private collaboration. The basic dimensions of such network management are inclusion, institutional design and operative strategies of stakeholder involvement and coordination.

Inclusion and institutional design

The subject of inclusion in collaborative governance is subject to considerable debate, reflecting more fundamental controversy about the inclusion/exclusion-dynamics in the policy process. In general, however, stakeholders are typically organized interests such as business organizations, social partners and advocacy organizations. For the same reason, collaborative governance has sometimes been linked to more familiar arrangements such as corporatism and pluralism. While the core group of stakeholders may often look familiar, however, collaborative governance is less stable, less formalized and less focused on grand bargains with peak organizations than corporatism, and less market-based than pluralism. Collaborative governance may thus give more room to NGOs, social movements and community organizations, at least in principle. Most importantly, inclusion in public policy networks rests on the possession of information and knowledge about the problems at hand and the efficacy of possible solutions, as opposed to the large membership base and potential for social stability offered by the peak organizations of the industrial era. For the same reason, collaborative governance often includes individual scientific and technical experts to a larger degree than corporatism and pluralism.

Although collaborative governance is uniformly committed to networks as the basic organizational form, there are numerous variations. The type of networks supporting collaborative governance include: local networks anywhere between protest movements attempting to block urban development and support networks for refugees; national networks deeply integrated into all aspects of areas such as employment policy, enterprise and business development, environmental policy and so forth; and transnational networks such as those greatly influencing national educational systems in Europe and banking regulation in the case of the Basel Committee (Marcussen & Torfing, 2007). Collaborative networks also extend from the agenda-setting and development phase of public policy to implementation. In the former case, collaborative networks are often modifications of corporatist forums such as commissions and councils, supplemented by less formal and flexible meeting sessions, fast-paced working groups and narrow expert commissions. At the implementation and delivery side of public policy, collaborative governance networks include stakeholders in co-production and co-delivery (Pestoff & Brandsen, 2008). As such, there is no single organizational blueprint for collaborative governance. Examples may include EU expert groups and 'comitology' (Metz, 2015); public–private partnerships, which can be found on all levels of governance across a wide range of policy fields (Osborne, 2000); community groups, local councils, public hearings and new forms of engagement with local councils (O'Flynn & Wanna, 2008); and citizen involvement in urban planning, resource management and regeneration projects (McCarthy, 2007).

Operative strategies

Whereas institutional design concerns the basic attributes of the network, including overall goals, distributions of competence, authority, purpose and function in relation to a specific policy, the question of operative strategies pertain to the everyday management of interaction between network members. This, in turn, points to the role of a specific network manager, charged with keeping the network on track in relation to its policy objectives. Exercising a combination of hands-off and hands-on network management is usually considered the *sine qua non* of collaborative governance. Whereas hands-off network management is done through broad framing of policy objectives, in combination with institutional design, hands-on management involves active participation in the network, mediation, brokerage and conflict resolution, as well as the enhancement of communication, information sharing, resource pooling and trust-building among network members

(Kickert, 1997; Klijn & Koppenjan, 2000; Sørensen & Torfing, 2007; Yang & Bergrud, 2008).

Against this background, ICTs certainly provide a tool that can facilitate inclusion and support or even substitute institutional platforms for network interaction. Moreover, there is clearly also a broader communicative rationality at work in the operative strategies of network management. Indeed, network management is based on so-called procedural communicative tools – tools used to 'alter the behavior of policy network members involved in the policy-making process', including 'front-end' tools used in the agenda-setting / policy formulation phase and 'back-end' tools used in the implementation phase (Howlett, 2009: 26). In the terms of collaborative governance, such tools are endemic to overall network facilitation (Bressers & O'Toole, 1998; Salamon, 2002), network management (Edelenbos et al, 2013; Mischen, 2015; Cristofoli et al, 2017) and meta-governance (Klijn & Edelenbos, 2007). However, network management in collaborative governance is not inherently about management of technological networks or communication in the wider context of the hybrid media system, but rather about stakeholder involvement and partnerships.

For the same reason, collaborative governance may seem less obviously technocratic, at least insofar as it does not directly concern the implementation of new technology or the wider effects of the digital and informational revolution. However, collaborative governance plots a path towards the creation of a network state that is no less shaped by the idea of an imperative adaptation to the demands of the post-industrial network society. As stated clearly by Castells, inclusion of non-governmental actors is an integral part of the network state, and the implied animosity towards bureaucracy finds an even clearer expression here. Although the adage that the use of networks in public policy takes place 'in the shadow of hierarchy' has been a fixture of the new governance since its earliest days, the basic opposition between the operational logics of bureaucracy and collaborative network governance can hardly be overstated. Chronologically, collaborative governance coincides with the 'death' of NPM alongside DEG and communicative governance, but the more essential conflict at the level of rationality and practice is with bureaucracy.

By the same logic, collaborative governance and network management have consistently been seen to make the public sector more open, accessible, responsive and ultimately more democratic. Networks and public/private collaboration can, according to this line of argument, create new institutional spaces for participation and deliberation that supplements the basic framework of representative and electoral democracy (Mathur & Skelcher, 2007; Sørensen & Torfing, 2007; Edelenbos et al, 2013). However, this bid for democratic legitimacy tends to obscure the technocratic nature of collaborative governance. In this respect, the pervasive exclusion of ordinary citizens from governance networks and collaborative processes due to their lack of relevant information, knowledge and resources is only the most apparent expression of this problematic. Institutional design, for its part, remains largely suited to the demands of the policy process and largely top-down. Operative strategies of management are, correspondingly, meant to frame and guide networks towards improved policy solutions and implementation capacity. Hence, the claim to wider democratic legitimacy seems to confuse a decrease in bureaucracy with an increase in democracy.

State and state: multilevel governance

The final line of transition towards a network state concerns connectivity across the territorial borders of the nation-state, which is clearly the most essential component in Castells' outline of the transformation from governance to a form of governance based on the network state as the operating unit of political management in network society. In other words, this is where the new governance tackles the issue of transnational governance, regional governance and global governance as a response to the globalizing dynamic of network society. Transnational governance (ideally global but realistically regional) is seen here as a necessary solution to the control problems and asymmetries facing the political system in relation to a globalized network economy, as well as new reality of social identities and projects moving easily across national borders. The network state, in other words, is also a network *of* states where the nation-state has to accomplish the difficult feat of maintaining some form of identity while relinquishing and sharing sovereignty with other states and international institutions.

As such, the network state is not a state in the territorially delimited, culturally cohesive and hierarchically organized sense of the nation-state, but a state enmeshed in and permeated by networks horizontally *and* vertically. In addition to inclusion of stakeholders across the public/private divide, networks extend upwards to transnational and supranational levels of governance as well as downwards to the local level of governance. Whereas communicative and collaborative governance concern the 'interactive' dimension of networks, we now turn to the 'multilayered' nature of the network state. This is where the network state takes on a more recognizable face as an alternative political system, or rather a polity, decisively different from that of the nation-state. More generally, this particular form of polity is known as multi-level governance (MLG), that is, a system where supranational, national, regional and local governments are enmeshed in territorially overarching policy networks (Hooghe & Marks, 2001).

The concept of MLG was originally introduced to describe the particular attributes of the EU polity as a system of interrelated formal and informal decision-making at several territorial tiers in response to the increasing variations in the territorial reach of policy externalities (Hooghe & Marks, 2001). Although originally applied to the case of the EU, the core idea of MLG is a basic design principle with broader implications: matching the level, tier or sphere of policy development and implementation to the different scales, reach and horizon of policy problems and externalities. In order to distinguish this principle from instances of federalism or devolution, a distinction is often drawn between type I MLG (of federalist descent) and type II MLG, characterized by multiple and overlapping jurisdictions centred around policy problems rather than all-purpose jurisdictions build around political communities, intersecting rather than mutually exclusive memberships, functionally specific competencies rather than generic political authority, and flexible development of institutions and procedures rather than comprehensive system-wide architecture (Hooghe & Marks, 2003).

In a broader sense, MLG (type II) provides the basic design principles for a flexible and adaptive infrastructure of transnational governance under the conditions of network society. Since the network society enables economic and social action on all levels of action, the state has to develop a capacity to shift policy development and implementation to the proper level of action and engage the relevant array of stakeholders. More formally, this can be described as a polity based on a combination of horizontal and vertical mobility: MLG 'provides a more flexible mode of optimizing the policy making process by allowing multi-directional shifts both vertically and horizontally in decision-making authority and power' (Stein and Turkewitsch, 2008: 26). In order to allow for such multidirectional shifts, political authority in an MLG system is dispersed not only horizontally across different sectors of interest and spheres of influence, but also vertically between different levels or territorial spheres of action. Seen from the perspective of the state, this means that authority is shifted both upwards, downwards and sideways (Bache & Flinders, 2004). MLG is thus a variable geopolitical infrastructure of allowing for policy design and delivery across all levels and sectors of public policy-making and implementation.

While the EU may be the most apparent example of this line of transition to the network state, it also includes other forms of transnational governance associated with the UN, the OECD, the World Bank, the IMF and so on. Even though decision-making power has not been transferred to these institutions to the same degree as in the case of the EU, they still provide forums of interrelated formal and informal decision-making linking different territorial tiers of policy formulation and development. Taken to its extreme conclusion, the exercise of global governance based on the infrastructure of an MLG system can be seen to approximate a globally networked 'Empire' (Hardt & Negri, 2000). Although the notion of a global and 'informal' empire remains highly contested, it also presents an established and increasingly important view on the dynamics of globalization (Grewal, 2008). In contrast to the dynamics of territorial expansion, colonialism, centre/periphery relations and military dominance traditionally associated with empires, the new global empire is polycentric and deterritorialized, shifting laterally between decision centres all over the world and vertically between different levels of decision making in a system of shared sovereignty developed in response to the globally networked production of the techno-economic system. In other words: the fully realized polity of the network 'state' would no longer resemble statehood in any sense of the word, but rather a global empire displaying the basic infrastructure of an MLG system.

Short of a global empire fully materializing, however, it is the EU that provides the most apparent illustration of the link between the development of a multilayered network state and the rise of the new technocracy. EU has infamously been interpreted as the ultimate technocratic project, and the Brexit turmoil is often seen as one of the most clear-cut expressions of the conflict between technocracy and populism. Admittedly, the interpretation of the EU as a technocratic project has often been based on imprecise indicators such as the lack of popular participation, the democratic deficit, elite orientation or simply the image of a rampant bureaucracy removed from the democratic context of the nation-state (Wallace & Smith, 1995; Kurki, 2011). While this characterization is not entirely wrong, it is not entirely correct either. The reason that the EU is indeed a fundamentally technocratic project lies rather in the attempt to create a multilayered and multidirectional polity, which is neither bureaucratic nor democratic, but designed to facilitate the development and implementation of necessary policy solutions as required by the structures and processes of network society.

Conclusion

Technocrats used to be very fond of large-scale bureaucratic organizations. From the original outline of the technostructure in the mature industrial enterprise to the technocratic takeover of bureaucracy and creation of techno-bureaucracies in the industrial state, the underlying trend seems to be that technocrats thrive in bureaucratic organizations and depend on bureaucratization for political influence. This logic has substantially changed in the new technocracy. The new technocrats have become ardent believers in the power of networks and prophets of network organization. Bureaucratic organizations are still a fact of life in the political system and society at large, as are market-style organizations based more or less exclusively on contractual relationships. In this respect, the new technocracy operates with an all-pervasive choice between bureaucracy, markets and networks, where it is the 'mix that matters' according to the new standard of flexible meta-governance. However, the organizational choice within this framework is neither symmetric nor ultimately free: the logic of the new technocracy prescribes an imperative but difficult transition to a network in response to the techno-economic and social structures and dynamics of network society.

This logic is played on the space between technology and organization, ranging from the most direct responses to the imperatives of the informational revolution (e-governance, DEG and more expansive forms of communicative governance) to collaborative governance and stakeholder involvement as well as the creation of flexible systems of MLG. Even if the new technocracy is still living with the apparent persistence of bureaucratic organizations, it is now guided by the idea of a deep and fundamental conflict between the demands of network society and the bureaucratic model of organization. This anti-bureaucratic stance is, in turn, supplemented by a technocratic preoccupation with a democratic promise of network organization and network society. The imperative but difficult transition to a network state not only involves a rejection of bureaucracy, but also a new technocratic embrace of democracy, openness, inclusion, communication and deliberation. This is, however, only the first dimension of the new technocratic reversal of the original formula of industrial technocracy.

6

Technocratic Regulation: Coping With Risk and Uncertainty

> The rationale for relying on resilience as the better strategy lies in life's inherent uncertainty.
>
> (Wildavsky, 1988: 92)

Other things that happened in the 1980s

The network society is the essential element of post-industrial society in the information age: it is the interplay between the latest truly pervasive technological revolution and network organization across economy, civil society and the state that defines the essential structures and processes of post-industrial society, substituting the industrial interplay between machine technology and large-scale bureaucratic organizations. The post-industrial society is, however, also a risk society arising from changes in the interplay of technology and regulation, or more generally technology and politically provided security. When viewed in this way, the epochal difference between industrial society and post-industrial society occurs the moment that the security provisions and compensation schemes of industrial society are nullified by the 'central paradox of risk society': that 'risks are generated by the processes of modernization which try to control them' (Beck, 1998: 10). When does moment occur? In the preceding chapter, I placed the emergence of network society in the 1980s, albeit keeping in mind that we are dealing with prolonged processes of social transformation. Based on the same logic, the 1980s is not the worst place to look for the emergence of risk society either.

Perrow published his reflections on the effects of living with high-risk technologies in 1984, the same year that the Bhopal chemical disaster occurred, but inspired mainly by the Three Mile Island nuclear accident in 1979. Two years later, Beck published the original German version of *Risk Society* in the horizon of the Chernobyl nuclear disaster. The same year, the Challenger Space Shuttle disaster occurred, bovine spongiform encephalopathy (BSE) was officially recognized as a disease and the publication of *Engines of Creation* announced the 'coming era of nanotechnology' (Drexler, 1986). What came to be known as the AIDS epidemic appeared in 1979. The first genetically engineered plant saw the light of day in 1983, although the first plant (a tomato) was approved for commercial release in 1994. In 1983, the Beirut barracks bombing occurred, killing 307 of the 659 people killed between 1982 and 1986 in 36 suicide attacks in Lebanon. The Exxon Valdez ran aground in the Alaskan Gulf in 1989. The Intergovernmental Panel on Climate Change (IPCC) was established in 1988 by the World Meteorological Organization and the UN (it was preceded by an international scientific Advisory Group on Greenhouse Gases set up in 1985). For good measure, it was recently discovered that the accelerating melting of the Greenland ice sheet started with a fundamental imbalance occurring in the 1980s.

Chemical spills, failure of experimental technology, environmental disaster, pandemics and terrorism were clearly not invented in the 1980s, but the decade does mark the beginning of a fundamental reconfiguration of the state/society in the image of these and other risks. The result is a 'non-industrial' risk society putting an end to traditional security and certainty (Beck, 1998). In contrast to network society, this development was largely unforeseen in Bell's original outline of post-industrial society. Or rather: Bell did include the increased preoccupation with technological innovation and control of its impact through planning and future orientation as one of the five basic dimensions of post-industrial society, but this approach to risk, control and security amounts to a form of 'linear technocracy' characteristic of industrial society and advanced industrialism in particular (Beck, 2009: 110). The transition from industrial society to risk society, however, means exactly *the end* of linear technocracy. Faced with the reality of risk society and the proliferation of manufactured, global and incalculable risk, the new technocracy has increasingly turned to a new form of risk management based on the *internalization of risk and the impossibility of insurance against harm and uncertainty*.

Risk management was always a quintessentially technocratic discipline (Dusek, 2012). Industrial technocracy sought to create a society of 'zero risk' through prudent risk management, a society where nuclear power plants become increasingly fail-safe, the economy can be set free of external limitations, genetic engineering really becomes just engineering and the occasional accident can be covered by some form of compensation scheme. Faced with the reality of risk society, however, the new technocracy has come to be defined rather by a reflexivity about risk that challenges and even reverses the staunch belief in the power of planning, management and control to harness the dangers and side effects of technological innovation, socio-economic development and humankind's use of natural resources. Against the earlier technocratic belief in the proportional relation between technical expertise and problem-solving capacity, the new technocracy rather suggests that every attempt to control risks will inherently fail and most likely become a source of unintended side effects, in effect cancelling the underlying rationale of industrial security guarantees and compensation schemes. Indeed, this form of risk management has increasingly been elevated to the status of a pervasive policy paradigm by the new governance, battling an ever-growing list of wicked problems.

The internalization of risk and the impossibility of insurance against harm and uncertainty thus adds a second and distinct logic to the transition from government to governance. Risk management constitutes an equally important (albeit sometimes less apparent) component of the new governance, expressed both as a preoccupation with (im)possible solutions to the increasingly wicked problems across most policy sectors, and as a more general concern with the demands of risk and uncertainty on public policy. Although risk management provides the new technocracy with a distinct dynamic in this way, there is clearly also a certain degree of overlap and cross-fertilization with the imperative but difficult creation of network state. This intersection of risk management and network governance is the essential formula in the emerging field of risk governance: here, the use of networks for purposes of knowledge accumulation and flexible coordination in the development and implementation of public policy is seen as the best possible response to the increasing complexity, uncertainty and unintended consequences of risk society.

The commitment to reflexive risk management adds additional fuel to the anti-bureaucratic stance of the new technocracy. The internalization of risk and the rejection of safety and certainty is fundamentally incompatible with bureaucracy and its underlying form of rationalization. Indeed, Beck goes so far as to claim that risk 'stands for a type of social thought and action that was not at all perceived by Max Weber' (Beck, 1994: 9). This argument applies not only to Weber's original outline of bureaucracy, but also to the fully developed techno-bureaucracy of advanced industrial society and the welfare state. Thus understood, linear techno-bureaucracy is a type of bureaucracy defined through and through by the logic and principles of industrial risk management: risk calculation, security guarantees, insurance and compensation. Risk society, however, fundamentally undercuts this type of techno-bureaucracy. This development is then interpreted by reflexive risk managers, and not least by Beck himself, as a potential for democratic renewal through the 'enlightenment function' of risk society. Before we arrive at this version of the new technocratic formula of anti-bureaucracy and pro-democracy, however, it is necessary to take a closer look at the fundamental attributes of risk society.

A different kind of industrial revolution: manufactured, global and incalculable risk

Risk should not, as is always emphasized by risk specialists, be confused with infliction of damage or occurrence of harmful events. Rather, risk involves an orientation towards the potential occurrence of harmful events in the future, and is thus a complex function of probability, scale of effects and vulnerability. Risks are always threatening events somewhere in the future, but once the event materializes, it becomes a catastrophe or crisis rather than a risk, while risk has 'already moved elsewhere' to the anticipation of new events (Beck, 2006: 332). While the negative connotations of risk clearly dominates here and elsewhere, the distinction between anticipation and actual occurrence of events also means that risk leaves the future essentially open as a potential for harm *or* safety, loss *or* gain (Wildavsky, 1988; Giddens, 1998). In one respect, this clearly means that risk is as 'old as the human race itself' (Beck, 1992a: 97). However, much as with the drastic proliferation of networks, clearly a form of organization as old as the human race itself, risk society emerges with an exponential increase in the potential for harm caused by technological development, and in a broader sense by *'hazards and insecurities induced and introduced by modernization itself* (Beck, 1992b: 21, original emphasis). This development can be understood as the proliferation of manufactured, global and incalculable risk.

Manufactured risks

In one sense, risk society involves a shift from danger to external risk and ultimately to manufactured (internal) risk. This sequence is premised, first, on a distinction between danger and risk, meaning two fundamentally different anxieties about a potential for harm, the former being completely unrelated to decisions and the latter completely intrinsic to them. Danger involves events outside of one's control, whereas risks are always taken, minimized and maximized. Pre-industrial societies thus conceived of potentially harmful events as dangers, and their actual occurrence as strokes of fate, divine intervention or simply bad luck raining down on humankind from God, demons or Nature (Beck, 1992a; Luhmann, 2005). Through industrialization and rationalization, however, the symbolic and material reality of such dangers are largely eradicated: the attributions of causes to the supernatural or an uncontrollable nature are done away by scientific rationalism and material protection from poverty, starvation, floods and so on steadily increased. Through this process, old dangers are gradually domesticated, tamed and rationalized as 'external' risks attributable to discernible decisions and causes, subject to calculation and prediction, preventive measures and insurance.

This eradication of old dangers through provident management of external risks is endemic to the 'first two hundred years of existence of industrial society' and concepts of risk calculation, protection and insurance culminating in the welfare state (Giddens, 1998: 27). However, this epoch comes to an end with the displacement of external risk by manufactured risk and uncertainties, originating not from the outside but from within the very dynamics of human progress itself, and in particular by scientific and technological innovation. In this second step from external to internal risk, threats are no longer a matter of 'outside risk but a risk generated inside each person's life and inside a variety of institutions' (Beck, 1998: 10). This paradox of internal, manufactured risk sets risk society decisively apart from industrial society and its corresponding form of risk management, deeply entrenched in the idea that both natural and industrial risks can be predicted, reasonably controlled and fairly compensated where prevention fails. By contrast, the increasing awareness and reflexivity about the inherent paradox (or at least problem) of manufactured risk means that risk society is 'increasingly occupied with debating, preventing and managing risks that it itself has produced' (Beck, 2006: 332).

Global risks

This internalization of risk coincides with the expansion and spread of risk to all domains of human life. By this logic, risk society emerges the moment global destruction becomes the normal horizon of risk, shaped and approximated by the reality of harmful events increasingly transgressing spatial, temporal and social borders (Beck, 2006). This development challenges the industrial idea of risk as an acceptable and manageable side effect of technological innovation and industrial production. This conflict reaches a critical point, if not before, when industrial society is 'confronted with the historically unprecedented possibility of the destruction through decision-making of all life on this planet' (Beck, 1992a: 101). The simplest demarcation line for this development is arrival of industrial 'mega-technologies' producing 'mega-hazards' on a potentially global scale. Three Mile Island and Chernobyl are thus key events in the history of risk society because they were caused by the first technology with the potential for global destruction (Beck, 1992b). While neither of the two accidents were global, the scale and transnational span of effects made any pretences of containment and control impossible. While post-war industrial society largely viewed the danger of nuclear Armageddon through the prism of the bomb and warfare, Three Mile Island and Chernobyl manifested the destructive potential of nuclear technology in the domain of industrial and manufactured risk.

Since then, the global horizon of risk has become all the more apparent with innovations in technologies that were only coming into view at the time of those two nuclear disasters: chemical technology, genetic technology, nanotechnology and the like. Today, pandemics, uncontrollable genetic mutations, artificial intelligence or tampering with the 'engines of creation' through nanotechnology seem bigger risks than nuclear technology. In addition to the risk of leaks and spills, chemical risks are now related to everything from toys to foodstuffs and medicine. The risk of a global breakdown in the ecological system, only coming into view at the point of transition from industrial to risk society, has since become *the* global risk with the acceleration of global warming and climate change. The threat of terrorist attacks without clear geopolitical limits or even origins is also part of the global horizon of risks, regardless of their objective probability and impact. The threat of terrorists or 'rogue states' getting their hands on weapons of mass destruction still looms large, while the memory of malfunctioning nuclear plants fade quickly (although the 2011 meltdown of the Fukushima Daiichi reactor did produce significant responses in several countries and the abolition of nuclear power in Germany).

The global nature of risk clearly also has to do with a certain overlap between network society and risk society, which is in turn reflected in their corresponding policy paradigms. Digital ICTs and the increasing integration of other technologies in informational networks have accelerated and magnified industrial risks related to nuclear, chemical or biological technology. Moreover, ICTs have produced a new set of risks barely considered in the earliest stages of risk society. One set of risks pertains to the hardware and software keeping the global information system running, such as cyber attacks, hacking and viral infections. Another set pertains to the content of the global information system, the financial crisis of 2008 being the example par excellence. While 2008 was in one sense just another entry in a long list of more or less global economic crises, it was the first of its kind to be driven by financial markets and products operating almost exclusively on the basis of informational networks. In this latter sense, 2008 signified a historically unprecedented combination of concentrated economic power and rapid distribution of effects made possible by informational networks.

Incalculable risks

Whereas the development of risk assessment and risk management in industrial society was firmly entrenched in a belief about the predictability of harmful events aided by more sophisticated techniques for calculation of probabilities and 'future orientation', risk society is defined by an increasing number of risks that cannot be predicted or calculated with any degree of certainty – risks that reside in the terrain of so-called 'unknown unknowns'. This point gained widespread popular attention in 2011 when then US Secretary of Defense Donald Rumsfeld invoked the concept of unknown unknowns in response to questions about governmental knowledge about weapons of mass destruction and links to terrorist groups in Iraq prior to the US invasion in 2003. Amid popular amusement about the blatant admission of lack of evidence supporting the invasion, it was also recognized that unknown unknowns are indeed a standard concept used widely by technical planners, and in particular by NASA and other so-called high-reliability organizations (HROs) specializing in management of industrial risks at the cutting edge of technological development (Boin & Van Eeten, 2013).

HROs inherited the concept from engineering and technical sciences, but it was given one of its earliest and most decisive formulations in economics. More specifically, John Maynard Keynes and Frank Hyneman Knight drew a distinction between largely predictable and calculable contingencies and fundamentally non-predictable and non-calculable contingency, the latter meaning fundamental uncertainty and 'simply not knowing' (Chow & Sarin, 2002). This distinction broadly corresponds to the distinction between known unknowns and unknown unknowns, and was used by Knight specifically to separate the domain where calculation of risk and probability can be done meaningfully from a domain where it cannot. More generally, the concept of unknown unknowns represents the limit of scientific certainty. While scientific certainty is always a body of accumulated knowledge situated exactly on the limit between known knowns (scientifically proven facts) and known unknowns (margin of error, statistical uncertainty, contextual factors unaccounted for, next steps and so on), unknown unknowns are squarely and decisively on the other side of scientific certainty of any kind.

The proliferation of incalculable risk and unknown unknowns means that risk society is faced with a fundamental dilemma or problem of taking decisions meant to provide security based on more or less admitted not-knowing. As Beck states, this means that Rumsfeld was, whatever else one might say, making a fully consistent statement based on the logic of risk society: to the extent that the US invasion of Iraq was indeed meant to prevent terrorists from acquiring chemical or nuclear weapons, the admission of not-knowing is as much a reason to act as reason not to act, since terrorists could possibly acquire weapons of mass destruction, and indeed do so precisely because we believe in 'not being able to know and hence do nothing' (Beck, 2006: 335). In this sense risk society brings about an age of speculation (Wilkinson, 2002). Non-calculable risk and unknown unknowns are speculative, hypothetical and ultimately imagined. Nevertheless, incalculable risk and unknown unknowns constitute a fundamental premise of decision making and security mechanisms in risk society: the worst possible, more or less improbable scenarios, will have to be imagined and taken into account. Decisions of risk management are thus taken in a grey zone between rationality and hysteria where knowledge drawn from experience and science is mixed with 'imagination, suspicion, fiction, fear' (Beck, 2006: 335).

The blurring of risk and hysteria is further exacerbated by the potentially irreversible nature of technological development in risk society. Decisions in risk society are also about unknown unknowns in the sense that technological development itself has become rife with unknown thresholds, tolerances and points of no return. Climate change and global warming are known knowns with a certain span of unknown knowns surrounding model predictions, but the precise point of irreversible ecological breakdown still remains a largely unknown unknown. When exactly will terrorists or rogue states acquire weapons of mass destruction? What is the tolerance of traditional crops for genetic engineering? How much manipulation does the human genome tolerate? If we are past any of these points, it is already too late and, with a formulation encapsulating the new genre of rational hysteria, we are already dead. Decisions in this terrain are always potentially irreversible decisions about life and death, taken completely in the dark. Trial and error cannot be applied here and there is no such thing as a controlled experiment. Every intervention runs the risk of unwittingly stumbling past the point of no return.

Risk society and the end of linear technocracy

Taken together, the proliferation of manufactured, global and non-calculable risk provoke a 'self-confrontation with the effects of risk society that cannot be dealt with and assimilated in the system of industrial society – as measured by the latter's institutionalized standards' (Beck, 1994: 6). This moment of self-confrontation, in turn, marks the end of the first modernity and the onset of reflexive modernity where the immanent contradictions of modernity and counter-modernity in industrial society takes centre stage. As such, reflexive modernity is not the end of modernity, but the beginning of 'modernity *beyond* its classical industrial design' (Beck, 1992b: 10). Nowhere is this felt more immediately and directly than in the state and the political system more generally. This is not saying that the techno-economic system and civil society are left unaffected by the self-confrontation and risk reflexivity. However, it is in their effects on the state and the political system that structures and dynamics of risk society set themselves more fundamentally apart from the new economy and social transformations already associated with network society.

The 'economy' of risk

The new economy of post-industrial society is more or less universally seen to hinge on the new role of networks, information and knowledge, as elaborated by Bell, Castells and a host of more popular entries about the new economy. The proliferation of manufactured, global and incalculable risks does not change this logic on the level of organization, key factors of production, sources of wealth and growth, global competition, the accelerated rise and fall of big businesses, the division of labour or other established dimensions of the economy in the normal sense of the term. The principal economic 'effect' of risk society is rather the superimposition of a new mode or logic of production on the post-industrial economy. This is what Beck describes as a fundamental shift in the primary mode of production from a logic of wealth production/distribution to a new logic of risk production/distribution (Beck, Beck, 1992b: 70). Post-industrial society obviously still produces goods, services and ultimately wealth, but the particular post-industrial mode of production is defined not only by the importance of information, knowledge and network organization, but also by the fact that the production and distribution of wealth is increasingly overtaken and reshaped in the light of the threats and hazards that were previously suppressed, limited and understood as acceptable side effects.

Risk society thus involves a reversal of the hierarchy between the two logics: whereas the logic of wealth production dominates risk production in industrial society, the reverse holds true for post-industrial society, and the gains of techno-economic progress are increasingly overshadowed by its risks. In other words, the production/distribution of 'bads' are increasingly superimposed on the basic economic production/distribution of goods (Beck, 1992b: 73). This reversal depends on two historical conditions. For one, the (partial) realization of the promise of emancipation from immediate material needs, the dictatorship of scarcity, undeserved poverty, social dependence and so on through techno-economic progress: the success story of industrial society and modernity. The second and darker historical condition, however, is that hazards, potential threats and destructive forces have been unleashed to an extent previously unknown or unseen through the process of industrialization. The conjunction of these two conditions means that the former is relativized and overridden by the latter: as industrial society surpasses the point of emancipation from a society of scarcity (albeit this point is still not reached for substantial parts of the world) and turns to overproduction, the basis of legitimatization for unchecked production and techno-economic progress gradually erodes, which in turn brings the fact that the sources of wealth are 'polluted' by growing and increasingly disastrous side effects into full view (Beck, 1992b: 20).

Risk exposure and individualization

This new logic of risk production and distribution is, in turn, complemented by new social and cultural uncertainties and insecurities in risk society, which amount to a process of 'social transformation within modernity, in the course of which people will be *set free* from the social forms of industrial society – class, stratification, family, gender status of men and women' (Beck, 1992b: 87, original emphasis). At this point, risk society and reflexive modernity add a further push to the erosion of civil society as a meaningful system of institutions and identities set in motion by the proliferation of informational networks. However, the dynamic here takes on a distinct logic of uncertainty and insecurity produced by the end of traditions and institutions associated with industrial civil society: 'risk society begins where tradition ends, when, in all spheres of life, we can no longer take traditional certainties for granted. The less we can rely on traditional securities, the more risks we have to negotiate' (Beck, 1998: 10). This argument, which bears strong resemblance to Giddens' analysis of reflexive modernity (1991), suggests that roles, institutions and social forms of civil society are being fundamentally recast according to new logics of reflexivity, individualization and risk exposure.

This logic is most apparent in the case of social class and stratification. On the one hand, the emancipation from the fixed class positions of industrial capitalism increases the potential for individual and meritocratic mobility. On the other hand, social inequality and stratification remains an obvious fact of life in risk society. The result can be called 'individualized social inequality' in the sense that inequality abstracted from social background and bonds, in principle at least, is replaced by the formation of new class distinctions based on a 'new inequality, the *inequality of dealing with insecurity and reflexivity*' (Beck, 1992b: 98, original emphasis). This argument assigns particular relevance to the labour market as a motor of individualization and thus adds a further attribute to the flexible workforce of the new economy. Partly related to this development, traditional gender roles and the institution of the nuclear family have also been submitted to the forces of individualization and risk exposure. On the hand, this means increased equality between the sexes and emancipation from the institutionalized system of inequality inscribed in the family in industrial society. On the other hand, however, it is also submits each individual to a new 'freedom of choice' between the family and the profession, which brings with it new risk exposures and inequalities (Beck, 1992b: 123).

Beyond the provident state

The new economic and social importance of risk production, distribution and exposure leads to a fundamental transformation of politics and the state under the conditions of risk society (Beck, 1995). Indeed, the 'entry into risk society occurs at the moment when the hazards that are now decided and consequently produced by society *undermine and/or cancel the established safety systems of the welfare state's existing risk calculations'* (Beck, 1999: 76, original emphasis). On this point, Beck draws on Ewald's analysis of *L'État providence* from the perspective of risk (1986). Ewald's analysis is, in turn, heavily inspired by Foucault's later work on governmentality, which had pointed to a clear connection between the 'biopolitical' management of the population and insurance technology, actuarial forms of calculation and ultimately the new importance of risk for this new art of government. From this perspective, Ewald suggests that the French welfare state is essentially defined by its regulation of the population as a 'risk group' based on a dialectic of risk calculation and insurance – calculation of accident statistics and probabilities and a generalized exchange principle of money for damages. The formative moment in this history is the first French law on accidents at work from 1898, seen as nothing less than the foundation of political modernity and philosophical event surpassing even the French Revolution in importance (Ewald, 1986).

This analysis pits the dialectic of risk and insurance against the more conventional interpretation of the welfare state from the perspective of class struggle, progressive politics and/or ideological compromises in the interest of the social and/or economic order. Instead, Ewald interprets the provision of welfare services (health care, education and the like), the creation of insurance schemes and social benefits, and ultimately the entire regulation of the economy and the environment 'in terms of the creation of security' (Beck, 1998: 20). This view of the welfare state as the expression of yet another step in the ongoing development of newer and ever more refined arts of government, as opposed to the emphasis on the emancipatory, progressive and egalitarian potential of welfare state policies, has generated substantial controversy about Ewald's analysis. This controversy has been further fuelled by Ewald's professional affiliation with the insurance industry and more or less official commitment to liberalism. Regardless of Ewald's choice of profession and personal politics, however, his analysis of the provident state is deeply loyal to the one consistent methodological principle exercised by Foucault: 'his single-minded insistence on the centrality of power to any serious analysis of history and society' (Behrent, 2010: 586). There is no other side of power, and even the welfare state – accomplishments notwithstanding – shapes life in particular ways that can and should be brought to light (Esmark, 2018).

Perhaps wisely, Beck largely avoids such controversies and focuses instead on the principal point: the simultaneous development of industrial society and the welfare state was overseen by a coalition of industry, science and state administration, centred around the dialectic of risk calculus and insurance (Beck & Holzer, 2007: 4). The result, at least in its Continental and Northern variant of the welfare state, can to some extent be seen as an 'Eldorado of bureaucratically organized care and caution' offering an unprecedented level of security founded on the perfection of 'techno-bureaucratic norms and controls' and 'highly developed safety bureaucracies', orienting society 'from top to toe toward security' (Beck, 1992a: 104). In other words: viewed as the essential institutional apparatus of the provident state, the techno-bureaucracy of the golden technocratic years can be understood as a highly developed safety bureaucracy and a form of 'linear' risk management inherent to advanced industrialism and the welfare state, operating through 'accident scenarios, statistics, social research, technical planning and a great variety of safety measures' (Beck, 1999: 76).

Thus understood, the advanced industrial technocracy is inseparable from the security pact of the welfare state and the 'security dream of the first modernity', based on the 'scientific utopia of making the unsafe consequences and dangers of decisions ever more controllable', and the principle that 'accidents could occur, as long as and because they were considered compensable' (Beck, 2006: 334). The material expression of the security dream and the security pact of the welfare state is a 'linear model of technocracy' underpinning the risk management of industrial society under the assumption that technical knowledge and proper planning could ensure full protection, or at least compensation, and thus a society of 'zero risk' (Beck, 1999: 82). The proliferation of manufactured, global and non-calculable risk and the onset of reflexive modernity, however, effectively put an end to the linear model of technocracy and its idea of zero risk, the underlying security pact of the welfare state and ultimately the very security dream that defined industrial society and the first modernity. The systematic cancellation and nullification of the risk calculations and safety systems inherent to the emergence of risk society, simply put, is equal to '*the invalidation of linear models of technocracy*' (Beck, 2009: 110, original emphasis).

On the one hand, the end linear technocracy suggests a decreasing capacity for industrial forms of risk assessment and management in risk society, as the safety bureaucracies of the welfare state are confronted and overrun by the spread and challenge of new hazards, threats and potentials for destruction. The proliferation of manufactured, global and incalculable risk systematically erodes the industrial dialectic of risk calculus and insurance: accidents and catastrophes lose their delimitations in time and space, generating an 'open-ended festival' of permanent and mutating crisis where damage becomes irreparable, unlimited and non-compensable; hazards cannot be precisely anticipated or monitored; and existing standards and procedures for calculation are abolished as calculation turns into obfuscation (Beck, 1992a: 102). Seen from the perspective of risk, the welfare state is a collective and institutional response to localized and externally attributable risks, based on actuarial principles of risk calculation, legally guaranteed compensation, and collectively shared and rule-governed responsibility. With the proliferation of manufactured, global and incalculable risk, however, 'these modes of determining and perceiving risk, attributing causality and allocating compensation have irreversibly broken down, throwing the function of bureaucracies, states, economies and sciences into question' (Beck, 1998: 16).

On the other hand, the new reflexivity about risk that invalidates linear technocracy also brings with it a potential 'enlightenment shock' seen to hold a potential for cosmopolitan democracy as well as extensive politicization of risk (Beck, 2006). The self-confrontation and reflexivity of risk society, in this view, involves 'a compulsion to open oneself' to outsider perspectives and knowledge, which challenge established technocratic prerogatives such as the authority of scientific and technical standards based on expert consensus and closed circles of decision making (Beck, 1999: 126). Thus, reflexive risk management not only implies the end of linear techno-bureaucracy as we know it, but supposedly also the 'liberation of politics, law and the public sphere from their expert patronization by technocracy' altogether (Beck, 1999: 61). Here, risk reflexivity appears not only as the impossibility of linear technocracy, but also approximates a standard of democratic (or at least political) legitimacy, centred around the idea of a '*second Enlightenment* which opens up our minds, eyes and institutions to the self-afflicted endangerment of industrial civilization' (Beck, 1998: 21, original emphasis). This argument parallels and reinforces arguments for the democratic virtues of network governance: self-confrontation and reflexivity 'compulsively' opens up the closed techno-bureaucratic apparatus to new agents and conflicts over questions, methods, scenarios and evaluations of risk.

As with network governance, however, less bureaucracy (including techno-bureaucracy) does not necessarily mean more democracy. At least any claim to such a development would have to stack up against the more likely result: the development of a new and more reflexive technocracy, fully embracing the enlightenment shock of risk society through the internalization of risk, uncertainty and the impossibility of insurance and protection. Although this form of technocracy may be risk reflexive rather than linear and stuck in a security dream of zero risk, it is not exactly democratic. Rather, risk reflexivity adds another crucial dimension to the new technocratic alliance with democracy against bureaucracy, thus adding a further push to the transition from government to governance in the shape of the informational, inclusive and multilayered network state. In contrast to the network state, risk reflexivity is not about the organizational transformation of the state per se, but rather the perpetuation and expansion of risk management working with the grain of the manufactured, global and incalculable nature of risk. Even if this endeavour may well call for the use of networks, it is ultimately about the exercise of reflexive risk management through the pursuit of wise policies and smart regulation in response increasingly wicked policy problems.

Public policy and wicked problems

In a society defined by the proliferation of manufactured, global and incalculable risk, policy problems become increasingly 'wicked' as opposed to 'simple' or 'tame', which is to say malignant, tricky, aggressive and caught in vicious circles. More generally, such wicked problems are defined by attributes such as, inter alia, the absence of definitive interpretations, limits, causes and solutions, essential uniqueness, chains, links and complex waves of repurcussions making every problem the symptom of another problem, irreversibility of decisions, the impossibility of correcting for unintended consequences and the imperative 'not to get it wrong', since 'interventions are social experiments that cannot go wrong without detrimental effects to society and citizens' (Rittel & Webber, 1973: 158). Although the broader context and causes of wicked problems were only explored rather superficially in Rittel and Webber's now canonical list, it did invoke a 'new social context' of 'post-industrial society', defined by increased differentiation, openness of social systems, interdependence and complexity (Rittel & Webber, 1973: 167).

With the benefit of hindsight, we can now recognize this as a provisional outline of what we know now as risk society. Rittel and Webber thus observed the proliferation of manufactured, global and incalculable risk from the perspective of public policy well before sociological inquiry gave us a fully developed analysis of risk society. The (re)interpretation of public policy problems as wicked policy problems, and the managerial challenge such problems pose, is in this sense a concrete expression of the internalization of risk and impossibility of insurance against dangers and hazards by governments reshaping security and regulation in risk society. While most of the key examples provided as evidence for this development were originally drawn from urban planning and social policy in a broad sense, including tax rates, school reform and crime, wicked problems were seen to potentially include nearly all public policy issues (Rittel & Webber, 1973:). This proclamation has proved more than a bit prophetic, as the list of wicked problems has grown steadily to the extent that few or no problems of public policy are currently considered simple or tame.

The realization that public policy was increasingly faced with wicked problems also captured the emerging conflict between risk society and linear technocracy more than a decade before Beck completed the argument. The conflict was originally framed as a 'dilemma' for the general theory and practice of social planning, but also more fundamentally by the claim that 'the classical paradigm of science and engineering – the paradigm that has underlain modern professionalism – is not applicable' to wicked policy problems (Rittel & Webber, 1973: 160). Indeed, the challenge of wicked problems were extended to the then dominant managerial paradigm in business and government in its entirety, that is, the paradigm forged 'in the industrial age' and based on combination of planning and a cognitive and occupational style of professionalism derived from modern science, mechanistic physics, classical economics and efficiency, where 'each of the professions has been conceived as the medium through which knowledge of science is applied ... in effect, each profession has been seen as a subset of engineering' (Rittel & Webber, 1973: 158). Given this argument, it is impressive that Rittel and Webber actually managed to avoid using the word technocracy. However, the point is clear enough: the type of social planning and engineering exercised by industrial and linear technocracy will only exacerbate wicked policy problems. Whereas Rittel and Webber could not yet gauge the alternative emerging out of this conflict, we can now give a fuller account of the result: the risk-reflexive technocracy of the new governance.

The new technocracy and the governance of resilience

While technical risk management and governance are to some degree still separated by practical and disciplinary boundaries, they have also increasingly merged. This development can be observed from both sides of the table. From the viewpoint of risk management, the turn to governance signifies an attempt to apply the framework of the new governance to the 'identification, assessment, management and communication of risks' (Renn & Walker, 2008: 11, see also Renn, 2008). This line of argument of revolves around the idea of collaborative governance and the use of networks as an integral part of good risk management. Networks are, according to this line of argument, ideally suited to ensure critical components of risk management such as collaboration, coordination, accumulation of knowledge and the flow of information (Conklin, 2006; Syrett & Devine, 2012; Helbing, 2013). While forms of organization and modes of governance associated with state and market remains part of the package, networks are often seen as indispensable due to their capacity for information and knowledge sharing, stakeholder inclusion and flexible scaling (Daniels et al, 2006: 8). Moreover, networks are seen as a way to minimize organizational failures in response to old and new threats (Perrow, 2007), as well as an essential component of resilient and learning organizations (Weick, 2012).

Conversely, and more importantly, the new governance has also increasingly been interpreted as a generalized form of risk management under conditions of uncertainty and complexity (Koppenjan & Klijn, 2004; Jessop, 2011). Beyond more or less explicit connections between risk and governance, however, this link is maintained by the ubiquitous references to wicked problems demanding new policy approaches and smart regulation in the new governance. Within the all-pervasive organizational choice between bureaucracies, markets and networks, this had led to the general conclusion that 'traditional hierarchical forms of organization and systems of control, focused on input monitoring and process compliance, substantially limited the opportunities to think expansively about the policy issues of the type that might be thrown up by wicked problems' (Head & Alford, 2015: 719). Market organization, for its part, is also deemed insufficient to deal with wicked problems due to fragmentation, turf wars and, in cruder forms of NPM, an idealization of private business practices that tend to reinstate bureaucratic planning systems cloaked as corporate strategies. Hence, we arrive at network organization, involvement of stakeholders and leadership styles tailored to the demands of network management as the optimal response to wicked problems (Koppenjan & Klijn, 2004; Weber & Khademian, 2008; Head & Alford, 2015).

However, the principal implication of this convergence between the new governance and risk management does not concern organizational choice, although it does provide an additional rationale for the widespread preference for networks. The more important implications have to do with security, responsibility and ultimately regulation. The breakdown of the security dream of the first modernity and its embodiment in the security contract of the welfare state not only challenges the organizational form of the bureaucracy, but also the broader logic of traditional regulation. The regulatory rationale of the welfare state, viewed as a provident state tackling risks, was essentially that discernible and properly calculated risk could be met with a combination of legislative measures and financial tools such as insurance and compensation, thus providing adequate security and certainty. Risk society, however, throws this logic into disarray and questions if and how risk can be regulated and managed. In general, we can distinguish between three responses to this predicament: precaution, laissez-faire and resilience. This distinction roughly mirrors the idea of bureaucracy, markets and networks as broader modes of governance, but applied specifically to the problem of risk. In this respect, precaution, laissez-faire and resilience constitute what has been called 'risk regulation regimes' (Hood et al, 2001). All three options are on the table for the new governance, but as with networks, the more or less univocally preferred solution is the latter one: the creation and management of resilient citizens, organizations, infrastructures, communities, buildings, cities and so on.

Precautionary principle

In regulatory terms, precaution means that unless something is conclusively demonstrated to be safe, it should be forbidden. The principle thus confers an obligation on policy makers to ensure public safety through prohibition under conditions of scientific uncertainty about the potential for harm. By extension, the precautionary principle implies an assumption of guilt (harm) until proven otherwise, and shifts the burden of proof from the victim or accuser to the potential perpetrator. As such, the precautionary principle can be seen as the natural extension of the protective ambitions of linear techno-bureaucracy under the new conditions of the risk society. The basic logic of the precautionary principle is that manufactured, global and incalculable risk necessitates harder regulation, legislative measures and prohibitions. This is all the more so because the other instrument in the toolbox of the provident state is no longer available: regardless of whatever public expenditure is allowed, it cannot provide adequate insurance and compensation for the effects of crises and catastrophe in risk society. Precaution has, of course, always been a possible approach to risk, but in the face of risks that are not tolerable, manageable nor logically or practically insurable, precaution increasingly appears to be the only possible way to ensure certainty and safety. As such, the precautionary principle is essentially an attempt to maintain the security dream of zero risk and the claim that political solutions and safety bureaucracies are, even in a risk society, capable of maintaining safety and certainty.

In its attempt to anticipate and prevent harm, the precautionary principle suggests a way to navigate the conflict between the reality of manufactured, global and incalculable risk and the unabating pressure on government and safety bureaucracies to ensure safety and certainty. The precautionary logic of better safe than sorry corresponds to a 'hierarchist' risk regulation regime that retains, to the largest extent possible, the essential responsibility of government to develop anticipative solutions for the whole of society based on a justice model of aggregated social welfare (Hood et al, 2001: 14). In addition to the use of prohibitions as the essential regulatory tool, precaution and the hierarchist risk regulation regime relies on extensive use of expert forecasting, quangos and committees to assess risk. The precautionary principle demands comprehensive and exhaustive anticipation of harm and the provision of public safety through bans and prohibitions, which can only be lifted with the support of conclusive scientific evidence. In this way, the precautionary principle raises the bar of technical and scientific evidence to a standard of conclusive evidence of harmlessness that is almost always impossible, thus creating a situation where technical and scientific expertise is called on to assess ever more risks, while also being subjected to higher levels of political suspicion and doubt.

Laissez-faire

The polar opposite to precautionary principle is laissez-faire. Used specifically as a principle of risk management, laissez-faire states that everything that has not been proven dangerous is safe. In legal or quasi-legal terms, the principle thus parallels the normal assumption of being innocent until proven otherwise, and reverts the burden of proof to the potential victim, or more generally to those claiming risk or harm. More specifically, laissez-faire implies an obligation to abstain from regulation (or to deregulate) in lieu of absolute proof of harm. Moreover: even when intervention and regulation is called for, laissez-faire takes bans and prohibitions to be a last resort, preferably avoided by the use of soft law such as safety standards, threshold values, quotas, licences and permissions, financial tools such as polluter-pays and/or attempts to reduce information asymmetries or deficiencies. The laissez-faire principle is thus the core of the 'individualist' risk regulation regime, placing risk management in the hands of individual citizens and firms relating through markets and courts, based on a justice model of free choice, minimal legal intrusion and taxation of behaviour (Hood et al, 2001: 14). This use of the principle clearly builds on the usual meaning of the principle in liberal economic theory and practice, and the (re)interpretation of laissez-faire specifically in the context of governmental risk management has, correspondingly, gained ground through liberal critiques and revisions of the precautionary principle (Sunstein, 2002b).

Viewed specifically as a response to risk society, however, the laissez-faire principle embodies a form of 'hazard technocracy', which is to say a form of intervention where expansive threshold values, the demand for absolute proof of harm and compensation through private settlement lead to a situation where the potential for harm is materially increasing but politically, legally and economically decreasing (Beck, 1992a: 103). Taken to its radical conclusion, the demand for decisive evidence of harm will mean that even causes of harm supported by normal scientific balances of probability will be disregarded as evidence for culpability and demands on compensation. As with the precautionary principle, hazard technocracy arises out of the conflict between security claims, concepts and recipes developed in the industrial era (in particular those related to private insurance and settlement) and the reality of risk society, but with the opposite result: rather than an attempt to match new threats through anticipation and prevention, hazard technocracy maintains its security claims through rejection and nullification of threats. In the individualist risk regulation regime of hazard technocracy, 'dangers are being produced by industry, externalized by economics, individualized by the legal system, legitimized by the sciences and made to appear harmless by politics' (Beck, 1998: 16).

Resilience

Both precautionary measures/hierarchist risk regulation regimes and laissez-faire/individualist risk regulation regimes are readily observable responses to the challenges of risk society. However, they are also at odds with the basic lesson of risk society: accidents and disasters will happen, probably sooner than later, and attempts to deal with this situation are likely to create new accidents and disasters. The problem, in a nutshell, is that both principles fall short of adequate risk reflexivity: precautionary measures suggest that security is possible by finding and removing the root cause of harm, whereas the laissez-faire principle suggest that security is possible because the threat of harm is negligible or even non-existent. Both claims, however, are continuously undercut with each occurrence of crisis or catastrophe, or even the mere suspicion of potential harm, showing the failures and inadequacies of political risk management. The result is always and everywhere crisis management (logically the result of failed risk management), damage control, blame games and buck-passing. In risk society, 'not only accidents, but even the suspicion of them, can cause the facades of security claims to collapse' (Beck, 1992a: 105).

It against this background that the principle of resilience has gained traction as a more consistent response to the reality of risk society and the demand for adequate risk reflexivity. The principle of resilience offers a way out of the impasse of risk society: rather than having security claims constantly exposed and undercut, the principle of resilience is inherently based on the assumption that crisis, failure and catastrophe is inevitable, but nevertheless maintains that some form of security is possible in risk society through reflexivity, awareness, adaptation, innovation and recovery (Rogers, 2015). This enterprise corresponds to a rather particular combination of the 'fatalist' and 'egalitarian' risk regulation regimes (Hood et al, 2001: 14). The fatalist risk regulation regime, for its part, stresses the unpredictability and unmanageability of risk, the unintended consequences of policy solutions, thus substituting governmental anticipation and prevention for ad hoc and post hoc responses to crisis and catastrophe as they occur, based on a 'chancist' justice model. The egalitarian risk regulation regime, in turn, emphasizes local and community participation in the development of adequate responses to risk. Both types of risk regulation are endemic to resilience building as a form of social engineering – the creation of individual and collective subjects with a capacity for continuous change, innovation and adaptation in the face of risks and uncertainty.

The concept of resilience originates in technical engineering where it is used as a measure of material constancy or elasticity, meaning the amount of energy that can be stored or absorbed by a material without permanent distortion. However, the concept was significantly revised from a definition of material efficiency to a concept of 'systemic recovery' in the field of ecology, where it is defined as the 'capacity of a system to absorb disturbance and reorganize while undergoing change so as to still retain essentially the same function, structure, identity and feedbacks' (Walker et al, 2004: 66). While this definition is premised on an interplay between disturbance and equilibrium, the emphasis on reorganization also implies that systems can function under multiple states, which is to say that resilience is closely connected to adaptive capacity, change and disturbances that can switch systems from one equilibrium state to another. Through this reorientation towards external shocks and capacity to maintain stability and balance in ecosystems, resilience becomes a more dynamic and complex processes than the 'linear application' in engineering resilience (Rogers, 2017: 15). Indeed, 'systems are seen as complex, non-linear, multi-equilibrium and self-organizing; they are permeated by uncertainties and discontinuities', making causal predictions difficult if not impossible (Berkes & Folke, 1998: 12).

Another important source of resilience thinking is the structure and culture of so-called HROs, defined by their ability to overcome external shocks and crisis normally thought to threaten organizational functions and survival, often at the forefront of technological and industrial risk (LaPorte & Consolini, 1991). More generally, 'high reliability theory' provides one of the two major paradigms of organizational theories of risk, the other being the 'normal accident theory' about the inevitability of organizational failure (Perrow, 1984). The resilient organization, combines so-called 'precursor resilience' – the ability to absorb external shocks and maintain operational capacity during crisis and catastrophe – and 'recovery resilience' – the ability to bounce back, returning to normalcy after crisis (Boin & Van Eeten, 2013). Moreover, 'adaptive resilience' denotes a capacity to emerge even stronger after disruptions, learning from crisis rather than engaging in blame games (Boin et al, 2014; Duit, 2015). The culture of resilience in HROs has also been viewed as distinct value system in the public sector, based on standards of success such as reliability, adaptation and robustness vis-à-vis standards of failure such as risk, crisis, breakdown and collapse, all within the overall 'currency' of security and survival (Hood, 1991: 11).

Reflecting the design principles of HROs, the value system of resilience in the public sector is in turn associated with a type of organization based on loose coupling, multiple and negotiated goals, high degree of redundancy (or slack), open channels of information and knowledge sharing. Notably, the values and design principles of resilient organizations was highlighted by Hood as a contrast to the values and design principles of the then dominant NPM reforms, as well as the values and design principles of bureaucracy. A more direct analysis of resilience as a risk regulation regime is found in Wildavsky's analysis of safety paradigms in public policy, which draws a direct contrast between the precautionary principle and hierarchist risk regulation on the one hand and a resilience-based approach to risk on the other. Here, the latter denotes a capacity to cope with unanticipated dangers when they become manifest – 'learning to bounce back' rather than relying on anticipation and prevention (Wildavsky, 1988: 85). In addition to systemic and ecological resilience, this understanding also draws on the psychological concept of resilience, which denotes a capacity to deal with stress and turn adverse circumstances into positive (or at least normal) human development (Richardson, 2002).

From these various points, resilience has gradually come to occupy a more fundamental position as the principal response to the 'the governance of complexity' in risk society (Chandler, 2014). In contrast to precaution and laissez-faire, resilience does not seek to maintain traditional security thinking and guarantees under the conditions of risk society, but rather encapsulates an attempt to exercise adequate 'self-reflective awareness' about the 'unintended consequences or secondary effects (side effects) of any securitizing measure', of the 'internal capacities and attributes and the need to be constantly adaptive', and of the 'relational vulnerabilities' reproduced through complex systems and relations of interdependence (Chandler, 2014: 11). As the new governance has developed, resilience has become increasingly influential in a number of external and material policies concerned with the creation of resilient citizens, businesses, communities and systems in response to risks and wicked problems such as international conflict and development, terrorism, cyber attacks, climate change and socio-economic development (Comfort et al, 2010; Aldrich & Meyer, 2014; Chandler, 2014; Chandler & Coaffee, 2017).

The principle of resilience thus takes us decisively from old, industrial and linear technocracy to a new and reflexive technocracy, based on the internationalization of risk and the impossibility of insurance against dangers and hazards. Indeed, resilience thinking reflects a more basic shift from 'mechanistic and linear metaphors of command-and-control' (Head & Alford, 2015: 724), and from the liberal modernist ontology of linearity and discrete subjects, to a relational ontology of complex system dynamics and the 'rise of non-linearity or of our awareness of contingency and complexity' (Chandler, 2014: 11). Correspondingly, an art of government shaped fundamentally by non-linearity and reflexivity is seen by its proponents to reside in fundamental conflict with traditional government, instead demanding 'a different set of strategies and processes of governance', based on recognition of the fact that complex relational systems cannot be governed or directed 'from above', that unintended outcomes are inevitable and that 'failing better' should be the key goal in the development and adjustment of wise policies (Chandler, 2014: 12). In other words, the development and implementation of public policy based on the resilience principle and its fatalist-egalitarian risk regulation regime is the key addition of reflexive risk management to the new governance. I conclude this chapter by discussing two examples of this development.

Resilience and ecological governance

Resilience and fatalist-egalitarian risk regulation have undoubtedly had the biggest impact on environmental policy, which is not to say that this approach reigns supreme in this area. Environmental policy has also seen a consolidation of the precautionary principle in the UN charter for the protection of nature, the Montreal Protocol for protection of the ozone layer, the Rio Declaration, the Kyoto Protocol, the Treaty of the European Union (article 191) and in a number of state-level environmental policies. Moreover, environmental policy is rife with a form of regulation closer to the ideas of the laissez-faire principle such as tradeable quotas systems, licences and polluter-pays (Hepburn, 2010). However, socioecological resilience has been essential to the ongoing development of environmental risk management as an inclusive and overarching form of 'ecocentric' management, environmental governance and climate change governance (Shrivastava & Hart, 1995; Bernauer & Schaffer, 2012).

The history of environmental policy is comparatively short and intrinsically related to the changing perception of industrial production and risks that underlie the transition from industrial society to risk society. The recognition of potentially irrevocable environmental damage provides a practical and operational standard for the reality of manufactured, global and incalculable nature of industrial risk, leading to a surge of various national constellations of ministries and agencies devoted to the environment and industrial risk producers (energy, nuclear safety, mining, agriculture, transportation and so forth) from the 1970s onwards. The switch from a primary logic of wealth production/distribution to a primary logic of risk production/distribution, and, of course, the continuing tensions between the two, is thus reflected with particular clarity in the domain of environmental policies. In contrast to the protection of individuals through social policies, workplace regulation, food and drug regulation and consumer protection, environmental policy was from the outset concerned with the identification and limitation of industrial risks at the level of ecological systems.

Environmental policy is in this sense born with techniques and practices of risk assessment and management influenced by, inter alia, ecology, natural resource management, environmental economics and engineering (Power & McCarty, 2002). It is in this context that the concept of resilience was introduced as a paradigm for the interpretation and management of ecosystems based on a fundamental preoccupation with 'measuring the probabilities of extinction' (Holling, 1973). Ecological resilience is a composite measure of four variables: latitude (the threshold or point of no return after which recovery becomes impossible); precariousness (proximity to the point of no return); resistance (the ease of change in a system, or lack thereof); and 'panarchy' (the level of cross-scale interactions, or more informally the interconnectedness and complexity of the system) (Gunderson & Holling, 2002). While the original application of resilience to ecosystems was to some degree focused on external management of natural systems, subsequent development of the approach has resulted in a more integrated view of 'social ecology' that shifts the focus to the adaptive capacity of social *and* environmental system, in either 'contestation or cooperation' (Rogers, 2017: 16).

Although socioecological resilience has been available as a concept of environmental risk assessment and management for some time, more widespread use of the principle in environmental policy has largely followed the arrival of climate change as an all-pervasive problem and the corresponding understanding of human impact on ecosystems. The reframing and reinterpretation of existing environmental policies in the horizon of global climate change and the Anthropocene have in this sense found a common focus point in the principle of socioecological resilience and the complex interplay of human systems and ecosystems working either in contestation or cooperation. For one, this development includes established policies related to the measurement and control of environmental impact, including pollution and waste management, protection of natural resources and biodiversity, control of agriculture, deforestation, fishing and, of course, nuclear waste, chemicals, toxins, biotechnology and other industrial risks. While such concerns form the historical nucleus of environmental policy, the focus on resilience here implies a more pervasive strategy of environmental governance where environmental concerns are embedded in all levels and sectors of decision making, social systems and individuals are viewed as a subset of ecosystems and strong standard of zero environmental impact is maintained through innovative use of technologies and whole systems management.

Second, socioecological resilience been introduced to existing policies on sustainable growth and development, which relate more directly to the interplay of economic progress and the environment, originally premised on the idea that the latter provides the former with definite 'limits to growth' (Meadows et al, 1972). Building on this idea, sustainability and sustainable development have developed through various incarnations and variations, ranging from early conservation efforts past the infamous Brundtland Commission and its ensuing framework of 'three pillars' and the 'triple bottom line' (environment, economic growth and social fairness) (United Nations, 1987), Agenda 21 and the Rio Protocol, the Millennium Goals and the most recent iteration in the '2030 Agenda', which lists 17 Global Goals for Sustainable Development (United Nations, 2015). In this process, socioecological resilience has been used to emphasize that the distinction between social (including economic) and ecological systems are fundamentally linked or even integrated (Berkes & Folke, 1998), which in turn calls for integrated and adaptive environmental management focused on the need for learning and continuous change. In the more radical version of this argument, socioecological resilience is understood as a necessary alternative to the 'weaker' principle of sustainable development that does not take the ultimate limits of Earth's resilience into account.

Behind these developments, however, lies the third and more pervasive use of resilience in relation to the challenges of global warming and climate change. Here, resilience is now used as the 'third pillar' of responses to global warming together with climate change mitigation and adaptation. More to the point, socioecological resilience provides a common framework of 'climate-resilient pathways' that highlights an integrated approach to the mitigation of and adaptation to short- and long-term effects of climate change (IPCC, 2014). Mitigation includes efforts to reduce emission of greenhouse gases (currently the goal is a reduction of 40 per cent by 2030 per the Paris agreement) through interventions in production and transportation, to the transition to renewable energy, as well as geoengineering and use of carbon-binding ecosystems. Adaptation, for its part, includes measures intended to cope with the effects of climate change, including changing weather patterns and natural disaster as well as economic effects. In this context, the introduction of resilience implies a rejection of the opposition between mitigation and adaptation 'camps' in climate change policy and debate (a battle over whether to deal with the causes or the effects) in favour of a dual perspective where mitigation and adaptation appear as two sides of the same coin. Although 'climate resilience' is to some degree and extension and modification of adaptation (Nelson et al, 2007; Nelson, 2011), the broader implication is a two-pronged strategy including mitigation as well as adaptation in an effort to close the 'resilience gap' of socioecological systems (Union of Concerned Scientists, 2016).

Climate change is the quintessentially global risk and socioecological resilience is the quintessentially holistic and systemic perspective on risk management. However, the emphasis on resilience has also served to break up the global challenge into discrete and possible actions taken on different levels of decision making. This development involves the standard tiers and scales of the MLG system, thus linking global resilience to regional, national and local resilience. In this framework, metropolitan areas and cities have emerged as a particular crucial locus of action and a type of integrated socio-economic system in their own right. Building resilient communities and cities has thus become a key priority for the new urban governance and the 'smart growth' paradigm in local planning and development (Bahadur & Tanner, 2014; Brunetta et al, 2019). The latter development is part of the process of 'glocalization', which is the prevalence and interconnectedness of global and local horizons of action, and the potential 'bypass' of the national and regional levels and scales in between (Bulkeley & Betsill, 2003). In one sense, cities are of course part of the local level in the multilevel system of governance. On the other hand, however, cities also constitute a particular socio-geographical locus subject to its own particular dynamics of urbanization, concentration, growth and complexity.

While the recent and rapid proliferation of strategies, projects and policies related to the development of resilient communities and cities originated in environmental policy and responses to climate change, it has since come to include all manner of risks and threats. The recently concluded project '100 Resilient Cities' (100RC) launched under the auspices of the Rockefeller Foundation in 2013, defines resilience as the 'capacity of the individual, communities, institutions, businesses and systems within a city to survive, adapt and grow no matter what kinds of chronic stresses and acute shocks they experience' (see: www.100resilientcities.org/). Together, chronic stresses and acute shocks cover a wide array of risks and wicked problems, or 'resilience challenges', identified by the 100 cities taking part in the project: climate change, flooding, earthquakes, extreme cold and heat, energy insecurity and outages, ageing populations, crime, food insecurity, corruption, infrastructure protection, unemployment, overpopulation, terrorism and so on. The objective, correspondingly, is to develop projects and policies that address multiple challenges at the same time and pay a 'resilience dividend', that is, the benefits of applying the forward-looking, risk aware and inclusive 'resilience lens'.

The 100RC project was privately funded, but implemented by city authorities and embedded in a network of local governments, the private sector and NGOs with an overall aim of facilitating the global development of resilience practices. Moreover, the 100RC project was part of the Medellin Collaboration for Urban Resilience together with, among others, the World Bank, Cities and UN-Habitat. The World Bank, supported by the Global Facility for Disaster Reduction and Recovery, runs its own 'city resilience program' linking urban resilience to disasters, climate risks and poverty. With its particular emphasis on project development and funding, the programme covers more then 40 cities in developing regions (see the section on the city resilience program at the World Bank website, www.worldbank.org). UN-Habitat, the UN's programme for human settlements and sustainable urban development, runs projects, campaigns and a 'resilience hub' dedicated to urban resilience. UN efforts on urban resilience reflect a broader preoccupation with the development of an integrated analytical framework of 'risk and resilience', and 'risk management and resilience building' in order to promote coherent and holistic analysis and joint planning, and to maximize effectiveness and impact of policies, thus connecting the different pillars of the UN and the overall objectives of sustainable development (Askim et al, 2017).

Resilience and economic governance

Environmental policy and climate change have been the main conduit for resilience thinking and practice in public policy, but the paradigm has migrated well beyond the original notion of socioecological resilience. This development is already visible in urban resilience projects and policies, where an expansive list of risks is developing around the core risks related to climate change and natural disasters. This process is also found in other areas of governance and changes the interplay between risk and resilience on both sides of the equation: more risks are added to an expanding list of resilience challenges, and socioecological resilience is substituted with a broader concept of socio-economic resilience. Ecological and natural systems still produce risks, and these are often highlighted in available risk profiles, but there is also an increasing emphasis on risks that do not carry a distinctly ecological component. Correspondingly, the original concept of socioecological resilience is increasingly linked to established standards of well-being and welfare of the population found in social and economic policies and sciences.

'Economic resilience' is now broadly defined as the capacity of national economies to contain potential vulnerabilities, reduce the probability of crises and enhance the capacity of the broader economy to cope with shocks and crisis. Resilience is, correspondingly, associated with standard measures such GDP and growth rates (OECD, 2015), as well as broader measures of social welfare (Briguglio et al, 2009). While the causes and dynamics of crisis, and available responses, are of course issues of long-standing interest in economic theory and policy, the integrated focus on exposure to shocks, mitigation of their impact and ability to recover is of more recent date, spawned in no small measure by the financial crisis of 2008 (OECD, 2016). The result is a particular emphasis on the general risk of being affected by external shocks and the attributes of national (or regional) economies that determine the level of exposure or vulnerability to such shocks. Economic policies and measures are, correspondingly, assessed in light of their ability to offset vulnerabilities by increasing the coping ability and enabling countries to withstand or bounce back from adverse shocks. This, in turn, draws attention to the trade-offs between economic growth and vulnerability as the central standard of economic policy choice (OECD, 2016). Achieving growth without exposure or vulnerability thus becomes the ultimate goal of macroeconomic risk management.

While this form of risk management maintains exogenous shocks (man-made or natural disasters, climate change, refugee crisis and the like) in the risk profile, emphasis is on crisis (currency, banking, debt crisis) and shocks (downturns) intrinsic to the economy. On the one hand, possible responses to the threat of economic crisis include detection and early warning systems based on selected macroeconomic indicators of economic imbalances and vulnerability (Hermansen & Röhn, 2017). Such efforts are concerned with risk assessment, identification of key vulnerabilities that expose national economies to shock and development of forecasting models – predicting the next crisis – thus enabling preventive steps or avoidance of shock or crisis altogether. However, economic resilience policies and tools are associated more strongly with coping capacity and the ability to bounce back. Here, institutional quality and stability, interventions in favour of competitive product markets and the development of flexible labour markets are seen as preferable, while support and liberalization of financial markets generate growth at the cost of increased fragility (the 2008 global financial crisis), and the reverse holds true for 'macro-prudential' measures putting loan caps, reserve requirements, liquidity demands and so forth on financial markets (OECD, 2015).

In addition to the OECD, the focus on economic resilience and corresponding policy measures has been central to recent initiatives by G20, the IMF, European Central Bank and the EU in general (European Commission, 2018). In what is perhaps the most consistent effort to make resilience and overarching policy objectives so far, however, the Rome Declaration (which can reasonably be seen as the key document on the future response of the EU to recent crises and challenges, not least that of Brexit), introduced a 'stronger and more resilient' union as the principal response to the 'new and unprecedented challenges' such as regional conflicts, terrorism, migration and socio-economic inequality (Council of the European Union, 2017). The introduction of resilience in high-level proclamations has, in turn, been mirrored by an attempt to develop a systemic and integrated framework 'operationalizing resilience for policy and monitoring purposes' and placing 'resilience sensors' on all member-states so as to be able to track and regulate the 'behaviour of various *entities* such as people, communities, cities, regions or countries' (European Commission, 2018: 9, original emphasis).

Conceptually, the EU resilience framework identifies resilience with a scale of capacities in response to the intensity of shocks and their duration: absorptive capacities, adaptive capacities and transformative capacities. The framework distinguishes between the 'engine', 'assets' and outcomes of national systems, as well the economic 'core' measures across these dimensions and the broader 'non-core' measures. Whereas the former include standard economic measures such as investment, government deficit, employment rate GDP and so on, the latter include broader societal standards of welfare such as fairness, trust, social activity happiness and life satisfaction in an effort to 'ensure that not only economic, but natural, social and environmental resources are also harnessed in an efficient, sustainable, fair and responsible manner' (European Commission, 2018: 5). All said, the framework includes 34 systems variables that can be combined into aggregated resilience indicators in order to assess system-wide behaviour. Taking the latest global financial, economic and sovereign debt crisis as an opportunity for a 'unique natural experiment for the study of resilience' (European Commission, 2018: 6), the framework has so far been put to the test by ranking the ability of EU member-states to bounce back or even 'bounce forward' (performing better than pre-crisis levels) between 2007 and 2016 (European Commission, 2018: 15).

Conclusion

Risk management was always a quintessentially technocratic enterprise. In its original form, risk management has been integral to industrial production, society and state. It originated as a standard of good engineering and grew with industrial production and its increasing effects on society, citizens and consumers. As a form of governmental rationality and practice, it has been integral to the welfare state and the techno-bureaucracies charged with upholding its security and compensation schemes. However, this form of industrial risk management has been completely overrun and undercut in risk society, which spells the end of linear technocracy, the security dialectic of risk calculation and risk insurance and, according to Beck, the end of bureaucracy and rational modernity as conceived by Weber altogether. In its place, risk society has supposedly heralded in a new era of reflexive modernity invoking a promise of a possible enlightenment shock and a new cosmopolitan moment.

However, the enlightenment shock and cosmopolitan moment of reflexive modernity have, more than anything else, created a more risk-reflexive technocracy fully immersed in the new reality of manufactured, global and incalculable risk. In more or less direct opposition to linear technocracy, the new technocratic principle is the internalization of risk and the impossibility of insurance and protection against dangers and uncertainty. This, in turn, suggests a new approach to risk regulation in response to the proliferation of wicked problems everywhere in public policy. Conceived as risk regulation, policy programmes and interventions can follow a precautionary principle (the hierarchical risk regulation regime), laissez-faire (the individualist risk regulation regime) or resilience (the fatalist–egalitarian risk regulation regime). Faced with this choice, risk–reflexive technocrats will more or less univocally opt for the latter and focus on building resilient citizens, organizations, communities, societies and systems. Although this choice is coherent by the standards of risk reflexivity, it is far from inherently democratic. The new technocratic approach rather draws its appeal from the contrast with the old bureaucratic principle of precaution and prohibitions, as well as the hazard technocracy of laissez-faire. However, a technocracy informed by the enlightenment shock of risk society is not a cosmopolitan democracy, but rather a new type of risk reflexive and recursive technocracy.

7

Technocratic Calculation: Economy, Evidence and Experiments

> Cost-benefit analysis reflects a firm (and proud) commitment to a *technocratic conception of democracy*.
> (Sunstein, 2018: xi, original emphasis)

The last (and first) piece of the puzzle

This chapter concludes the analysis of the three basic paradigms of the new technocracy by looking in more detail at the search for scientific results and evidence in public policy, conducted under the broader label of performance management. Historically, performance management has been developed through a steady accumulation of concepts, practices and standards such as quality management, management by numbers, evidence-based policy, evaluation practices, auditing and inspection. The common denominator, however, is a fundamental commitment to improve public policies through measurement of effects in ways that make it possible to confer the status of quantifiable and objective evidence on these effects more or less directly. The core idea of performance management is thus to make the policy process part of, and ideally identical to, the scientific process of discovery. As such, the chapter tackles what is often considered the first and last dimension of technocracy more directly: governmental scientism and the preoccupation with quantification, measurement and objective evidence as the foundation of political authority and effective social engineering.

This focus comes with a particular challenge: given the historical constancy of governmental scientism in technocratic rule, what is then new about the new technocracy in this respect? Whereas the paradigms of network organization and reflexive risk regulation introduce rather clear shifts and reversals in technocratic rationality and practice, the current attempt to provide a scientific basis for public policy through performance management seems rather to confirm the idea of eternally recurring Saint-Simonism: the claim that technocracy has remained largely unchanged since its initial conception. This degree of historical permanence is certainly part of the equation when it comes to performance management. As much as I would like to list more decisive events of the 1980s in the spirit of the two preceding chapters, such an exercise would not make much sense. If anything, this would be where the interpretation of the 1980s as the decisive decade in the rise of neoliberal hegemony becomes relevant, at least when it comes to the question of the econocracy and the influence of economic knowledge and expertise on public policy.

In some ways, the current technocratic exercise of performance management is as close to an affirmation of Bell's baseline hypothesis about the belated realization of technocracy in post-industrial society as we can get: performance management thrives because our current society is still a knowledge society based on the continued 'centrality of theoretical knowledge as the source of innovation and policy formulation in society' (Bell, 1999: 14). Whereas network society and risk society both comprise dimensions of post-industrial society that did indeed only come into full view roughly around the 1980s, Bell's axial principle, *primus inter pares* among the five basic dimensions of post-industrial society, turned out be the most prescient part of his social forecasting. Together with the ancillary development of new intellectual technologies, the axial principle still has significant purchase on the current state of affairs in public policy. Performance management is to some extent the most recent result of the mutual constitution of knowledge society and a form of political management exercising social control and engineering on the basis of theoretical knowledge for the purpose of directing innovation and change.

However, knowledge society has also, in important ways, become a learning society, an experimental society, an evaluation society and an audit society. The structures and dynamics underlying all of these developments have occurred in the interplay between technology and methods for the production and calculation of knowledge. The common denominator between the various extensions and permutations of the knowledge society, correspondingly, is that they challenge the importance of purely theoretical knowledge and its ancillary intellectual technologies originally observed by Bell. The new technocracy has changed accordingly: rather than a univocal commitment to theoretical knowledge, the new technocracy is guided by a broader and more inclusive principle of *learning from evidence and the continuous improvement of policy*. On the one hand, this principle clearly reflects the historical continuity with earlier technocratic versions of technocratic scientific government and policy. On the other hand, however, the principle also reflects a significant degree of change in the span and purpose of knowledge applied in public policy and in the way evidence is collected and calculated. This, however, has only served to make current performance management a broader and more influential policy paradigm, in contrast to the limited influence sometimes attested to by its forerunners.

This success is largely due to the efforts of the new governance. Performance management is widely seen as one of the cornerstones and lasting contributions of NPM, even among those inclined to declare NPM dead. In the NPM version, performance management largely comes down to a focus on quantification, measurement and calculation of individual and organizational performance for the broader purpose of mimicking the informational flows and signals of the market in the public sector. The result is the pervasive spread of accounting systems designed to calculate efficiency and, by the same token, enable auditing, inspection and public accountability. However: although NPM reforms have certainly had a bigger impact on performance management than network governance and risk management, the NPG version of the new governance has brought its own version to the table. The NPG version of performance management calls for better (quasi-)scientific procedures of data collection, calculation and dissemination in order to find out 'what works' in public policy, often with the help of engaged citizens. The result is a form of evaluation systems designed for the creation of public value, problem-solving, experimentation, innovation and public participation. Although the accountability and evaluation systems are rather different in intention and potential effects, they can be hard to disentangle in practice and they share certain fundamental features such as a commitment to hard evidence, comparison, ranking and cost/benefit calculation, broadly understood.

Both versions of performance management exacerbate a conflict with bureaucracy that was always inherent to the technocratic reliance on quantification, measurement and scientific evidence in the pursuit of public policy. Although this conflict may have been moderated by the compromise of techno-bureaucracy, current performance management is less inclined to strike a compromise with bureaucracy. Regardless of whether performance is viewed as a matter of increased efficiency and accountability or innovation and problem-solving, bureaucracy is largely understood as an obstacle to improved performance. And, following a now familiar pattern, this anti-bureaucratic stance more or less invariably correlates with a new claim to democratic legitimacy, be it through efficiency and improved accountability or improved public value and social welfare. Either way, the democratic gain in performance management comes down to a matter of output legitimacy. This is how, as represented by Sunstein's proud commitment to a technocratic conception of democracy discussed earlier, performance management contributes to the new technocratic alliance with democracy and simultaneous rejection of bureaucracy. In order to gauge this development, however, we have first to consider the interplay of technology and dominant methods of calculation and choice more fundamentally.

Still the age of econocracy? Technocratic knowledge and methods of calculation

In institutional terms, Bell's identification of post-industrial society as a knowledge society is based on a new alliance of science and technology under the auspices of a politically guided search for innovation (see Chapter 2). The specific axial principle arising out of this development, however, is at one and same time highly specific and extremely general: 'what has become decisive for the organization of decisions and the direction of change', he states, 'is the centrality of *theoretical* knowledge – the primacy of theory over empiricism and the codification of knowledge into abstract systems that, as in any axiomatic system, can be used to illuminate many different and varied areas of experience' (Bell, 1999: 20, original emphasis). In other words, the axial principle builds on a direct contrast between theoretical knowledge and empirical knowledge, or at least the amateur 'empiricism' that drove the major innovations of industrial society. The nature of this claim and its importance for the assumption about the rise of technocracy in knowledge society gives rise to a number of more specific questions at the heart of the belated realization thesis.

Scientific disciplines and fields of knowledge

First and foremost, what scientific fields and bodies of knowledge support technocratic power and influence? On the one hand, the axial principle clearly refers to the advent of 'hard' sciences in general and in public policy in particular. As Bell's later restatement of the axial principle makes clear, theoretical knowledge principally means the axiomatic and symbolic systems of mathematics applied to domains such as quantum theory, relativity theory, solid-state physics, materials science and so on (Bell, 1999: 39). In this way, the axial principle refers to the core academic disciplines at the heart of the new relationship between technology and science, that is, the involvement of physicists, chemists and mathematicians in the technological innovations of modern warfare, propelled by the Second World War but carried over to the peacetime operations of the military–industrial complex and institutions with a broader public policy agenda such as RAND. In other words, the proliferation and importance of theoretically codified knowledge is what draws the hard sciences into public policy and helps technocracy overcome its previous limitations as the rule of engineers.

However, the involvement of hard science and foundational research in technological innovation is not the most important implication of the axial principle for technocratic influence on public policy. For this, we have to look to the impact of the new primacy of theoretically codified knowledge in a 'less direct but equally important way', in the 'formulation of government of government policy, particularly in the management of the economy' (Bell, 1973: 22). More specifically, the axial principle of post-industrial society is brought most decisively to bear on public policy and social engineering through 'the attempted use of an increasingly rigorous, mathematically formalized body of economic theory, derived from the general equilibrium theory', resulting in a situation where 'managing the economy is only a technical offshoot of a theoretical model' and 'economic policy formulations, though not an exact art, now derive from theory and must find their justification in theory' (Bell, 1973: 25).

In other words, the axial principle is also the immediate source of the econocracy – a technocracy operating more or less exclusively through the body of knowledge nurtured by neoclassical economics (see Chapters 1 and 2), and the corresponding idea the idea that a background in economics, the quintessential form of 'technical' social science, is the most important indicator of a technocratic orientation (see Chapter 3). Bell's axial principle thus points us to an almost unbroken line of mutually reinforcing formalization of economics and involvement in economic policy since the economic discipline started its path to academic and political prominence more than 70 years ago: even the experience of the last great economic recession, largely unforeseen and by most accounts at least partially caused by economic experts, has done little to reduce the status of the neoclassical paradigm and its influence on public policy (Chang, 2014; Earle et al, 2017). However, the econocracy is also a 'changeable beast that has evolved with economic knowledge but that always values this knowledge above all else and always involves experts in turning political problems into purely "economic" ones' (Earle et al, 2017: 17).

The major changes in the nature of the econocratic beast include additions to the neoclassical paradigm such as (new) institutional economics, behavioural economics and, to a lesser degree, ecological economics. Indeed, these traditions have been welcomed into the economic mainstream: key representatives of institutional economics such as Coase, North, Ostrom and Williamson have all received the 'memorial' Nobel prize, as have representatives of the behaviouralist school such as Kahneman and Thaler, the latter being one of the principal architects behind the nudging agenda that rose to prominence in the United States under Obama's tenure, although it was represented at the governmental level even earlier in the United Kingdom by the so-called Nudge Unit. Simon, who received the prize in 1978, is a key figure in both traditions. Nordhaus, a recent laureate, received the price for integrating climate change into standard economic models, thus providing official recognition for one of the economists 'flirting with the idea of moving away from GDP as the central measure of economic success' (Earle et al, 2017: 16). The question is, then, whether outcrops such as institutional economics, behavioural economics or ecological economics signal deeper changes in the established body of economic knowledge or its influence on public policy.

On the one hand, it is clear that none of the more recent additions represent a fundamental break with the dominant paradigm. Although they proceed from observations of certain limitations in basic assumptions of neoclassical economics, their ambition is still to improve and expand on the basic axiomatic system of economics. Moreover, they remain firmly committed to the image of economics as a form of hard or technical science, even if advanced mathematics is sometimes used more sparsely. On the other hand, institutional economics and behavioural economics also place greater emphasis on the 'layered' or 'bounded' rationality of individuals and their interplay with institutions as an important part of the economy. Correspondingly, proponents of new institutional economics and behavioural economics will typically take a more flexible stance on government interventions and, more importantly, look to a wider range of policy domains as areas of intervention rather than the traditional reliance on macroeconomic policy levers.

This development can also be seen to suggest the new technocracy is in some sense more pluralist or even cross-disciplinary than a straightforward econocracy. Institutional economics is situated somewhere between political science and economy in a manner akin to a revised form of political economy. Kahneman and Tversky, the godfathers of behavioural economics, where both trained as psychologists. The creator of the British nudge unit, also a psychologist, has suggested that the real revolution in behavioural public policy lies in bringing psychologists to the heart of public policy (Halpern, 2015: 30). Taken to its radical conclusion, this suggests that the use of behavioural economics in public policy amounts to a 'psychocracy' rather than an econocracy (Feitsma, 2018). Although economists still maintain a substantial grip on public policy, the econocracy has in this sense also experienced pressure from other disciplines with their own particular version of formal and technical social science. These disciplines have to a large extent been incorporated into the econocracy, which has in turn begun to offer policy advice based more on experiments, empirical studies and data, in addition to the purely theoretical knowledge traditionally provided by economic model simulations and calculations.

Intellectual technologies and methods

In addition to the axial principle itself, the fifth and last dimension of post-industrial society pointed to the rising importance of a set of ancillary 'intellectual technologies', enabling the 'substitution of algorithms (problem-solving rules) for intuitive judgements', and projected in the original forecast to be 'as salient in human affairs as machine technology has been for the past century and a half', if not sooner then by 'the end of the century' (Bell, 1973: 29). In essence, this suggests that the influence of theoretically codified knowledge captured by the axial principle extends to different techniques or methods of decision making and 'algorithmic' problem-solving based on the abstract and formal system of mathematics and logic. These technologies include, inter alia, cybernetics, systems analysis, game theory, decision theory, utility theory and, in mathematics, advanced set theory, probability theory and stochastic processes.

The proliferation of such intellectual technologies clearly has an intimate relationship with the opportunities offered by the calculative power and programming language of computer technology. The terminology of algorithms and technology thus lends itself easily to the idea that intellectual technologies can be equated with computer software, programmes and models in relation to the hardware of information technology. Indeed, Bell's revisiting of the original forecast confirms that this is the most important aspect of the informational revolution: the proliferation of intellectual technologies is greatly helped along by the transition from mechanical machine technology to information technology, but this is merely a development subsumed under the axial principle of knowledge society (Bell, 1999: 38). Current preoccupation with Big Data and machine learning clearly testifies to the continued enthusiasm for the power of algorithms in this respect. However, the new intellectual technologies ultimately invoke a broad and dual 'methodological promise' for the second half the century: the 'management of organized complexity (the complexity of large organizations and systems, the complexity of theory with a large number of variables)'; and 'the identification and implementation of strategies for rational choice in games against nature and games between persons' (Bell, 1973: 28).

Techniques and methods for the management of complex organizations and systems generally fall under the province of systems theory and cybernetics, both cross-disciplinary approaches loosely structured around the attempt to understand mechanical, biological, cognitive and social systems under the assumption that these display the same basic properties of organized complexity such as emergent and spontaneous order, self-organization, recursivity, feedback loops, learning and adaptation, which is then taken as a starting point for the pursuit of more adequate tools of management, steering and control (Wiener, 1961). The implied idea of a technical social science of steering and control based on the attribution of formal system properties to social systems has led some to view cybernetics and systems theory as the technocratic intellectual technology par excellence (Meynaud, 1968; Fischer, 1990). While cybernetics and systems theory do indeed bridge between mathematics, computer science, engineering, biology, psychology, sociology, law, organizational studies and management, however, they have also failed to consolidate themselves scientifically largely for the same reason. This is particularly pronounced in social science, where the approach is associated with functionalism and thus largely out of fashion, save for a stronghold in theories of organization and leadership. Moreover, direct influence on public policy has always been debatable.

To some degree, the intellectual technologies related to the identification and implementation of strategies for rational choice originate in the same branches of mathematics as cybernetics and systems theory. However, their development has also been defined by a much closer alignment with the econocracy and its core body of knowledge. Game theory, in particular, originates from the basic axiomatic system of the neoclassical paradigm (Earle et al, 2017: 96). In general, however, game theory is not a theory or model of markets or any particular object, but a method for the calculation of optimal choices under different strategic conditions of cooperation and conflict, probability and availability of information, which lends itself easily to a wider set of applications outside the market context or the economy understood in more narrow terms. In the domain of policy and politics, this logic is archetypically represented by public and social choice theories, which specifically attempt to develop a unified framework for economic and political science, based on the application of economic tools to political choices and decisions.

However, the more recent development and application of game theory and the wider set of intellectual technologies for identification and implementation reflect the same basic ambiguity observed on the level of economy as a field and body of knowledge more broadly. On the one hand, the success of game theory and rational choice can be seen as an essential component in the steady expansion of economic reasoning to non-economic fields and ultimately to everything (Chang, 2014). Moreover, current use of computer models and simulations to determine optimal choice is often taken straight out of Bell's playbook for intellectual technologies, only now with exponentially increased powers of calculation. On the other hand, however, we also find signs of pluralism, cross-disciplinary interaction and, in particular, a renewed focus on empirical variation and experimentation, intertwined with institutional economics and behavioural economics. In relation to the former, the use of game theory, evolutionary algorithms, agent-based modelling, simulation and lab experiments have thus been seen to provide institutional economics with new tools to tackle core issues such as interdependence and complex interaction (Elsner et al, 2015).

The same line of reasoning lies behind 'design economics', which has been involved in the construction of markets for, inter alia, labour and professional services, education, electricity, telecommunications bandwidth and, not least, financial markets since the 1990s. As defined by Roth, one of its principal proponents (and yet another Nobel laureate), design economics involves the use of game theory, experimentation and simulations in the comprehensive construction of specific markets, in contrast to just analysing naturally existing markets, which means that the design economist cannot simply rely on 'the simple conceptual models used for theoretical insights into the general working of markets' (Roth, 2002: 1341). Rather, design economics envisions 'the economist as engineer' in relationship to the core neoclassical body of knowledge identical to the 'relationship of engineering to physics, or of medicine to biology' (Roth, 2002: 1343). Looking at economics from the outside, the simple conceptual model of the neoclassical paradigm obviously already places the economist in the role of a social engineer. However, design economics nevertheless suggests a more direct and experimental approach to social engineering.

Cost-benefit analysis

The most influential 'intellectual technology' of decision making used by econocracy, however, is not particularly theoretical or formal, but rather the potentially simple calculation of costs and benefits. The centrality of cost–benefit analysis (CBA) was highlighted in the original analysis of econocracy as a 'vice worse' than any form of technocracy run by experts in hard or technical sciences: CBA is viewed here as the 'supreme example of econocracy', based on the broader point that 'much of the rationale of economic science is, or is supposed to be, that of bringing a diversity of factors into the common language of accounting' (Self, 1975: 44). Thus understood, CBA has been the key source of economic influence on public policy and the primary tool for the expansion of welfare economics to a wide array of policy domains. In a decisively less critical vein, this is also the essence of Sunstein's more recent argument for the development of a *Cost-Benefit State* (2002a) and the 'triumph of the technocrats' based on a 'silent cost-benefit revolution' from Reagan's presidency onwards (2018: 7). Maybe the 1980s is also a watershed in the case of performance management after all.

At its core, CBA is a simple and flexible form of addition and subtraction determining whether the benefits outweigh the costs, based on values assigned within a more or less developed system of data collection. The basic operation of CBA thus remains simple, flexible and can be applied to practically any decision with a variety of data and more or less advanced methods of calculation. In this respect, the idea that CBA is the quintessential econocratic intellectual technology presents a slightly different view of econocracy than the emphasis on the dominance of the neoclassical paradigm and its highly abstract and theoretical model-building. Although CBA is still a part of econocracy from this perspective, it plays a rather marginal role (Earle et al, 2017: 10). In other words, the two versions of econocracy are not necessarily strongly linked: the common language of accounting and CBA can be applied with little or no theoretical or practical connection to the econocracy of mainstream economics and the neoclassical paradigm. The use of CBA may of course also rely more directly on theoretical assumptions and models, but a key to its success is also that it can be broadly applied without such refinements.

This is to say that the use of CBA cannot be seen as an extension of the axial principle or its ancillary intellectual technologies per se: CBA may be economic in a broad sense, but it does not require the possession or use of advanced theoretical knowledge. In a broader sense, this has to do with fact that CBA predates modern econocracy. Indeed, CBA can be viewed (anachronistically) as the historical *raison d'être* for the development and use of statistics and accounting systems in public policy more generally (Porter, 1995: 115). Historically, economic quantification has been 'closely allied to accounting', as has 'much of economics itself, especially the parts of it that has [sic] been created or mobilized to aid in management, planning and regulation' (Porter, 1995: 114). As Porter goes on to say, this creation and mobilization of economic quantification as an extension of accounting practices is integral to both the French and American technocratic revolutions, albeit in different ways. This view places CBA in the broader historical sociology of statistics, or more generally the development of statistics as the 'knowledge of the things that comprise the very reality of the state ... of the forces and resources that characterizes a state a given moment' (Foucault, 2007: 274).

This is a history that precedes post-war econocracy by centuries. Compiling and calculating statistics in this way is a matter of accounting, which is simply to say placing values on the various dimensions of the population as an object of regulation and then counting (setting aside for now the massive practical obstacles to this operation throughout much of its early history). As such, statistics and accounting is a historical precursor to modern economics, embodied for example by the first ever 'modern' model of interacting economic forces ('the economic table') developed by the French physiocrats (Foucault, 2007: 342). This ancestry is reflected by the modern discipline of econometrics and the development of national budgets aggregating economic data into relevant categories for statistical analysis, used for historical and structural analysis of the economy, forecasting and policy advice (Bell, 1973: 24; Earle et al, 2017: 97). Econometrics thus provides the econocracy with a pervasive statistical apparatus for the collection and analysis of empirical data, historically rooted in accounting but also lending itself to various tests of the theoretical model of the neoclassical paradigm. Econometrics has resulted in a steady expansion and refinement of statistical data on national economies accumulated both by states themselves and various international organizations. However, the new technocracy is less about econometrics than the use of CBA, accounting and calculation of value in a much broader sense, but usually also on a smaller scale. This, in turn, has to do with more fundamental changes in the role of knowledge at the intersection of state and society.

Beyond knowledge society? Audit society vs learning society

The organization of post-industrial society around knowledge, in Bell's original version of the argument, has a dual purpose: directing innovation and exercising social control. More to the point, the political focus on the process of innovation in the newly fused system of technology and science leads to a broader demand on the ability to exercise social control and direct processes of change. The dual focus on innovation and 'commitment to social control', in turn, 'introduces the need for planning and forecasting into society', which is also to say a demand for the technocratic 'hallmarks' of rationality, planning, and foresight (Bell, 1973: 28). In an attempt to illustrate the implications of this development for public policy in more concrete terms, Bell provides a blueprint for a 'System of Social Accounts', meant to create a 'balance sheet that would be useful in clarifying policy choices' by providing a 'broader framework' for the use of economic accounting and CBA (Bell, 1973: 326). In addition to established data on the national economy, the system should include measures of the social cost and return of innovation, social gains such as opportunity and mobility, ills such as crime, family disruption and the like, and lead to the creation of 'performance budgets' in areas of defined social needs.

Such integration of social indicators and performance budgeting clearly resonates widely in current performance management. Indeed, current performance management has been seen as the result of a continuous development from scientific management to early performance budgeting and the social indicators movement in the 1960s and 1970s, onwards to NPM in the 1980s, evidence-based policy from the 1990s, and finally ongoing review and revision of accumulated practices since 2010 (Van Dooren et al, 2015: 42). In this interpretation, the major changes in the history of recurring 'quantification of government activity' are new technological tools making the reinvention and/or realization of old ideas possible (such as computational mapping of social geography and Big Data on health issues), and the increasing institutionalization, professionalization and specialization of production and use of performance data (Van Dooren et al, 2015: 55). While the link between current performance management and earlier attempts at quantification in the name of planning and accounting efficiency is certainly worth emphasizing, however, there are at least two possible historical ruptures that must be taken into account: the audit explosion and the experimental revolution.

The audit explosion

At the most fundamental level, the audit explosion suggests a mutation of knowledge society into an audit society, defined through and through by the principles of formalized accountability and practices of constant checking and verification, roughly since the 1980s, at least in the case of the United Kingdom (Power, 1999). In general, this development can be understood as a more or less subtle mutation of external powers of oversight, policing and surveillance into more indirect, but potentially also more omnipresent, forms of control and supervision based on the 'programmatic restructuring' of organizational life in order to make individuals and organizations accountable, that is, capable of giving auditable accounts, through the creation of performance criteria that set the standards of internal improvements and make such improvements externally verifiable and certifiable. There are certainly traces of earlier scientific management, planning and control of efficiency to be found in systems designed for purposes of accountability in this way. However, the audit explosion has less 'to do with policing or surveillance in the normal sense of external observation, although elements of this may exist; it has more to do with attempts to re-order the collective and individual selves that make up organizational life' (Power, 1999: 42).

Although rooted in earlier practices of budgetary accounting and auditing, the audit explosion thus represents a more or less subtle development from efficiency to accountability as the overriding standard of performance management, creating a demand for extensive collection of performance data, examination of such data and authoritative views, judgements and assessments based on the results (Power, 1999: 66). An important element in the audit explosion is thus the creation of auditing bodies with extensive independence and powers of oversight in domains such as health, environment, social services, education and ultimately public policy as such, turning public and private organizations into 'auditable' subjects. Broadening the geographical scope from United Kingdom to Sweden, the Netherlands, Finland and France, but limiting the analytical focus more to so-called supreme audit institutions (SAIs), the audit explosion can be said to have merged older forms of auditing and performance management in new formula of 'performance auditing' in the context of broader public management reforms and the new governance, roughly since the late 1970s and early 1980s (Pollitt, 1995).

Inspection and auditing have often been associated with technocratic influence. Indeed, the three 'administrative' (non-engineering) Grands Corps (Conseil d'État, Cour de Comptes and Inspection des Finances) of the institutionalized French technocracy are all, in various degrees and ways, 'supreme' audit institutions or inspectorates. However, the audit explosion is not merely a quantitative extension of older forms of public auditing and inspection of financial and regulatory compliance. What is at stake here is, rather, a new centrality of performance auditing in public policy and a foundational shift towards more or less systematic development of internal planning, control and/or accountability systems that facilitate continuous self-inspection and self-evaluation under the auspices of general audit institutions and systems of accreditation and quality assurance. Through this development, narrower concepts of CBA, efficiency and compliance are taken over by a broader standard of accountability and expansive systems of performance measurement designed to ensure governmental, organizational and individual accountability.

The experimental revolution

The second potential rupture in the otherwise continuous history of performance management is a new focus on empirical and experimental knowledge, the kind of knowledge explicitly rejected by the emphasis on the scientifically codified and validated theoretical knowledge following from the axial principle of knowledge society. This experimental revolution, however, is not an argument for a return to the 'amateur' empiricism of the industrial era, but rather the result of a competing vision for the role of social science in public policy. Roughly around the time of Bell's forecasting, David T. Campbell, noted psychologist, godfather of programme evaluation and a prominent advocate of experimental methods in social science and public policy, presented a rather different vision of post-industrial society as an experimental society. This society, although 'nowhere yet an actuality', would be more properly scientific, active, honest, non-dogmatic, open to criticism, accountable, decentralized, responsive and voluntarist than the thoroughly programmed and planned knowledge society. Briefly put, it would be an *'evolutionary, learning society'* (Campbell, 1991: 224, original emphasis).

This agenda was pitted explicitly against the 'dogmatic' and 'non-experimental' extrapolations from established theories for purposes of 'optimal social organization design' conducted by 'governmental and industrial planners everywhere', that is, the 'economists, operations researchers and mathematical decision theorists' that 'trustingly extrapolate from past science and conjecture, but in general fail to use the implemented decisions to correct or expand knowledge': the experimenting society, by contrast, means a *scientific society* in the fullest sense of the word ... distinguished from an earlier use of the term scientific in social planning' (Campbell, 1991: 225, original emphasis). This all-out confrontation with social planning and engineering clearly suggests that technocratic influence on public policy based purely on theoretical knowledge and intellectual technologies of decision making should be viewed as a failure. However, the problem is not technocratic influence per se, but rather a failure to truly live up to the goal of technocratic scientism and conduct proper social engineering by treating 'reforms as experiments'. In order to achieve this goal, technocrats should be recruited from the full array of social sciences and act as frontrunners for the experimenting society, taking it on themselves to ensure that the public policy reforms and ameliorative programmes be used as an opportunity for social experiments (Campbell, 1969).

This vision has to a wide extent been realized with the subsequent development of evidence-based policy, identification of best practices and evaluation systems. In particular, Campbell's vision of social engineering as experimentation and the corresponding idea of the experimental learning society have gained traction with the widespread commitment to evaluation and evidence-based policy in most advanced democracies since the 1990s. Indeed, this development amounts to an experimental revolution and a new commitment to finding 'what works' in public policy, or, in the fuller version: 'what works for whom under what circumstances and why?' (Sanderson, 2002: 19). While evidence-based policy and evaluation are rooted in ideas about extensive use of economic and social measures and indicators as touchstones of public policy, they also shift the underlying idea of social engineering fundamentally to social experimentation and continuous innovation in order to ensure adequate solutions to policy problems and optimal individual and collective welfare (Sunstein, 2018). In other words, learning from evidence and the continuous improvement of public policy becomes a matter of sufficient experimentation.

The combined result of the audit explosion and the experimental revolution is a basic duality in the current rationality and practice of performance management. This duality can be described in terms of distinction between the nature and function of the evidence provided. The systems created in and through the audit explosion are designed to provide evidence of accountability in a way that still harks back to the search for evidence of governmental efficiency to guide public policy decisions found in programme planning budgeting systems and other planning systems. Although the standards of performance are wider and the reach of inspection deeper, the principal function of accountability systems is still to provide documentation for results and overall political legitimacy. By contrast, evaluation systems seek to provide more experimental evidence of how well policies and programmes work under different circumstances (Sanderson, 2002: 33). This is sometimes viewed simply as a difference between the mere provision of performance information and actively *using* such information (Berman, 2006). However, the schism between efficiency and experimentation in performance management emphasizes that, viewed from the latter perspective at least, a more fundamental difference between forms of evidence and the systems that produce them are at stake. Nowhere has this been more evident than in the development of the new governance.

The new technocracy and innovative governance

The difference between performance management as a search for increased efficiency vis-à-vis innovation has been a matter of considerable attention in the new governance, broadly reflecting the respective positions of NPM and NPG. While variations in specific reforms under the NPM label remain a matter of ongoing discussion, they are widely seen to share a preoccupation with government efficiency, explicit and quantifiable measures and indicators of performance, output control and accountability (Hood, 1991; Christensen & Lægreid, 2011; Van Dooren et al, 2015). Indeed, improved performance management stands out as the lasting effect of NPM reforms in the landmark analysis declaring the death of NPM, including extensive valuation of public assets, systematic comparison and publication of performance results, and rewards for improved performance (Dunleavy et al, 2006). A more recent critical review also highlighted the performance-enhancing approach to public policy and management by numbers as the crucial component of NPM reforms in the United Kingdom since the 1980s, albeit with the particular point that the reality of NPM reforms is a paradoxical combination of 'evidence hunger' and 'evidence destruction', the latter being the result of shifting systems of measurement, volatile indicators and data breaks that make accumulation and comparison of data over time difficult or even impossible (Hood & Dixon, 2015: 45).

Correspondingly, analyses of the audit explosion and the rise of performance auditing also point to NPM as a decisive factor. For one, the emphasis on more indirect mechanisms of steering, output controls and organizational autonomy gives accounting practices and systems a central role in operationalizing the administrative ideals of NPM, aptly summarized in the characterization of the basic NPM formula as 'autonomous entities with financial reporting and audit requirements' (Power, 1999: 44). The audit explosion can be seen as a crucial and necessary part of NPM governance reforms insofar as the emphasis on increased accountability, output controls and government spending lead naturally to the common language of accounting, intensification of financial and non-financial information flows and the use of CBA as a generalized method of calculation. In other words, as the state becomes increasingly and explicitly committed to an indirect supervisory role, auditing and accounting practices assume a decisive function. Correspondingly, the performance audit appears as the result of direct and indirect influences back and forth between earlier auditing practices and NPM reforms modernizing, streamlining, and some cases minimizing the entire state apparatus (Pollitt et al, 1999: 22). Other effects notwithstanding, the principal legacy of NPM is performance management, and even if NPM is presumed dead on most other accounts, performance management is generally assumed to be alive and well.

It would appear then, that the new technocracy is more defined by NPM than network governance and NPG when it comes to performance management. Compared to network organization and risk regulation, the influence of NPM on the new technocracy is certainly also more apparent. However, post-NPM reforms and NPG are clearly not without effects in this case either. The central issue at stake in this version of the NPM–NPG debate essentially comes down to diverging perspectives on how to generate and use knowledge as a source of innovation and of policy formulation. On one level, the issue has to do with the underlying standard of public value. In this respect, NPM tends to equate value with efficiency in a manner that broadly resembles earlier planning, programming and budgeting systems of performance management. In the narrowest sense, the underlying standard of efficiency is 'value for money' or similar concepts of basic economic efficiency and productivity. In a slightly expanded version, the basic values of NPM have been defined as the so-called 'three Es': economy, efficiency and effectiveness (Pollitt et al, 1999; Power,

1999; Kickert, 2011). However, this also introduces a distinction between the two first Es and the last one (Pollitt, 1995). Whereas the former two remain a matter of input and output, broadly speaking, the latter involves a change of focus to quality or more specifically to outcomes and impact on users of public service and citizens in general. This schism is particularly evident in outcrops from the NPM paradigm such as 'entrepreneurial governance' (Osborne & Gaebler, 1992) and management of 'public value' (Moore, 1995) that aims to shift the focus from efficiency to outcome, impact and innovation in the development of public services.

This schism has then been further exacerbated by post-NPM criticism calling for 'wider' and 'deeper' understanding of performance information and broader standards of public value such as utility and sustainability of policy solutions and programmes (Van Dooren et al, 2015: 21). The post-NPM approach thus moves decisively beyond the three Es to a standard of problem-solving capacity, innovation and learning, thus defining the ultimate objective of performance management as 'effectiveness in tackling the problems that the public most cares about; stretching from service delivery to system maintenance', and the use of knowledge to improve public policy as a matter of 'reflection, lesson drawing, and continuous adaptation' (Stoker, 2006a: 44). Rather than efficiency or effectiveness, the post-NPM approach thus ties innovation to learning, either in the sense of instrumental (first order) learning with the aim of improving policy effectiveness through evidence of what works, or in the broader and more disruptive sense of (second order) 'reflexive social learning' associated with more paradigmatic changes and shifts in preferences, identities and foundational beliefs (Gilardi & Radaelli, 2012).

A related aspect of the NPM–NPG debate over the collection and use of knowledge as a source of policy innovation concerns the use of evaluation and the role of evidence-based policy. Although largely coinciding with the gradual transition from NPM to NPG, proliferation of evaluation and evidence-based policy, in one interpretation, can be seen as a consolidation of the kind of performance management set in motion by NPM reforms (Van Dooren et al, 2015). Thus understood, evaluation effectively functions as an extension of the audit explosion and its particular form of steering and control for purposes of accountability, in effect turning audit society into an 'evaluation society' (Dahler-Larsen, 2012). However, the turn to evaluation and evidence-based policy can also be seen to present a rather different version of performance management and a way of learning from evidence more in line with the experimentalist agenda, that is, a form of performance management invested less in the provision of performance information for purposes of measuring efficiency and providing accountability than in the pursuit of experimental evidence as part of a process of policy innovation based on instrumental and/or socially reflexive learning. While these two approaches can remain hard to disentangle in current performance management, the latter can reasonably be seen as part of the post-NPM development of the new governance and NPG in the broad sense.

In addition to the emphasis on policy innovation and learning on the level of public values and evaluation systems, the post-NPM approach to performance management is also a project to some degree of cross-fertilization with risk management. On a more general level, this reflects the logic that performance management often functions as a powerful tool of risk processing (Power, 1999). The more operational expression of this coupling of risk and performance management can be called change management or change governance, focused on the need for management of change and innovation created by technological, economic, political and social changes (Osborne & Brown, 2005). The focus of change management and governance, correspondingly, is the development of individual, organizational and systemic capacities for change, learning and adaptation under circumstances of unpredictability and uncertainty, parallel to the search for individual, organizational and societal resilience in risk management. However, a more apparent and pervasive connection has been established between the NPG version of performance management and the involvement of stakeholders.

This intersection of network governance and performance management revolves around an attempt to develop an adequate post-NPM 'management response' that combines an 'evidence-based approach' to policy innovation and effectiveness with the idea of 'stakeholder involvement' as a basis for efficient and legitimate decisions and the pursuit of active citizen 'involvement' in, and 'endorsement' of, public policy solutions (Stoker, 2006a: 49). The result is embodied in the idea and practice of performance governance – an 'interactive' and 'hyper dynamic' form of performance management, based on a recognition of the need to 'organize the public sector to allow for citizens and customers of public services to participate in the whole policy cycle. This means that citizens are involved in co-designing, co-deciding, co-producing and co-evaluating public services in society' (Bouckaert & Halligan, 2008: 189). Such performance governance ranges from 'co-production' of public services (Brandsen & Pestoff, 2006) to 'collaborative innovation' in public policy more generally (Sørensen & Torfing, 2016; Torfing et al, 2019). This approach clearly draws on broader ideas about networks as a source of critical information about policy problems and services vital to learning, innovation and the development of sustainable policy solutions in a wider sense (Goldsmith & Eggers, 2004; Eggers, 2005; Agranoff, 2007; Ansell & Gash, 2008; Goldsmith & Kettl, 2009; Ulibarri & Scott, 2016).

However, performance governance also links stakeholder inclusion and citizen involvement more directly to innovation and ongoing improvement of public policies and services. Indeed, performance governance can be seen as a model for policy innovation and improvement based on a combination of the experimental method and citizen involvement (Stoker & John, 2009; John et al, 2013). This model, in turn, rests on a claim about a natural affinity between the role of evaluation and experimentation in the improvement of policy design and the need for strategic guidance of governance networks under conditions of increased complexity and uncertainty, placing significant responsibility 'upon policy experimentation and evaluation as key institutional practices in interactive governance to provide the basis for reflexive social learning' (Sanderson, 2002: 99). In addition to the focus on stakeholder involvement, the emphasis on policy learning in the NPG version of performance management also overlaps significantly with the broader design principles of MLG, which can thus be seen as mechanisms for 'policy transfer' on and between all levels of the MLG system (Evans & Davies, 1999). I conclude the chapter by discussing two examples that reflect both the internal logic of performance management and its intersection with risk regulation and network organization in the new governance.

Experimentalist governance: the EU and beyond

One of the more apparent expressions of the new governance approach to policy innovation, learning and experimentalism is so-called experimentalist governance. Experimentalist governance revolves around the idea of a distinct architecture for systematic policy learning and design based on three general design principles. First, experimentalist governance architectures combine centrally stated goals, frameworks and targets with autonomy for locally developed solutions in order to accommodate diversity of particular conditions. The second design principle of experimental governance architecture is the provision of a mechanism for coordinated learning from local experiences through regular and systematic comparison of locally adopted solutions, based on more or less extensive lists of measures and indicators, peer review, supervision and plans for improvement. Third, both means and ends are considered provisional and subject to change in the light of new evidence and experience, thus allowing for instrumental policy learning within existing goals as well as socially reflexive or 'double loop' learning where fundamental goals, values and frameworks are questioned and potentially revised (Zeitlin, 2015: 10).

Originally extrapolated from features of policy coordination and development in the EU associated with the so-called 'open method of coordination' (OMC), the architecture of experimentalist governance rests on the institutional features of the MLG system (Szyszczak, 2006). However, the focus is on the iterative process of policy innovation and learning within the basic structure of any 'tiered' or 'nested' governance system with two or more levels of decision-making power and autonomy. For the same reason, experimentalist governance is by no means exclusive to the EU, although it can be considered an early and leading adopter of experimentalist governance due to the particular combination of policy expansion, uncertainty and internal diversity (Sabel & Zeitlin, 2008). More generally, however, the development of experimental governance architecture can be seen as a 'widespread response to turbulent, polyarchic environments, where strategic uncertainty means that effective solutions to problems can only be defined in the course of pursuing them, while a multi-polar distribution of power means that no single actor can impose her will on other without taking into account the views of others' (Zeitlin, 2015: 11). While this description increasingly also fits national governance, architectures of experimentalist governance have been identified and studied mostly in the transnational realm.

In the case of the EU, experimentalist governance has developed well beyond the OMC and its use in areas such as macroeconomic policy guidelines, the European Employment Strategy and social inclusion. In the current state of affairs, experimentalist governance architecture has become an institutionalized feature of the EU across a variety of policy domains such as environmental policy (in particular water management and industrial emissions regulation), consumer protection, food, drug and water safety (genetically modified organisms, for example), energy and telecommunications, finance, justice, security, data privacy and fundamental rights (Sabel & Zeitlin, 2008; Zeitlin, 2015). Moreover, the EU more or less systematically seeks to extend experimental governance architecture to non-member states as part of its external and extended governance efforts. Outside the EU, a number of 'transnationalist experimentalist regimes' with architectural features similar to the EU have developed across a similarly wide policy spectrum. Examples include the Montreal Protocol for the protection of the ozone layer, the Forest Stewardship Council for sustainable foresting, the Financial Stability Board, the UN Convention on the Rights of Persons with Disabilities and the Global Food Safety Initiative (Zeitlin, 2015).

As is clear from these examples, there is a considerable overlap between the development of experimentalist governance architectures and core risk policies such as environmental protection, consumer protection and critical infrastructures. Indeed, experimentalist governance architecture is in this sense an attempt at risk regulation in a situation where strategic uncertainty has overwhelmed the capacities of traditional regulation, in some cases drawing direct inspiration from systems of risk management and risk regulation regimes (Sabel & Zeitlin, 2012). In line with the original debate on the OMC, the design principles of experimentalist governance architecture are often viewed as a form of 'soft law', albeit in various combinations with hard law. However, experimentalist governance remains rather indistinct as a form of regulation and a risk regulation regime in a narrower sense: there is no overarching regulatory strategy or distinct orientation towards precaution, laissez-faire or resilience building in response to risk, uncertainty and turbulence. What is distinctive about experimentalist governance is its particular architecture and iterative procedure of policy innovation and learning from diversity, based on continuous and systematic evaluation, comparison and supervision.

Although there is an element of scoring, identification of top performers and so-called naming and shaming to experimentalist governance, the principal purpose is not measurement of efficiency or formal accountability, but rather effectiveness in dealing with (wicked) policy problems. Information is not compiled for purposes of broad publication or legitimation of government performance to the general citizenry, but for supervised peer review and exchange. Moreover, data compilation and calculation are relatively simple. Although the list of indicators according to which particular solutions are measured and compared can be extensive, experimentalist governance does not rest on complex models, advanced calculation methods or formal intellectual technologies of decision making. Rather, governance processes are designed to 'systematically provoke doubt about their own assumptions and practices; treat all solutions as incomplete and incorrigible; and produce and ongoing, reciprocal readjustment of ends and means through comparison of different approaches to advancing general common aims' (Zeitlin, 2015: 3). This approach is experimental, so the argument goes, in the manner of American pragmatism and John Dewey (Sabel, 2012). Extending this point, Campbell's experimental learning society is certainly also an ideational forefather of experimental governance.

In the manner of performance governance more generally, this emphasis on evaluation and experiments goes hand in hand with a focus on stakeholder inclusion and collaborative governance. Indeed, experimental governance is viewed as a decisively post-NPM approach, relying on the vertical and horizontal links of the MLG architecture (Sabel & Zeitlin, 2010). This means that networks are, first and foremost, networks of public authorities formally included on the national and/or local level of MLG systems. Correspondingly, private stakeholders included in the wider networks of transnational experimentalist governance are more or less always high-level interest organizations, business interests and well-organized NGOs within the particular policy domains in question. While ordinary citizens may, of course, be involved in local experimentation with policy solutions, they are generally completely absent on the higher levels of the MLG system.

In this respect, experimentalist governance is subject to the well-known problems of democracy beyond the national level and the democratic deficit in the EU. Nevertheless, experimentalist governance also reflects the broader claim to 'near-democratic' legitimacy advanced by the new governance. Although experimentalist governance conforms neither to the 'traditional canon of input nor output legitimacy', it is deemed 'normatively attractive' due to the ability to accommodate diversity and provide 'policy space' for local solutions (Zeitlin, 2015: 11). More generally, experimentalist governance is seen to provide a form 'directly deliberative polyarchy', based on a deliberative procedure where administrative authorities are forced to justify their solutions in light of comparable choices made peers and richer performance information about possible alternatives than is available in traditional forms of hierarchical governance (Sabel & Zeitlin, 2008; 2010). Ultimately, however, such claims reflect the basic legitimation strategy of the new technocracy: equating less bureaucracy with more democracy.

The focus on MLG systems means that experimentalist governance architectures have rarely been analysed in the national context, and then mostly in federal systems such as the United States. However, experimentalist governance is broadly comparable to processes and mechanisms of performance governance on the national level associated with co-production, public sector innovation and collaborative innovation. Although coined in a somewhat different terminology, the basic architecture of experimentalist governance is clearly visible in the image of policy innovation as a 'design process' where ideas and solutions are 'tested and redesigned until they work in a satisfactory way and produce desirable outcomes' through 'pragmatic methods of experimentation and trial and error' and 'iterative rounds of inspiration, ideation, selection and implementation' (Ansell & Torfing, 2014: 44). In contrast to the emphasis on systematic evaluation, this design process is clearly more open-ended and focused on creative and reflexive learning vis-à-vis instrumental policy learning (Stoker & John, 2009; Stoker, 2010). However, the basic objective is still problem-solving capacity, utility and sustainability. Being an extension of collaborative governance and NPG, this approach to policy innovation and change places greater emphasis on stakeholder involvement and the creation and management of collaborative forums around the design process that broadly reiterates the logic and institutional design and hands-on management of networks (Torfing et al, 2019).

Experimenting with citizens: nudging and the construction of choice architecture

A rather different but highly significant variation of experimentalist governance can be found in the nudging agenda spearheaded by Thaler and Sunstein's widely debated manual on the improvement of 'health, wealth and happiness' through the use of 'nudges' and the design of 'choice architecture' around individual welfare choices across a wide array of domains such as health, environmental policy, savings and investment, education (2009). In a broader sense, the nudging agenda is merely an expression of a broader movement towards behavioural public policy, meaning that it can aptly be described as 'the basic manual for applying behavioral economics to policy' (Kahneman, 2011: 372). On the one hand, the success of the nudging agenda and the underlying discipline of behavioural economics can be taken as evidence of the changeable nature of econocracy and the fact that the 'role of economic experts has been expanded beyond simply designing policies to influencing the decisions of citizens' (Earle et al, 2017: 17). In other respects, however, the nudging agenda is also so far removed from the original parameters of the econocracy that the only remaining link is a vague connection with the cost-benefit 'revolution' (Sunstein, 2018). The other revolutions claimed by the nudging agenda, however, have less to do with econocracy.

Nudging is, first and foremost, part of the behavioural revolution and the broader movement towards 'behavioural public policy' (Oliver,

2013; Shafir, 2013). Indeed, key proponents of nudging have associated themselves rather straightforwardly with this agenda (Halpern, 2015; John, 2016). Behavioural economics has thus been instrumental in developing and testing the core claim of the nudging agenda: that public policy can by significantly improved by substituting standard assumptions about rational choice with consistent attention to the psychological heuristics, biases and mechanisms affecting individual welfare choices (Halpern, 2015; John, 2016; Madrian, 2014). In the place of rational choice, the nudging agenda operates with a distinction between two systems of cognition and decision making called the 'automatic system' and the 'reflective system' by Thaler and Sunstein (2009: 21), but known more generally as 'system 1' and 'system 2' in behavioural economics (Kahneman, 2011; Thaler, 2015), and 'dual process theory' in psychology (Evans & Stanovich, 2013). The cognitive processes of system 1 are fast, uncontrolled, unconscious, effortless, associative and skilled, but also based on heuristics, cues and shortcuts responsible for a plethora of biases and cognitive mistakes. The processes of system 2 are slow, controlled, effortful, logical, calculating and rule-following, and in this sense a precondition for reflection and reasoned decision-making.

The distinction between system 1 and system 2 has been aptly described as 'a simple dichotomy common to all variants of behavioural theory: that we possess both "reflective" (rational) and "automatic" (emotion-driven) "systems", arguing that the automatic system repeatedly wins out' (Leggett, 2014: 5). In behavioural psychology and economics, the distinction serves as a common reference point for experimental research generating an ever-expanding list of biases and cognitive problems created by system 1 (Kahneman, 2011; Shafir, 2013). Concrete nudging interventions may or may not include specific assumptions about such biases, but in general the distinction between systems 1 and 2 serves to distinguish two modes of nudging relying on rather different techniques. The ideal path of intervention for choice architects is activation of system 2 in order to correct for the cognitive flaws of system 1 and generate more deliberate, reflective and reasoned welfare choices. In this group we find three techniques allowing for different degrees of free choice and free 'thinking': mapping, feedback and social influence. Nudging can, however, also target the various biases, heuristics and shortcuts of system 1 directly and thus seek to programme choices and thinking with increasing degrees of automation through priming, framing and gaming, as is more or less routinely done in electoral and commercial campaigning (Esmark, 2019).

The application of such techniques in public policy is clearly not limited to the traditional domain of economic policy, nor do these techniques rely extensively on economic knowledge, data or forms of calculation. The more formal variants of behavioural economics do make use of game theory to some degree, but at its core behavioural public policy simply attempts to design policy in accordance with the assumed existence of cognitive flaws and biased decision-making leading to suboptimal welfare choices about, inter alia, food consumption, exercise, education, savings, energy conservation and pro-environmental choices more generally. In other words: 'just as an engineer with a better understanding of air flows and wind resistance can use this knowledge to design a more economical car, a better turbine, or faster plane, so we try to use behavioural insights to improve the design of lots of different policy levers' (Halpern, 2015: 318). Good policy design, thus understood, also requires application of CBA where both costs and benefits are understood and calculated broadly, including material wealth, security, health and happiness (Halpern, 2015; Sunstein, 2015).

This approach to policy design displays is both generally and specifically linked to risk regulation based on the principle of resilience (Sunstein, 2002b). Nudging and the construction of choice architecture involves the use of policy instrumentation and tools in a way that is highly adverse to traditional regulation, legislation and prohibitions. This is reflected in the very definition of a nudge as 'any aspect of the choice architecture that alters people's behaviour in a predictable way without forbidding any options or significantly changing their economic incentives' (Thaler & Sunstein, 2009: 6), and 'a means of encouraging or guiding behaviour, but without mandating or instructing, and ideally without the need for heavy financial sanctions … It stands in marked contrast to an obligation; a strict requirement; or the use of force' (Halpern, 2015: 22). More generally, the nudging agenda is in this sense based on a government–citizen relation modelled on the idea of reflexivity (Leggett, 2014). Policy design as nudging and construction of choice architectures is essentially meant to correct the flaws in the risk calculi exercised by individual citizens in their welfare choices. In this way, nudging trains 'self-reflexivity' and strives to build resilient citizens that constantly assess and change behaviour based on continuous assessment and calculation of risks.

Second, nudging is also part of the informational revolution. Nudging is akin to established communicative policy tools such as notification, moral suasion, persuasion, exhortation and indeed more or less traditional public information campaigns (Vedung & van der Doelen, 1998; Howlett, 2009; Rice & Atkin, 2013). However, nudging applies such tools as a form of 'smart information provision', adding behavioural insights *and* new media to well-established tools such as the public information campaign and canvassing (John, 2013, 2016). In similar fashion, nudging has been characterized as a form of 'behaviourally shaped informing', meaning a revision of established tools aided not only by behavioural insights, but no less so by new media, digital government and big data 'shaping and enhancing the power of nudges' (Halpern, 2015: 180). As such, nudging is clearly a form of communicative governance displaying all the hallmarks of a network state operating in the informational flows of network society (Esmark, 2019). Indeed, the job of a choice architect consists in the deliberate construction of informational networks and flows around specific welfare choices within particular policy domains.

The intersection between nudging and network governance also extends, albeit to a lesser degree, to collaboration and the inclusion of stakeholders. Although most nudging interventions are designed specifically to correct welfare choices and thus target individual citizens as objects of regulation, the broader expansion of the broader nudging agenda into the domain of so-called 'think' strategies accurately reflects the ambitions of collaborative governance in its application of behavioural insights political participation and deliberation rather than individual choice (John et al, 2013). In contrast to the choice-correcting function of most nudging interventions, the purpose of 'thinking' interventions is to create institutional spaces for participation and deliberation, shared policy platforms and learning in a manner that largely equates democratic network governance, citizen-driven innovation and co-production (Mathur & Skelcher, 2007; Edelenbos et al, 2013).

Last but not least, the nudging agenda has positioned itself as the spearhead of an 'experimental revolution' in public policy (Halpern, 2015). The experimental approach of the nudging agenda is inherited from the roots of behavioural economy in cognitive psychology, leading to an even split between laboratory and field experiments among the 156 nudging studies carried out so far (Szaszi et al, 2018). In more practical terms, the source of the experimental revolution is the development and consolidation of evidence-based policy in the field of health and medicine. Referring to the case of the United Kingdom, the consolidation and spread of the 'what works approach' from health policy (starting with the creation of the National Institute for Clinical Excellence in 1999) to other policy domains have been described somewhat programmatically but aptly as the 'rise of experimental government' based on a commitment to 'radical incrementalism', and as a process of 'industrializing the experimental approach' (Halpern, 2015: 281). The 'industrial' aspect refers to the creation of so-called 'clearing houses', which collect, compare and disseminate accumulated evidence on the impact of different types of intervention and policy tools. Reflecting Campbell's vision of public policy as social experimentation more or less to the letter, experimental government involves a commitment to plan, execute and evaluate all policy interventions, big or small, as experiments to the greatest extent possible. Where the gold standard of randomly controlled trials cannot be applied, the experimental logic should be applied as much as practically possible (Stoker & John, 2009; Stoker, 2010).

This is a rather different version of learning, from evidence and continuously improving policy rather than social engineering and planning based on an axial principle of purely theoretical knowledge and corresponding technologies for calculation of optimal choices. Optimal choices are certainly still being calculated by proponents of the nudging agenda and choice architects, and they may indeed rely to some degree on old mainstays of earlier techno-bureaucracy such as game theory. Moreover, the use of CBA, albeit in a broad and flexible sense beyond efficiency and value for money, is more or less endemic to the nudging agenda and the broader movement towards behavioural public policy. However, the nudging agenda also adheres to a very specific understanding of scientific public policy as design of interventions based on and providing experimental evidence in a continuous search for better solutions, public value and general welfare. This logic ultimately runs counter to the axial principle of knowledge society and suggests a reconfiguration of the state/society nexus in the image of an experimental learning society. The consolidation of experimental government, correspondingly, does not depend on large-scale systems ensuring value for money, but rather on the expansion of the experimental logic beyond the various 'nudge units' to more and more policy interventions and on the creation of systems for the accumulation and dissemination of experimental evidence. The result, as indicated by Sunstein, will be decisively technocratic, but also less bureaucratic and more democratic.

Conclusion

The preoccupation with learning from evidence and the continuous improvement of public policy in current performance management goes to the core of the technocratic scientism, measurement, calculation and the culture of objectivity. Although the technocratic idea of government by science has is roots in engineering and was pushed further with the new role of physics, chemistry and mathematics with the post-war alliance of science, technology and politics, economic knowledge and forms of calculation have been most instrumental to technocratic influence on public policy. In this dimension at least, industrial technocracy was first and foremost an 'econocracy'. The kind of performance management exercised by the new technocracy, however, is not just an extension of the econocracy. For one, this has to do with the fact that the econocracy, at least understood restrictively, is to some extent limited to the domain of economic policy. Even understood more expansively as a form of decision making based on the application of CBA, however, the new technocracy has moved beyond the formula of industrial econocracy.

On the one hand, the basic principle of cost-benefit calculation is used more pervasively (and proudly) than ever, even to the extent that we are in the midst of a cost-benefit revolution, according to some. On the other hand, however, CBA is simply an anchor point for processes of performance management that are not based on economic knowledge or techniques in a narrow sense, if it all. The new technocratic use of performance management has in this sense moved beyond industrial econocracy in two ways. First, through the creation and management of systems designed to calculate efficiency and enable auditing, inspection and public accountability. Such systems may be considered an extension of earlier econocracy in the domain of accounting and budgeting practices, but they are also much more expansive and push further into every aspect of organizational life. Second, performance management can be pursued more as a matter of creating and managing evaluation systems designed with an eye to public value, problem-solving, experimentation, innovation and public participation. Here, we have moved more decisively beyond the scope of econocracy and into the avant-garde of the new technocracy: experimentalist governance treating social engineering as a matter of social experimentation in the learning society.

8

New Populism vs New Technocracy

Can the governance paradigm survive the rise of populism?
(Stoker, 2019)

The populist explosion

Populism lived a marginal existence in Europe for the better part of the 20th century. It is only from the late 1990s onwards that populism became a significant political phenomenon. In the time since then, populist parties have become an endemic and often dominant feature of European politics. A majority of countries now have at least one successful populist party and one of these is among the three largest parties in one third of European countries. While some of these parties were already consolidated at the turn of the millennium, the surge in European populism has also seen an array of new parties and movements. By comparison, populism has a longer history in South and North America, originally carrying connotations of progressive politics and democracy. In spite of this history of 'normalized' populism, however, the Americas are also facing new populist challenges. Taken together, all of these developments amount to what has been called a populist 'explosion' (Judis, 2016).

The populist explosion spans various national experiences with populism and the entire spectrum from Left to Right, including 'both Trump and Sanders and both France's National Front and Spain's Podemos' (Judis, 2016: 11), and it has propelled the issue of populism and its causes to the top the agenda in both political science and practical politics since the turn of the millennium. Getting to the root cause of the populist explosion has thus become a top priority in order to understand this mounting threat to the political order and democratic politics. The puzzle of populism and its causes has, however, provoked extensive debate but no universally accepted answer. Following a brief overview of some of the more widely discussed reasons for the populist explosion, the chapter is dedicated to exploring one possible explanation: that the new populist challenge has to a large degree been caused by the new technocracy. The purpose here is not to find *the* single cause of the recent rise of populism, but it does follow from the preceding chapters that technocracy should at the very least be seen as a key contributing factor.

In other words: how has the new technocracy and the substitution of governance for government contributed to the rise of populism, and what is the nature of the populist response to this development? This is, albeit with a slightly different twist, also the question posed by Stoker in this chapter's epigraph, concluding a rehearsal of the point-by-point attack on the core principles of the new governance mounted by populist movements. The rise of populism is, thus understood, the unintended and until recently unforeseen effect of the new governance. Based on the preceding chapters, we can identify a more specific dynamic in this development: populism aims for radical repoliticization in the face of technocratic depoliticization. However, the mechanisms of this dynamic also vary considerably between network management, risk management and performance management.

Populism and its causes

One of the more direct and widely discussed responses to the question 'what is populism' points to a combination of anti-elitism, anti-pluralism and a form of identity politics that poses a major threat to democracy (Müller, 2016). Alternatively, populism can be seen as a particular strategy of personalized leadership and mobilization, based on a direct relation to a group of largely unorganized followers (Taggart, 2017; Weyland, 2001). Yet another definition interprets populism as a blurring of fascism and democratic government, resulting in a 'transfiguration' of representative democracy where populists, once in government, challenge democratic fundamentals more or less radically (Urbinati, 2018). The notion of a populist explosion rests on a definition of populism as a particular type of political language that pits the noble people against the corrupt elite (Judis, 2016). This emphasis on the antagonistic relationship between the people and the elites is also the core of the widely used definition of populism as a 'thin-centred ideology', also referred to as 'the populist Zeitgeist' (Mudde, 2004), that considers society to be ultimately separated into two homogeneous and antagonistic camps, '"the pure people" versus "the corrupt elite," and which argues that politics should be an expression of the *volonté générale* (general will) of the people' (Mudde & Kaltwasser, 2017: 6).

The argument developed here proceeds from the latter definition. I do not, however, take this starting point to preclude aspects of other definitions, even if they are sometimes seen to represent more fundamental differences between economic, regime-oriented, strategic, discursive and ideational approaches (Kaltwasser et al, 2017). Although the interpretation of populism as a thin-centred ideology focuses on the ideational and discursive antagonism between the people and the elite, the importance and style of strong individual leaders, anti-pluralism, identity politics and the inherent conflict with democracy are all compatible with this approach. The key upshot of considering populism a thin-centred ideology, however, is the focus on its inherent incompleteness: populism in itself is not sustainable as a political force without the support of additional concepts and ideologies. In other words, populism always latches itself on to 'host' ideologies and ideas in order to sustain mobilization and pursuit of political power. This lack of an inherent strong ideology is the reason that populism can be found on either end of the political spectrum and slide back and forth along the axis between autocracy and democracy.

European populism has been predominantly right-wing, or, more specifically; latched on to the host ideologies of nationalism, conservatism and nativism, including the strong anti-pluralistic and more plainly anti-democratic sentiments of such ideologies (Mudde & Kaltwasser, 2017: 34). The prototypical European populist party, on this view, is Front National (renamed Rassemblement National in 2018), which came to embody the direct confrontation between populism and technocracy in the 2017 French presidential election that eventually sent Macron to the Élysée Palace. However, this type of populism is broadly represented across Europe, including FPÖ in Austria, AfD in Germany, Party for Freedom in the Netherlands, the Danish People's Party, the Progress Party in Norway and so on. A particularly strong authoritarian version is found in post-communist countries such as the Polish Law and Justice party and Fidesz in Hungary. However, left-wing populists attached to host ideologies of socialism, or perhaps rather social anarchism, have also become prominent, in particular after the financial crisis in 2008 and mostly in the European south that suffered the most from the crisis and the ensuing political measures. As exemplified by *Indignados*, *Podemos* and more recently the Yellow Vests in France, the left-wing current in the populist explosion tends to be more as movements than parties, or at least somewhere in between. Finally, parties such as UKIP and Forza Italia represent a form of populism working more in conjunction with crude laissez-faire liberalism and entrepreneurism similar to historical currents of populism in the United States. More recent outcrops of populism in the United States include, at opposite ends of the political spectrum, Occupy Wall Street and the Tea Party, Sanders and Trump (Judis, 2016).

The political influence of populist parties and movements varies, but they have become recurring participants in government in Europe, the Americas and elsewhere (Kaltwasser et al, 2017). Moreover, populist parties outside of government exercise considerable influence in a number of national parliaments. What produced this surge in populist parties and movements across the major regions of the globe? In one interpretation, explanations generally come in one of two forms: more sociological explanations interpreting populism as a reaction to loss of identity in the globalized 'mass society' and a type of explanation leaning more on the main staple of comparative politics – the specific properties of political and electoral systems (Hawkins et al, 2018). A more theoretical answer is that populism is a 'parasitic' movement, a 'shadow' or a 'spectre' that follows logically and historically from the inherent problems of representative democracy (Canovan, 1999; Arditi, 2004; Crick, 2005; Kaltwasser, 2012; Urbinati, 2013; Müller, 2016). For others, the key explanation is the decline of party politics and the transformation of political parties (Mair, 2002; Kriesi, 2014).

The ideational approach to populism as a thin-centred ideology, by contrast, leads to a distinction between, on the one hand, demand-side explanations that focus on structural conditions for the rise of populist attitudes and/or salience of populist ideas and, on the other hand, supply-side explanations that focus on the agenda of populist parties and movements and their performance in the political arena (Mudde & Kaltwasser, 2017: 99). The former group of explanations include, inter alia, the general prevalence of populist attitudes in the population, the occurrence of (primarily economic) crisis, corruption and scandals as windows of opportunity, and increasingly unresponsive political system focused on economic responsibility (austerity measures) rather than representation. Moreover, structural conditions include the changing media landscape, increased availability of information and the increasing independence and self-consciousness of the population. Supply-side explanations, for their part, include the ability of populists to act as outlets for social grievances, the flexibility of their thin ideology, the effectiveness and simplicity of populist rhetoric, as well as the degree to which populist ideas are part of mainstream politics and the broader political culture.

The focus on technocracy as a cause of populism clearly connects with certain aspects of such explanations, most notably the idea of an unresponsive political system and an increased political focus on responsibility rather than representation among mainstream parties. More generally, however, the focus on technocracy as an explanation for populism points to a more general and fundamental mechanism underpinning the entire relationship between demand and supply: the interplay of depoliticization and repoliticization. On the demand side, 'elites have used the growing influence of unelected bodies and technocratic institutions to depoliticize contested political issues' (Mudde & Kaltwasser, 2017: 117). In Europe, technocratic decision-making has been on the rise both in the long run and since the euro crisis in particular (Müller, 2016: 96). The demand created by technocratic depoliticization has, in turn, been met with an ample supply of populist repoliticization. Populists aim to 'moralize the political debate and try to (re)politicize disregarded issues and groups' (Mudde & Kaltwasser, 2017: 118), and have even become 'real experts in politicizing issues that deliberately or not have been ignored by the establishment' (Kaltwasser, 2017: 501). Action creates reaction, and technocratic depoliticization has now been met with populist repoliticization. We thus arrive at a rather clear-cut explanation for the new populist challenge: 'Populists attempt to restore political control over society in an age of technocratic depoliticization' (Rummens, 2017: 568). What is needed now is a fuller exploration of this dynamic.

Depoliticization and repoliticization

Parallel to the emerging rediscovery of technocracy as an explanation for the new populist challenge, depoliticization has been explored in more detail by critical (and predominantly British) observers of the new governance and Third Way politics. Although originating in political economy, this approach has laid the groundwork for the interpretation of depoliticization as a broader 'governing strategy' more or less directly linked to the new governance and the transformation from government to governance (Burnham, 2001; Flinders & Wood, 2014; Hay, 2014). As such, depoliticization amounts to a form of politics that places key socio-economic decisions above and beyond political contestation and responsibility by increasing managerial control and submitting political power to techno-economic forces and imperatives (Flinders, 2008; Burnham, 2014). In order to do so, the politics of depoliticization relies on a combination of 'institutional' (delegation of decisions to unelected bodies and agencies), 'rule-based' (binding agreements) and 'behavioural' (discursive and rhetorical framing) tactics and tools (Flinders & Buller, 2006). More generally, depoliticization has been described as stepwise removal of decisions from the governmental sphere to the private and societal sphere (Hay, 2007). With a recent summary definition, depoliticization comprises the 'processes (including varied tactics, strategies, and tools) that remove or displace the potential for choice, collective agency, and deliberation around a particular political issue' (Fawcett et al, 2017: 55).

As noted in the same volume, the relatively smaller and specialized group of contributions on depoliticization has gradually been connected more or less systematically with the larger and less specialized island of contributions on 'anti-politics', dealing with citizen dissatisfaction with government, disengagement or outright rejection of politics, low levels of trust in politicians, declining voter turnout, falling levels of party membership and so on (Schedler, 1997; Hay & Stoker, 2009; Flinders, 2015; Stoker, 2019). Such anti-politics is widely considered a vital threat to democracy insofar as it drains formal democratic institutions of their meaning and substance (elections without voters, parties without members, politicians no one trusts and so forth). Although depoliticization and anti-politics were initially used somewhat interchangeably, it is now common to view the former as an explanation for the latter. A particularly decisive argument here has been Hay's analysis of depoliticization as a reason for 'why we hate politics' (Hay, 2007). The consolidation of this cause–effect relationship is also notable if one compares the second and much revised edition of Stoker's *Why Politics Matters: Making Democracy Work* (2017) with the original version (2006b), which placed anti-politics on the agenda more than any other single contribution.

The explication of the link between depoliticization and anti-politics has, however, taken place without much sustained attention to the issue of populism. Stoker did include a brief reflection on the 'perils of populism' in the original outline of anti-politics, but has also acknowledged more recently that the rise of populism to some degree caught observers off guard (Stoker, 2019). More substantially, populism is in fact a rather different kind of response to depoliticization from anti-politics. Anti-politics, at least as originally conceived, was clearly slanted towards defeatism and passivism, and populism is clearly anything but. Whereas the logic of anti-politics is disengagement, withdrawal and rejection of politics, the logic of populism is engagement, attack and reclaiming power for the people. As such, the new populist challenge represents an important addition to the original formula of anti-politics, which can be seen as a more active and mobilizing form of anti-politics and/or a new phase in the development of anti-politics, depending on temperament. Either way, populism brings with it an element of sustained and even aggressive repoliticization missing from disengaged anti-politics. The one thing that populism does not lack is engagement and mobilization.

With this budding recognition of populism as an amendment to anti-politics, the emerging literature on the link between depoliticization and anti-politics offers a productive entry point to the interplay between technocratic depoliticization and populist repoliticization, thus providing an important addition to the more general search for an explanation to the new populist challenge. A particular strength of this approach is that it points to the new governance as the principal source of technocratic depoliticization, although in a way that clearly requires further elaboration. In a landmark analysis, the politics of depoliticization is thus seen as a child of Blair's Third Way, but also of the managerial state, privatization, regulation, NPM, public/private cooperation, user groups, accountability systems and Good Governance (Burnham, 2001: 129). Broadening the point, the transition from government to governance provides the missing link between depoliticization and anti-politics: the new governance is key to understanding if and how depoliticization results in anti-politics and, for some, how to avoid that very dynamic (Fawcett et al, 2017). My emphasis here is on the former part of this equation, the question of the new governance as the material expression of the dynamics, mechanisms, strategies and tools of depoliticization that result in anti-politics and more specifically in populist repoliticization.

On this point, however, the analysis of the new technocratic governance in the preceding chapters results in a somewhat revised line of argument than that in the existing literature. Since the turn of the millennium, the main 'culprit' in the analysis of depoliticization has been NPM, marketization, consumerization of the citizen, privatization, deregulation, the managerial state, public choice and ultimately the assumed hegemony of neoliberalism (Hay, 2007; Stoker, 2017). According to this line of argument, anti-politics is a problematic yet understandable response to, inter alia, the formalized cynicism of public choice theory that has defined and legitimized politicians and civil servants as self-interested utility maximizers, the willing relinquishment of political control through deregulation and privatization, public spending cuts and austerity measures, the restriction of policy choice in the name of free markets and the creation of competitive states, and the overall state sponsorship, misrepresentation and strategic utilization of globalization in the staging of responsible political choices.

This approach aligns the analysis of the new governance with a critique of ideology that ultimately leads back to the narrative of neoliberal hegemony since the 1980s. The decisive point about the technocratic depoliticization achieved through the new governance, however, is not a particular ideological affiliation, but rather that it does not have such an affiliation. Of course, technocratic depoliticization has functioned in lockstep with various configurations and agendas of liberalism and continues to do so. However, technocratic depoliticization is not simply a cover-up for a liberal agenda, but an art of government based on post-industrial management, techno-progressivism, social engineering and scientism operating at its optimum beyond ideology. Once we approach depoliticization from this angle, it becomes clear that NPM reforms and the broader liberal agenda to which they are attached are not the only part, nor even the most important, of the new governance: the subsequent development of network-based approaches, meta-governance and NPG are as, or more, vital to technocratic depoliticization. We can of course also submit this to an ideological interpretation and point to the affiliation between NPG and Third Way liberalism and its various incarnations of social liberalism and ordoliberalism. However, this should not cloud the crucial point that the technocratic attraction to this position is not caused by whatever ideological asymmetry is assigned to the Third Way, but in the possibility of moving beyond ideology.

Indeed, the limits of the ideological interpretation of depoliticization has to some extent been brought to the fore by the new recognition of an emerging crisis in the encounter between governance and populism. Here, it becomes clear that populism is not just a reaction to the market fundamentalism of NPM and neoliberalism, but an indirect and direct attack on the new governance in its entirety, including post-NPM practices, NPG, meta-governance and associated claims to democratic legitimacy (Stoker, 2019). To understand this populist attack on the new governance better, however, it is necessary to look at the particular contributions of network governance, risk management and performance management to technocratic depoliticization in more detail. In doing so, I do not propose to come up with a new general theory or framework of depoliticization. The ensuing analysis incorporates various mechanisms, strategies, tactics and tools of depoliticization discussed in more general frameworks. Taken together, however, the policy paradigms of network organization, risk regulation and performance calculation sheds new light on the broader dynamics of technocratic depoliticization and populist repoliticization as a counter-reaction this development.

Network organization: populism against partnerships and the empty place of power

The guiding principle of connective governance and network management is the imperative but difficult transition to a network state in accordance with the challenges and opportunities of the information age and the network society, that is, a transformation of statehood and political institutions based on the organizational morphology of networks. More concretely, the transition to a network state rests on the extensive creation, utilization and management of networks in order to increase the overall connectivity and problem-solving capacity of public policy. In general, such use of networks leads to depoliticization in the sense of an institutional removal of political decisions from government to the wider circles of public and private decision-making and ultimately the realm of non-political necessities (Hay, 2007). Network governance relocates key socio-economic decisions from the institutionalized arenas of democratic deliberation and decision making to networks of unelected stakeholders that come together for the purpose of solving all kinds of technical and socio-economic problems. As such, network governance also resembles an 'institutional' tactic of depoliticization, although it relies more on the creation of a hybrid network than the formal bodies and agencies originally highlighted by this term (Flinders & Buller, 2006).

This approach clearly runs counter to the characterization of network governance as a 'post-liberal' and 'pragmatic' deepening or radicalization of democracy based on extensive self-governance and opportunities for deliberation and participation (Sørensen & Torfing, 2009). Viewed in the context of technocratic depoliticization, such efforts are largely the result of the new technocratic partnership with democracy against bureaucracy, which creates a demand for new and flexible democratic standards under the heading of output legitimacy, adapted to the reality of selective stakeholder inclusion in the pursuit of effective solutions to wicked policy problems. Network governance is thus the essence of depoliticization as 'a process cloaked in the language of inclusiveness, democratization and empowerment', which 'capitalizes on the rejigging of domestic bureaucratic practices' (Burnham, 2001: 129), and a form of 'system governance' that 'borrows the language of radical democracy while missing its spirit' (Bevir, 2006:426. Even an otherwise committed defender of network governance admits that populists may have a point when it comes to issues such as the transparency and inclusiveness of governance networks (Stoker, 2019).

From secretive elites to open networks

At first sight, network governance simply seems to invoke the old technocratic aversion towards publicity and public involvement in politics and the image of the technocrat as a skilled hand at closed politics. Networks often carry strong connotations of secrecy, decision making behind closed doors and a general retreat from democratic arenas of decision making being subject to public scrutiny. This understanding of network governance is further reinforced by the association between networks and the notion of an isolated 'elite' running politics with complete indifference to the people. There is in this sense a rather direct line from networks and networking to a colluding or even conspiring elite running politics behind closed doors, which has always featured more or less prominently in critiques of network governance. Not surprisingly, then, this image of networks is also found in populist attacks on the existing political system as a collusive and petrified system of elite interests. Here, networks appear more or less straightforwardly as a synonym for a corrupt elite insulated from the real world of the people, for example in the populist discourse of M5S (Five Star Movement) in Italy (Stoker, 2019: 12).

Even if network governance sometimes does play straight into the hands of the populist antagonism between the elite and the people in this way, however, it is not necessarily the most important aspect of the interplay between technocratic depoliticization and populist repoliticization. Technocratic depoliticization through network governance does not rest so much on decisions taken behind closed doors by secretive elites as it makes political decisions disappear in the complex interplay and interdependencies among a multitude of actors in more or less formal governance networks. The institutionalization of industrial technocracy in the shape of a techno-bureaucracy did indeed involve a good deal of discretionary decision-making in the hands of bureaucratic elites and specific institutions insulated from public interference and, to some degree, also from political control. However, such decision making also remained rather formalized and centralized. Governance networks, by contrast, operate on a logic of weak (or at least variable) institutionalization and decentralization. Indeed, governance networks open up channels of influence on public policy absent from industrial technocracy. Network governance has made the policy process more open to international cooperation and agreements, stakeholder participation, exchange of knowledge and information, communication, and dialogue.

This is, however, part of the problem in the eyes of populism. Populists may always pit themselves against the image of a corrupt elite, but they are also (at least when it comes to right-wing populism) ardent believers in centralization and concentration of power in the hands of political leaders providing the simple solutions that the people are asking for. The problem with governance networks, from the perspective of populism, is not so much that they more or less consistently exclude ordinary citizens in spite of their openness to stakeholders in possession of knowledge and resources. Populists are not in favour of extensive participation in the tedious affairs of public policy, but support a strong and responsive government that delivers the right policies without unnecessary participation and bother on the part of the citizens (Mudde & Kaltwasser, 2017). Decentralization of decision-making power to networks of stakeholders, in other words, simply delays or hinders efficient politics. This mode of repoliticizing decisions attacks the very *raison d'être* of network governance, that is, the claim that the challenges and wicked problems of current public policy are so complex and interdependent that they require extensive coordination and collaboration between multiple actors with the required knowledge to come up with temporary and moderately acceptable solutions. Populists hold that there are simple solutions to perfectly understandable problems, and network governance simply makes political decisions unnecessarily complex and even contrived. The people, if only understood properly, speak with one voice that demands simple solutions.

The empty place of power

In more general terms, depoliticization through the relocation of decisions to technocratic governance networks can be described as the 'disappearance of the place of power altogether ... because of the decentralized nature of governance networks, power becomes illusive and invisible and citizens no longer know where to look in order understand who is deciding what on behalf of whom' (Rummens, 2017: 567). Pushing the point to its radical conclusion, this line of argument suggests that it is not the impersonal rule of bureaucratic officials that brings to life Hannah Arendt's infamous principle of rule by 'nobody' as a form of tyranny without a tyrant (1970), but rather decision making through governance networks. The populist counter-reaction to this development consists of a reassertion of a representational logic of a direct and unmediated relationship between leader and people. In other words, populist repoliticization counters technocratic governance networks and their empty place of power with its very opposite: centralization of decision-making power in the hands of the individual, strong and charismatic leader, incarnating the will and singular identity of the people. A sufficiently responsive government, in the populist logic, can only be ensured by a relation of direct representation, immediacy and close communication between the people and their chosen leader. Populists may point to a variety of institutions that stand in the way of such a relationship, sometimes including both electoral and parliamentary institutions, but governance networks represent its very antithesis.

This is perhaps most evident in the case of MLG and the multilayered dimension of the network state, associated most consistently with the EU. Indeed, the EU incarnation of MLG can be seen as an organizational infrastructure designed more or less specifically for technocratic depoliticization (Majone, 1996). Thus understood, the EU is the 'ultimate technocratic sphere' exactly because the very architecture of EU institutions was designed to shield the practical steps, 'day-to-day agenda', and incremental realization of 'limited projects of practical cross-border integration' from grand political visions, political interference and 'grandstanding for the national media' (Leonard, 2011: 2). Whereas the original version of this 'Monnet method' was based on the administrative discretion of relatively narrow and insulated techno-bureaucratic elites in the manner of industrial technocracy, attempts at democratization and more balance between technocracy and democracy has been a recurring issue ever since (Wallace & Smith, 1995). The erosion of the popular 'permissive consensus', if indeed it was ever there, and the widespread concern with the 'democratic deficit' of the EU has led to what is effectively the EU version of the general reversal from industrial to post-industrial technocracy: a dismissal of the extensive administrative elite discretion associated with the original Monnet method in favour of a new partnership with democracy, openness, inclusion and dialogue. This reversal is embodied, more than anything else, in the key technocratic institution of the EU: the Commission.

For decades (essentially since 'Eurosclerosis'), the Commission has attempted to find a balance between its basic technocratic mandate of depoliticized policy-making beyond national interests and concerns for the democratic deficit of EU policies. The result is that the Commission now exercises its institutional prerogative through a sort of meta-governor of extensive stakeholder inclusion, networking activities and the so-called comitology. The result has been characterized as a new and 'responsive technocracy' reacting to the increasing politicization of EU policy (Rauh, 2016), or as a transition from technocratic to 'reflexive' governance (Fischer, 2008). What is at stake here, however, is simply the transition from old to new technocracy. The Commission may be fully committed to network governance, but its mandate and practice have nothing to do with democratic inclusion or input legitimacy, but remains restricted to output legitimacy and the production of 'policies without politics', cloaked in the language of democratic deliberation and dialogue (Schmidt, 2013: 17). Indeed, network governance under the auspices of the Commission, in a particularly dismissive analysis, has been described as technocracy disguised as deliberation, 'where the whole paraphernalia of deliberation is employed as a cover for technocratic government ... a kind of super-deliberation is imagined in which very knowledgeable people, devoid of any interests except the interest in truth, talk together' (Martin, 2005: 351).

The place of power is not, however, left empty only by the upwards depoliticization of the embedded network stake. Political decisions can disappear into networks, stakeholder partnerships and collaborative governance on all levels of decision making, thus displaying the same fundamental traits of an inclusive and responsive technocracy claiming to support or even expand democratic deliberation and participation within a framework of output legitimacy. At a deeper level, this type of responsive technocracy rests on the exercise of communicative governance. Communicative governance links the ability to accommodate the media logics embedded in informational networks and hybrid media systems with stakeholder inclusion and the creation of a flexible MLG infrastructure of vertically and horizontally integrated policy decisions. In the face of all this, however, populist repoliticization simply drives a wedge between technocracy and democracy, reclaiming the latter for itself and exposing network governance for the inherent depoliticization of leaving the place of power empty. In doing so, however, populism always sets on a course that tends to substitute the tyranny of no one with the more familiar tyranny of an individual leader that 'is' the people.

Risk regulation: populism against fear and irony

The disappearance of political power into networks of interdependent stakeholders speaks directly to the spatial and institutional models of depoliticization and the view on the displacement of political choice and contestation in terms of a stepwise 'relocation' away from established political and democratic arenas. Risk management, by contrast, displaces the potential for choice, collective agency and deliberation of political issues in a manner more akin to behavioural and rule-based tools and tactics of depoliticization, although in broader sense. In general, technocratic depoliticization through the governance of risk operates through a simultaneous securitization and externalization of political decisions. Both aspects are captured by the observation that 'risk is always related to security and safety. It is also always connected to responsibility' (Giddens, 1999: 7). In relation to the first aspect, the governance of risks turns an increasing number of political decisions into a matter of security, while at the same time negating the very possibility of providing safety, protection or insurance through political interventions. In relation to the second dimension, the governance of risk externalizes responsibility for decisions to certain but unforeseeable threats, catastrophes, failures and unintended side effects, which at one and the same time leaves political interventions absolutely necessary and ultimately impotent. Indeed, the irony of this situation is the central insight of risk reflexivity and the enlightenment shock of risk society.

Securitization without security

The inherent relation between matters of national security and the 'powers of exception' has been extensively rehearsed in political, legal and constitutional theory. This approach points up the extreme form of depoliticization ingrained in various constitutional provisions, making it an executive prerogative to suspend the normal political order under conditions of war, siege and crisis. In the state of emergency, the rules of ordinary politics are effectively suspended and replaced by ultimate executive prerogatives and powers of intervention. The problems and paradoxes involved in this form of depoliticization have been further developed by governmentality studies, which have argued that politics is increasingly conducted in a generalized state of emergency, increasingly submitting all aspects of life to the power of exception and the use of extraordinary measures (Agamben, 1998; Hardt & Negri, 2000; Neocleous, 2008). In the field of international relations, the so-called Copenhagen School has pointed to an expensive logic of securitization, where new problems and policies beyond the narrow domain of warfare and security politics are submitted to the extraordinary logic of national security through various securitization 'moves' and 'speech' acts (Stritzel, 2007).

As understood by the Copenhagen School, securitization operates through a structurally fixed security grammar: a securitization move or speech act starts with the identification/construction of an existential threat to the referent object of ultimate value, which in turn creates a political imperative of defence against an external threat that legitimizes the complete suspension of ordinary politics and the use of extraordinary measures in order to ensure security, protection and ultimately survival (Buzan et al, 1998). In other words: there is a limited set of existential threats, but once encountered they call for ultimate measures and suspension of normal politics in order to ensure protection. Correspondingly, ordinary politics is defined simply as the absence of existential threats and immediate danger from the viewpoint of security grammar. Security concerns are clearly not absent from ordinary politics, but they are processed within the normal machinery of utility calculations, trade-offs, wealth (re)distribution, protection, compensation and insurance. In this way, the security grammars of ordinary politics and security politics converge in the material result: the extension of security guarantees and protection. The difference is whether to get there through standard regulation or extraordinary measures; through the normal machinery of politics or its suspension.

However, technocratic depoliticization through risk management relies *neither* on the security grammar of security politics, *nor* on the grammar of ordinary politics. Although the risk grammar of 'risk politics' is in some ways similar to that of conventional securitization, it also adds a distinct logic of 'riskification' (Corry, 2011). This particular logic of riskification has to do with dynamics and structures of risk society. Under conditions of manufactured, global and incalculable risk, the threat scenario of specific existential threats is increasingly supplemented by or even subsumed under a horizon of generalized risk and uncertainty. In contrast to a threat scenario of immediate danger and harm, the security grammar of risk management and the governance of risk operate in a scenario where the threat is located on the level of conditions of possible harm. This reconstructed threat scenario, in turn, opens up the field of possible subjects and objects 'at risk' of harm: whereas the referent objects or subjects of conventional securitization are a limited set of assets with existential value, archetypically defined by the parameters of the national interest, the threat scenario of risk grammar produced an open-ended list of 'governance-objects' exposed to risk and thus in need of increased resilience (Corry, 2011: 249).

Whereas the political imperatives of both security politics and normal politics are protection, safety, compensation and/or insurance, achieved respectively through extraordinary and ordinary measures, the political imperative of risk management is to increase the resilience of citizens, organizations, infrastructures, communities, cities and so on exposed to risk. In this way, the security grammar of risk management under the conditions of risk society securitizes political decisions while nullifying the possibility of politically guaranteed security. In risk society, everything is potentially dangerous, and nothing can ultimately be made safe. This goes against the shared logic of security politics and ordinary politics: that only some things are dangerous and protection against such things is indeed possible. Of course, security claims can be upheld by precautionary measures banning or limiting the perceived sources of harm or laissez-faire approaches denying the threat altogether. However, both approaches run aground with each crisis or catastrophe demonstrating that everything is indeed, objectively or subjectively, dangerous. Hence, the only solution consistent with the reality of manufactured, global and incalculable risk: a form of governance based on the interplay between risk exposure and 'precursor' and 'recovery' resilience in the face inevitable crisis and catastrophe.

With technocratic depoliticization increasingly turned to the security grammar of risk management and governance, it comes as little surprise that the populist counter-reaction goes to the heart of this grammar. Indeed, populism involves a pervasive and persistent reassertion of the logic that only some things are dangerous and protection is possible. Populists do not want to be told that everything is dangerous and react vehemently against the riskification of things such as food, smoking, the environment, driving their car, education and life in general. On the other hand, populists care deeply about the things that *are* seen as dangerous and call for reinstatement of strong security guarantees from political leaders. This form of repoliticization can involve a call for the return to normal politics or the extraordinary measures of security politics. A key example of the first dynamic is the populist call for a return to the forms of protection and insurance developed in order to cope with industrial risks. These are largely reactions to the risk exposure of the globalized economy and thus associated with anti-globalist and anti-capitalist sentiments. Here, populism demands that national political leaders reassert control and reinstate insurances and forms of compensation for risk exposure rather than bending the knee to global capitalism and its need for a mobile, malleable and disposable workforce.

The key example of the second and perhaps more pronounced dynamic, however, is where nationalist, nativist and straightforward xenophobic populist movements call for decisive and firm responses to issues such as immigration, refugee crises, multiculturalism and terrorism. Following a radical us/them distinction, populists define various ethnic and religious outgroups as an external, immediate and existential threat that places the 'true people' under siege, which in turn demands the deployment of extraordinary measures in order to ensure the survival of the people and the nation. For populists, the suspension of ordinary politics and the constitutional order, including its basic rights and liberties, is not even a sacrifice when the people are threatened by other groups. In one sense, this can of course be seen a call for further depoliticization rather than repoliticization, at least if we understood the latter as a return to normal politics. However, the state of exception can also be seen as an extreme form of politicization and the true political moment revealing sovereign power for what it really is – a power transcending the rule of the law and the constitutional order. In this way, the populist objection to the security grammar of risk management can be said to invoke sovereignty both as a constitutive power (at work in the state of exception and the use of extraordinary measures) and as a constituted power (at work in normal politics and the ordinary measures of insurance and compensation).

Responsibility, reflexivity and irony

Technocratic depoliticization through risk management also has a more direct bearing on one of the more widely discussed 'demand-side' explanations for the populist explosion: the increasing political preoccupation with responsibility and the corresponding interpretation of populism as a call for representation and responsive government against the logic of responsibility. The contribution of risk management and governance to this dynamic is that it imbues political interventions with a particular combination of absolute responsibility and absolute irresponsibility. The standard understanding of the political preoccupation with responsibility highlights the tendency for governments to interpret and present political decisions as responsible actions in relation to certain standards of necessity, thus displacing political choice and contestation with absolute necessities (that is, a politics of necessity), principally, of course, in relation to the economic system. This is, however, only half of the equation in risk management and governance. Under conditions of global, manufactured and incalculable risk, political decisions are bound to fail and failure is thus increasingly built pre-emptively into political decision-making. This creates a situation where political decisions are in one sense ultimately responsible for everything and at the same time completely devoid of responsibility.

Indeed, this is the principal political implication of risk society as a 'reflexive modernity' (Beck, 1996; Beck et al, 1994), the 'enlightenment shock' of risk society (Beck, 2006) and the idea that reflexivity should be seen as new democratic standard of political expert deliberation (Rosanvallon, 2011). In sum, the normative implications of acknowledging the transition to risk society amount to 'a *political theory of knowledge* of modernity becoming self-critical' (Beck, 1999: 81, original emphasis). Enlightened risk reflexivity involves self-aware and self-critical decision-making fully immersed in the reality of manufactured, global and incalculable risk. On the one hand, such reflexivity invokes an ultimate responsibility: every political decision can potentially create or contribute to disasters, crisis and catastrophe, making it politically imperative to demonstrate due diligence in consideration of this fact. This is where proper risk assessment leads to necessary decisions that must overrule representation and responsiveness if necessary. On the other hand, however, risk assessment is also bound to come up short in risk society. Any solution or measure will fail or even backfire, probably sooner rather than later: in the face of global, manufactured and incalculable risk, political solutions are at best temporary and at worst part of the (wicked) problem rather than the solution.

By the logic of risk reflexivity, this is simply a feature of risk society and not a failure of decision making. In other words: risk reflexivity not only places the grave burden of responsibility on political decisions, it also negates the very possibility of assuming full responsibility for the crisis, catastrophes and failures that are bound to happen. Of course, any crisis or catastrophe immediately produces the blame games and blame avoidance tactics that are as old as politics, but have become an increasingly important form of political manoeuvring in risk society (Hood, 2010). What happens when catastrophe does occur in risk society, however, is to some extent less important than what happens when it does not. Indeed, the attribution of guilt after the catastrophe is to some extent the very mirror image of the pre-emptive externalization of responsibility in between catastrophes. Such pre-emptive externalization is *not* a blame game, but rather a direct consequence of the political imperative of risk reflexivity. In the concrete process of heeding this imperative in the concrete governance of risk, risk reflexivity increasingly turns into a form of governmental irony in the face of the fact that definitive solutions are simply not possible in age of manufactured risk and wicked problems. All that is left is to try to fail a little less and/or a little better.

The more general association between reflexivity and irony has been well rehearsed by Beck (2006), but the relationship becomes more material when risk reflexivity turns into the 'irony' of risk management and governance. This is particularly pronounced in the interpretation of meta-governance under the conditions of manufactured risks and wicked problems as an art of government that can only be exercised through a certain measure of requisite irony (Willke, 1992; Jessop, 2011). Meta-governance, in this view, is not only a creative combination of bureaucracy, markets and networks, but more importantly also a 'reflexive orientation about an acceptable outcome in the case of incomplete success' and the exercise of 'self-reflexive "irony" such that the participants in governance recognize the likelihood of failure but then continue as if success were possible' (Jessop, 2011: 117). This is the irony of risk society translated into a guiding principle of meta-governance: political solutions are bound to fail, but we will proceed as though they actually work (and keep an eye on the outcome). In Jessop's view, such self-reflexive irony is the only viable alternative to stoicism, opportunism and cynicism, all of which remain readily available responses to the reality of manufactured risk and wicked problems in risk society. However, the unattractiveness of the alternatives does not mean that the case for self-reflexive irony should be overstated: reflexivity and irony may be the standards of a meta-governing technocracy subjected to the enlightenment shock of risk society, but they also involve a particular form of depoliticization that conflicts with representation and responsive government.

Putting it mildly, populists are generally not too keen on self-reflexive irony. From the populist standpoint, self-reflexive irony seems to be combining the worst of two worlds: political leaders that consider themselves omnipotent when it comes to overruling popular concerns with risk assessments and necessary interventions, but impotent when it comes to actually finding proper solutions. Populists would generally prefer the opposite: political leaders that humble themselves in relation to the will of the people, but appear omnipotent when it comes to actually finding political solutions and delivering the goods. Populists do not want to be told that there really are no solutions, but only the option of failing a little less or little better in the implementation of what are, on top of it all, absolutely necessary political decisions. Against the perceived arrogance of governmental irony, populist repoliticization asserts that 'politicians who know (rather than "listen to") the people' should be able to 'make their wishes come true' and provide the proper solutions (Mudde, 2004: 558). The only form of political responsibility that counts for populists is responsibility to the people.

Performance calculation: populism against scientific facts and accountability

Performance management is the most direct expression of technocratic scientism and the idea of government by science. This results in what is perhaps the most straightforward form of technocratic depoliticization: the substitution of political contestation, deliberation and mediation with political choice based on the best available scientific evidence. In this respect, current technocratic depoliticization through performance management reflects the basic inclination towards 'scientization' of policy and politics that has always been a constitutive dimension of the technocratic regime, often highlighted in standard definitions. However, evidence-based policy, policy and programme evaluation as well as the extensive use audits and inspections have all contributed an expansion and transformation of technocratic scientism. Scientific influence on public policy has become more pervasive with the new technocracy, as well as more empirical, experimental and multidisciplinary. Performance management and its core principle of learning from evidence in order to ensure the continuous improvement of policy have thus become a constitutive feature of current policy-making.

The common denominator between these practices is the idea of finding out 'what works' and the vision of public policy development and implementation as a process of radical incrementalism, innovation and learning, linking the phases, cycles and programmes of public policy together in the search for better solutions. Taken to its radical conclusion, this logic aims to redesign public-policy making as a form of social experimentation based on relevant indicator selection, data collection, analysis and reporting, and the subsequent use of the performance information by relevant decision-makers. This development includes elements of institutional and behavioural tactics and tools of depoliticization. Performance management involves a more or less systematic displacement of choice, collective agency and deliberation in favour of a pervasive transformation of a public policy to a process of scientific discovery and 'experimental governance' within and between states.

Facts vs feelings

While evaluation, evidence-based policy and institutionalized mechanisms of accumulation and diffusion of knowledge about 'what works' may be more entrenched in some fields than others, the scientization of policy and politics is a dynamic that affects all sectors and fields in most advanced political systems today. Economic science holds a particularly prominent place in technocracy, as evidenced by the notion of the econocracy. In some ways, economics is still the most influential science in public policy, not only in terms of its direct influence on economic and welfare policies, but also in the wide application of CBA, in more or less advanced forms, as method of calculating optimal policy choices. However, the current technocratic depoliticization is limited to economic knowledge and methods, but draws on a host of other social and hard sciences, and the various mixes thereof, in the pursuit of evidence-based policy across all major policy fields and domains, ranging from health policy and environmental policy to social policy and educational policy.

Against the political authority of scientific experts and evidence, populism advances the claim that the feelings and sentiments of the people are the only authentic basis of political decisions. This form of repoliticization is at the heart of the intimate connection between populism and what is sometimes referred to as post-factual democracy and post-truth politics. The people know and feel the truth, and no amount of scientific evidence can change this. Populist repoliticization is everywhere based on the reassertion of the authentic truth of the people against the idea that the ultimate foundation for political choice is the best available scientific evidence. In one version of the resulting conflict between facts and feelings, populists hold that scientific evidence is simply irrelevant and can be disregarded by political leaders with an innate understanding of what the people already know to be true. However, the populist stance towards the political authority of scientific evidence often goes one step further and suggests that supposedly 'scientific' evidence is simply part of false reality created by more or less conspiring elites. This line of critique is often extended to the media, which is seen only to represent the distorted reality of the alleged experts and submissive politicians. Mainstream media is thus rejected as being liars, borrowing the term *Lügenpresse* used by AfD in Germany, leading populists to establish their own 'alternative' media or social media forums where the authentic truth of the people is known and shared.

The truth of the people as defined and advanced by populists is composed of everyday experiences, anecdotes, mutually reinforcing storytelling, opinions, faith and moral judgements. In short: everything that is unscientific. More often than not, it is also based on what are simply fabricated 'facts', lies, distortions and moral sentiments in the form of racism and bigotry. The apparent dangers and undesirability of such communication, however, should not cloud the fact that the extensive technocratic depoliticization of political decisions to which populists loudly and explicitly object is in itself democratically ambiguous at best. From the technocratic viewpoint, the truth of the people is simply a matter of irrationality, hysteria and propaganda. This conflict between enlightened scientific rationality and the 'counter-enlightenment' of hearsay, manipulated facts and moralization is in some sense a completely accurate and consistent image of the current interplay between technocracy and populism.

Nevertheless, the increasingly antagonistic approach to this relationship, on the side of enlightened technocrats, too, tends to disregard the fact that technocratic depoliticization may to some extent also be part of the problem and not simply the solution. If this is not evident in principle, then it seems at least to be evident in practice: the host of experts explaining the scientific facts behind the logic of EU membership did little to curtail Brexit. This may of course be because of hard-headed people who are simply incapable or unwilling to understand scientific truths and thus need to be educated better. However, even if this approach may make some people better informed, it is also sure to add fuel to populist repoliticization. Moreover, the resistance towards scientific evidence about the merits of EU membership may also in part be because people are alert to the fact, which is also evident to most enlightened experts: that the value of EU is not simply determined by scientific truths, but also to a large degree by faith and beliefs.

Accountability and policy innovation

Although the opposition between facts and feelings is by far the most pervasive dynamic of depoliticization and populist repoliticization fuelled by technocratic scientism, the increased emphasis on accountability and co-production that performance management provides is also part of the equation. This dimension of performance management has to do more directly with the purported benefits of performance management to citizens. In systems of performance management designed mostly for the production of performance information and accountability, citizens figure as the ultimate accountability holder vis-à-vis the accountability 'holdees', ranging from heads of state to the local principal of a poorly performing school. By the logic of accountability, the value of such systems to the individual citizen is that performance information improves choices of political leaders, public service providers and everything in between. Where performance management is geared more towards experimental governance and innovation, citizens figure as potential participants in the co-production, co-design, co-implementation and co-evaluation of public policy, in principle gaining both experience, knowledge and influence.

It would be a stretch to say that populist repoliticization is a direct response to the proliferation of a system of accountability and experimentation in public policy. However, populists are not exactly keen on the idea that what citizens really need is more performance information in order to make better choices between politicians, schools and health services. The notion that ranking and scoring of comparative performance should be considered a measure of the quality of political decisions, big or small, and ultimately a source of political authority is highly contentious from the populist viewpoint. The accountability of performance measurement seems, rather, to be a way to sidestep true accountability, which is to say the accountability of political leadership directly to the people on standards that really matter: responsiveness, justice, moral purity and so forth. Citizen involvement in public policy experimentation, co-production and co-innovation, for its part, not only conflicts with the populist aversion to extensive participation and tedious incrementalism, but also adds a certain element of more or less direct co-optation. It is not the job of citizens to assist politicians in finding out what works and why, and in any event it is not simply what works that matters. Politicians should simply know and do what is morally right.

The increased amount of available performance information and opportunities for co-production may not be the most highly prioritized target of populist repoliticization, but it does capture an element of technocratic depoliticization in this aspect of performance management, too. For one, it is clear that accountability systems do not simply provide more or better information, but can also function as a 'hit-list' logic of scoring and ranking that restricts political choice at best and completely displaces other more politically relevant forms of information, deliberation and legitimization at worst. The inclusion of citizens in policy experimentation, innovation and co-production, likewise, should not be confused with democratic participation. Citizen involvement in such processes is based strictly on the standards of scientific evaluation, discovery, innovation and experimentation. Indeed, involvement of citizens in co-production, co-design and co-evaluation of public policy and service often involves efforts to teach citizens such standards and educate them in the production and use of valid knowledge in order to qualify their input and avoid irrelevant contributions.

Conclusion

Although the search for explanations to the new populist challenge and the 'thin-centred' populist ideology is still ongoing, it has become increasingly clear that technocracy should at the very least factor among the principal causes. The analysis of the new technocracy provides a further input to this line of argument in general and the emerging recognition of the interplay between technocratic depoliticization and populist repoliticization in particular. Armed with a comprehensive analysis of the new technocracy, it has thus been possible to map out the dynamics of this interplay in the areas of network governance, risk management and performance management: calls for centralization of power in the hands of popular leaders against the empty place of power and unnecessary complexity of technocratic network organization; simple solutions to simple dangers against the diffuse fear-mongering and irony of reflexive risk regulation; feelings and moral accountability against purported scientific truths and meaningless rankings of performance calculation. In this way, populist repoliticization systematically attacks and even reverses of all three constitutive policy paradigms of the new governance. This reversal points to a deeper structural symmetry between technocracy and populism with important implications for the issue of how to respond to populism, which is the central question of the ensuing chapter.

9

Reining Technocracy Back In?

Populism is a problem. Elitist technocrats aren't the solution.

(Berman, 2017)

What to do about populism?

Understanding populism and its causes is in a sense merely a precursor to the pressing issue of how to deal with the populist explosion. In this respect, a focus on structural, systemic and long-term causes of populism will probably lead to recommendations such as general state capacity building, strengthening the rule of law, anti-corruption measures, accountability for unethical conduct and transgressions (the type of accountability that concerns populists, not the accountability of a better ranking by the EU or OECD) and civic education in the values of democracy. An emphasis on actor-oriented explanations, on the other hand, will lead to reflections on the possible responses by mainstream parties, the media, human rights agencies and other specialized institutions that engage directly with populist parties and movements in everyday politics (Mudde & Kaltwasser, 2017: 108). A focus on populism as an integral problem of representative democracy will probably lead to a focus on ways to amend or alleviate the 'broken promise of democracy' and the problems of majority rule vis-à-vis minority protection in the practical construction of 'the people' (Müller, 2016: 75). Explanations that focus on the decline of party politics and the rise of mediated politics are likely to lead to a search for ways to reconnect political leaders and people that avoid the excesses of populist mobilization (Mair, 2002; Culpepper, 2014; Kriesi, 2014).

This chapter takes the same step from explanations to the more prescriptive problem of how to answer the populist challenge: having analysed populism as a response to technocracy, the question now is what kind of response to the populist explosion might be extracted from this analysis. In general, the answer follows directly from the interplay between technocratic depoliticization and populist repoliticization: if populism is, to some degree at least, an attempt at repoliticization in the face of technocratic depoliticization, one way to approach the populist challenge may be to rein technocracy back in and reduce the politics of depoliticization. This is not to say that populist movements and parties can simply be exonerated from their apparent excesses and more or less outright attack on democracy. Populism is not simply a symptom of the deeper problem of technocratic depoliticization. It is saying, however, that both populism and technocracy ultimately remain inherently undemocratic, even if one side can be viewed as a corrective to the excesses of the other. More to the point: populism is the inverted mirror image of technocracy, which is to say that overextension of technocratic depoliticization will always tend to produce a populist counter- and overreaction – and vice versa. Technocracy and populism are, in other words, apt to get caught in a destructive circle of mutually reinforcing moves and countermoves that pulls the political system apart and further away from democracy.

Reining technocracy back in is thus a matter of how to break this circle. This seems all the more important as a significant portion of responses to the populist explosion rather tends to assume that reinforcement and extension of the new technocracy and its claim to democratic legitimacy is key to overcoming populism. Indeed, technocratic responses to populism have become more antagonistic and moralized in their own right, depicting populist movements and parties as irrational and hysterical, if not plainly moronic. This is, however, a certain way to get caught in the circle of technocratic depoliticization and populist repoliticization. Technocratic responses to populism often lay claim to a position of enlightened understanding and moral superiority that is more than likely to feed further straight into populist self-understanding and mobilization, in effect making such responses akin to 'fighting fire with fire' (Kaltwasser, 2017). As farmers and firefighters will tell you, it is possible to fight fire with fire through 'back-burning', but that involves burning everything to the ground in order to prevent fires from starting or spreading. Hence the earlier reminder from Berman that technocracy cannot be the solution to the problem of populism. Instead, we have to start from a recognition of the fundamental symmetry between technocracy and populism in their attack on democracy.

The death spiral of technocracy and populism

The relationship between populism and democracy is in itself a matter of considerable debate. At one extreme, populism may not be viewed as threat to democracy at all, but rather as the realization of 'radical democracy' and 'revolutionary politics' that mobilize around the empty signifier of the people (Laclau, 2005). This line of argument is, however, the exception. A more common stance is that populism is both a potential threat and corrective to democracy (Kaltwasser, 2012). In this view, populists can be seen to take on different roles depending on regime conditions, such as the context of democratic regimes, authoritarian regimes and the steps between them (Mudde & Kaltwasser, 2017). Under conditions short of ideal democracy, the potential dangers of populism must be seen in conjunction with the fact that it poses uncomfortable but necessary questions about undemocratic practices, thus acting as a 'bad conciseness', a 'shadow' or a 'spectre' of democracy (Canovan, 1999; Arditi, 2004; Crick, 2005; Albertazzi & McDonnell, 2008). For some, however, the threat clearly outweighs any corrective function (Rosanvallon, 2008; Albertazzi & Mueller, 2013; Urbinati, 2013; Müller, 2016; Rummens, 2017). Even if populist repoliticization is an understandable reaction, it is also an overreaction that ends up being equally or more damaging than what it supposedly tries to correct.

Such democratic ambiguity obviously applies in equal measure to technocracy. However, the corrective function has clearly overtaken the image of technocracy as a threat to democracy since the new technocracy abandoned earlier postures and declared a new partnership with democracy. For some, this means that contemporary democracy cannot work with scientific expertise and some measure of technocratic depoliticization (Pettit, 2004; Schudson, 2006). The more ardent proponents of the new technocracy will, of course, go further and see technocracy as a way to deepen and advance democracy (Sunstein, 2018; Williams, 2006). In political and democratic theory, the latter line of argument is represented in particular by Rosanvallon's discussion of impartiality, reflexivity and proximity as the core standards of a contemporary democracy, thus defined essentially as a responsive technocracy (2011). Indeed, Rosanvallon has equally become a household name for a democratic defence for technocracy and a critique of populism as pure counter-democracy (2008). Any attempt to break the destructive circle of technocracy and populism, however, should start from the fact that they are ultimately equally undemocratic and apt to get caught in a dynamic of mutual reinforcement. Technocracy and populism are historically and logically opposed answers to the problem of politics based on an underlying structural identity.

I am certainly not the first to notice this inverse relationship. Indeed, the opposition between technocracy and populism has become a subject of considerable interest in the attempt to understand the new populist challenge. The most commonly noted identity between technocracy and populism is the adversarial stance towards party politics and party democracy (Bickerton & Accetti, 2017; Caramani, 2017). In this view, the ambiguity surrounding both technocracy and populism arises from the fact that they rigidly oppose factional politics and party democracy, although not necessarily other aspects of democracy. More generally, this aversion to party democracy is an expression of the anti-pluralism inherent to both technocracy and populism (Müller, 2016). Party democracy is an organized expression of a pluralist view on society and politics, and technocrats and populists are united in their rejection of this vision. Contrary to the pluralist idea of a decision about the common good based on aggregation, brokering, compromise and trade-offs, technocrats and populists hold that there is an objective common good that simply needs to be identified and implemented, to the good of all. Against the pluralist view of society as a field of legitimate interests competing for recognition rights and benefits, both technocrats and populists separate society fundamentally into the elite and the people, albeit for completely opposite reasons, which in turn leads to a trustee model of representation instead of the mandates issued through party democracy (Caramani, 2017).

There are other dimensions of this interplay between identity and difference in the relationship between technocracy and populism. Technocracy and populism are both premised on the idea of recruiting outsiders to positions of political leadership that are untainted by the party stigma of existing parties and party democracy in general, although the ideal type of outsider is, of course, recruited on the basis of expertise vis-à-vis being truly 'of the people'. Correspondingly, both sides may create new parties as vehicles for individual leaders when the machinery of party democracy is engaged. This may be more pronounced on the populist side of the table, but Macron's *En Marche!* certainly demonstrates the logic on the technocratic side too. Both technocrats and populists are generally in favour of strong executive power. Both sides are focused on outputs and the output legitimacy of political decisions. Or, in other words: both technocrats and populists opt for 'policy-politics' against the logic of 'politics-policy' of party democracy and pluralist interest aggregation, mediation and implementation. However, technocrats and populists interpret policy-politics as, respectively, responsibility to external imperatives and immediate responsiveness to the voice of the people. Moreover, technocracy and populism both seem to flourish in times of crisis and scandal, weakening the normal machinery of politics, but experience problems with accomplishing and/or sustaining long-term formal regime change. In the most general (and discourse theoretical) sense, the relationship between technocracy and populism has to do with the fact that they represent two structurally opposed principles of political articulation: a logic of pure difference and a logic of pure equivalence (Laclau, 2008).

In a more historical vein, the interplay between the opposing alternatives of technocracy and populism has also been observed in a variety of contexts. This is perhaps most apparent in the case of Latin America, where political history has for a long time been viewed in terms of alternation between technocracy and populism (Dargent, 2015). Indeed, the extensive and entrenched interplay between technocracy and populism, coupled with their shared opposition to party politics, can be said to have made 'technocratic populism' a dominant style of politics in Latin America (de la Torre, 2013). However, something similar occurred with the formation of the Italian 'government for change' in 2018, including M5S and Lega Nord under the leadership of Giuseppe Conte: although sometimes hailed as the first populist government of Western Europe, it represents, rather, a convergence of populism and technocracy in a European brand and 'family tree' of 'Techno-Populism' (Bickerton & Accetti, 2018). The interplay between technocracy and populism has also been seen as a key political dynamic in the United States (Fukuyama, 2014; Judis, 2016; Müller, 2016) and the post-war history of the EU (Leonard, 2011; Müller, 2016). The latter also illustrates the problems inherent to this interplay with particular clarity: decades of attempts to develop a more 'responsive' technocracy to alleviate the democratic deficit of the EU ultimately did very little to stop Brexit. And now, faced with the Brexit turmoil, disappointed responsive technocrats have increasingly turned to fighting fire with fire, launching moralized attacks on populists for their ignorance of the benefits yielded by the EU.

The images of the House of Commons in complete disarray over the attempt to negotiate an exit strategy from the EU are, however, only the most visceral illustration of a liberal democracy caught in the middle of the back-and-forth between technocratic depoliticization and populist repoliticization. The game of pure identity and opposition between technocracy and populism is not simply a theoretical exercise in structural symmetries, but everywhere and anytime a game with a high propensity to get caught in a vicious circle or even a death spiral spinning out of control. Indeed, any attempt to find appropriate answers to the populist challenge that does not start from a recognition of this fact is very likely to exacerbate the problem instead. The focus on the structural symmetries between technocracy and populism serves as a reminder that they 'are not simply opposite threats: they also seem trapped in mutually reinforcing dynamic with liberal democracy caught in the middle' (Rummens, 2017: 568). At the very least, the search for responses to the populist challenge needs to remain alert to this propensity. More fundamentally, however, the implication is that a key solution to the populist challenge is to rein technocracy back in: 'in order to break out of this vicious circle and preserve liberal democracy in the long run ... we will need to find new ways to curb the new technocratic governance regime' (Rummens, 2017: 568). Armed with a fuller analysis of the new technocratic regime, we are in a prime position to consider how this might take place.

'Militant democracy': reining the technocrats back in?

The search for answers to the populist explosion has given a new urgency to the traditional conundrum of 'militant democracy' (Malkopoulou & Kirshner, 2019): the possible responses to extremism and anti-democratic forces from 'within' democracy itself (Loewenstein, 1937; Capoccia, 2005, 2013). In general, possible strategies can be divided according to their time span (short term vs long term) and the measures used (repressive vs accommodative). The basic *militant* response is a short-term and repressive strategy that de jure or de facto curb democratic rights, essentially by placing bans on particular groups or activities. The strategy is often discussed, but has relatively few supporters as a defence against populism as it comes with significant legal difficulties and a heavy tax on the legitimacy of democratic regimes. However, a less radical militant strategy is the widely discussed option of a cordon sanitaire, which is to say a practice of non-cooperation and exclusion. The long-term version of the repressive response is to *purge* individuals associated with anti-democratic movements from positions of political influence, including everything from legal and political prosecution to hiring and firing. The short-term accommodative response consists in strategies of *incorporation* in the political system, intended to both weaken the extremist camp and increase the legitimacy of the existing regime – the opposite of a cordon sanitaire. The long-term accommodative response consists in strengthening democratic culture, value and beliefs through civic *education*, speaking directly to demand-side explanation focused on how receptive political cultures are to populism (Capoccia, 2005: 49; Kaltwasser, 2017).

While these responses have so far mainly been discussed as a possible response to populism, my aim here is, rather, to consider whether to present a possible course of action in consideration of the need to break the vicious circle of technocracy and populism and rein the former back in. In other words: does the political influence of technocracy require a 'militant' response, either in the form of legal and hard measures or in the form of practices and strategic responses by specific actors without constitutional squabbles, as reflected by the cordon sanitaire? And if the response should not be militant in either the hard or the soft sense, what is the alternative? Thus understood, the question of how to rein in technocracy primarily becomes a matter of how to rein the techno*crats* back in. Of course, technocracy has not been a clearly defined movement since the debacles of the second technocratic revolution in the United States, nor has it committed overtly to anti-democratic or extremist sentiments since the new technocratic partnership with democracy. It does, however, represent an anti-democratic force within democracy itself, present at all levels of political influence in the political system (see Chapter 3), and as such it can potentially be submitted to the same repertoire of more or less militant strategies of democratic self-preservation currently being discussed in relation to its populist mirror image. By the same token, however, the use of such strategies presents similar problems in the case of technocracy as in the case populism.

The hard militant response to populism effectively comes down to banning specific parties or movements, which is usually constitutionally difficult and requires that a fundamentally anti-democratic agenda can be proven, often in a test submitted to constitutional courts. This leaves the cordon sanitaire, exercised first and foremost by parliamentary party groups refusing to acknowledge populist parties as legitimate counterparts, in the most straightforward sense by refusing to include them in governmental coalitions. The standard example of this logic is Sweden, where the Swedish Democrats have been declared untouchable by mainstream parties. The verdict on the effects of a cordon sanitaire is still out. The Swedish case provides no definitive answer, as the country is, as at the time of writing, experiencing considerable civil unrest, extreme right-wing organizations and difficulties with finding stable governmental coalitions. In Denmark, Sweden's otherwise close neighbour, a strategy of incorporation has proved equally inconclusive, leaving the Danish People's Party with considerable electoral success and policy influence, albeit less so after the election of June 2019.

Beyond political parties, the most important actors in a position to choose between exclusion and incorporation are journalists, editors and owners of traditional media, either by taking an adversarial stance to their viewpoints or simply choosing not to cover them. In reality, most media provide populist leaders and movements with extensive attention and coverage. This is not necessarily an expression of support for populism, although political parallelism and control of the media may of course play a role, but rather the basic congruence between news criteria and populist politics. Populism meets media demands for drama, conflict, personalization and sound bites. In a nutshell, the radical nature of populist politics makes for good news, which is also to say that a highly mediatized society is rather conducive to populism (Caramani, 2017; Mudde & Kaltwasser, 2017). However, the media has also become increasingly aware of this congruence and in some cases implemented a more active stance against populism or a cordon sanitaire. For media, the cordon sanitaire can be applied at the level of news reporting, where populists can either be completely ignored or subjected to direct critique and delegitimization when reported on. Where formal demands on internal pluralism are in place, for example in the case of electoral debates, similar strategies of critique and delegitimization can be applied. Second, the media cordon sanitaire can be applied to opinion material where the media can choose not to give populists a voice, albeit the official reason will typically be guidelines excluding racism, hate speech, nationalism and the like. The voice of the media itself (through editorials) can also be used to take a more decisively anti-populist stance.

Although a general ban on technocrats remains even more difficult and questionable than banning populist groups, if not plainly nonsensical, it is in fact possible to consider a 'quasi-militant' response in the form of a ban on fully technocratic governments suspending party democracy. This may, of course, be seen as more of a long-term strategy if it involves constitutional reform, but a self-imposed ban on technocratic government by national parliaments and their members would rarely come into conflict with constitutional provisions. In contrast to a ban on specific groups or parties, a ban on technocratic government simply reasserts parliamentary responsibility, control and legitimacy against the installation of Monti-type technocratic government that represents the most formal expression of technocratic rule, which draws the most heated critiques and opens wide a window for populist counter-reactions. As with populist parties, it is also possible to consider a cordon sanitaire on technocratic parties or technopols. Technocratic parties are, of course, part of the political mainstream and neither inherently extremist nor overtly anti-democratic, making a strategy of exclusion in the actual sense of the term a largely irrelevant proposition. In a wider sense, however, a self-imposed cordon sanitaire limiting the number of technopols in political parties could probably help to avoid the mounting antagonism between technocratic and populist parties in many parliaments. Indeed, such a self-imposed cordon sanitaire is to some degree a precondition for a strategy of incorporation in relation to populism on the level of individual members and candidates. Simply put: fewer technopols and more ordinary candidates in mainstream parties.

As noted, the media has also found itself increasingly caught up in the back-and-forth between technocracy and populism. In spite of the basic congruence between news criteria and populist politics, traditional 'legacy' media have also started to reinforce traditional journalistic standards of objectivity and fact-checking and attack populist claims of the journalistic validity of alternative media more aggressively. Such measures all reflect a more or less explicit containment strategy towards populism on the part of traditional media in the face of the populist tendency to create alternative media and social media platforms that contribute to the creation of resonance chambers and post-factual democracy. In doing so, however, legacy media have also come to reinforce a function of pure fact-checking in manner that is highly uncritical of scientific knowledge and expertise. From a democratic perspective, the role of the media is also to test political claims against the horizon of values, interests and traditions rooted in practical experiences and the social lifeworld of ordinary citizens. This is, however, a job that easily gets lost in fact-checking and the battle against post-factualism, which in turn speaks to a more general submission of the media to scientific authority. The most immediate expression of this submission is the extensive reliance of scientific experience for even the most mundane forms of news reporting, even to the point where journalism is practically reduced to a matter of assembling quotes from scientific experts. Moreover, the media has also engaged in attempts to furnish itself with its own brand of scientific authority through data-driven journalism, scientific journalism and investigative teams organized more as research groups.

In other words, the media may have become self-critical and reflexive about its role in relation to populism and post-factualism, but this development also seems to reinforce the more or less complete lack of such reflexivity in relation to the problem of an excessively technocratic public sphere. The media may be increasingly willing to fact-check populism, but the preoccupation with fact-checking also provides even more impetus to the already existing preoccupation with scientific experts as the ultimate fact-checkers of everything. Journalism has become increasingly dependent on submitted scientific expertise. Setting aside more conventional problems associated with bias and political parallelism to the Left or to the Right, legacy media seem to have become subject to a new and potentially more important form of bias towards criticism of populist repoliticization vis-à-vis technocratic depoliticization. Whereas quality media assist widely and willingly in submitting claims, decisions and agendas to the test of scientific and technical expertise, the reverse test against the tradition-bound self-understanding of practical needs and experiences seems to be more lacking. Adopting a moderate media containment strategy on scientific expertise would, in this sense, be an important part of an attempt to rein the technocrats back in, outside the political system itself. The space freed up by a less one-sided focus on scientific expertise could, in turn, be used productively to focus on the test of purely 'factual' claims against the horizon of historically determined interpretations and expressions of practical needs and social interests. This is not a matter of finding more victims of or witnesses to the effects of political decisions and technological changes, but rather a matter of providing ordinary citizens with an actual proactive voice in the mediating function of the public sphere.

Short-term strategies are, however, likely to come up short without more fundamental attention to long-term responses. The long-term repressive strategy of purging, for its part, essentially implies the removal of technocrats from positions of political influence in the political system. As already hinted at in relation to the proportion of technopols in political parties, this strategy does merit some consideration, although the more draconian measures of prosecution and persecution alluded to by the term clearly have little relevance here. In particular, technocrats and their numbers feed directly into debates about the representativeness of parliamentary elites and the increasing influence of more or less professional politicians of a particular educational background. Moreover, the issue also extends to recruitment to bureaucratic elites and the number of techno-bureaucrats. However, any focus on the number of technocrats should not detract from the obvious fact that techno-bureaucrats and technopols neither can nor should be purged completely from the political system. Both technopols and techno-bureaucrats are here to stay, and long-term strategies should, rather, focus on the procedures and culture that regulate their position and influence. As conventionally understood, an accommodative long-term strategy of education does have potential bearing on the issue of how to rein technocracy back in insofar as civic culture can be made more or less resistant to technocratic overreach and scientism depending on its degree of critical attitude. However, the more important aspect of 'education' in relation to the issue at hand pertains to the domain of elite culture rather than civic culture. In sum, a comprehensive long-term response must engage the basic principles of the political system and its culture more fundamentally.

Back to the future? A decisionistic-pragmatic model of democracy

A search for alternatives to the current circle of mutually reinforcing technocracy and populism could reasonably return to the moment where this circle first started to spin out of control. In Habermas' analysis, this moment can be defined rather specifically as the point of transition from the decisionistic model outlined by Weber to a technocratic model that effectively reverses the hierarchical relationship between the politician and the expert, thus allowing the technocratic regime to exert a firmer grip on the political system (see Chapter 4). This raises the question: if this is essentially where the balance tips in favour of the technocratic regime, might not the solution be to revert to the decisionistic model? Some might object that this is a backwards approach. For one, Habermas clearly did not see the decisionistic model as attractive in and of itself: the transition to the technocratic model may signal a new and potentially even more problematic phase in the extension of bureaucratic domination, but this is clearly not to say that a return to an earlier form of bureaucratic domination is desirable. More generally: the decisionistic model is not an entrenched model of strong democracy, but rather a principle of division of labour between bureaucracy and political leadership, which has been subject to a variety of criticisms. Moreover, the change in the logic of bureaucratic domination also seems to suggest a gravitational shift in historical dynamics that would be difficult if not impossible to reverse, even if the decisionistic model is accepted. Nevertheless, the decisionistic model does offer some important clues about how the vicious circle of technocracy and populism gets started in the first place, and thus potentially also about how to break this circle.

In its basic form, the decisionistic model simply holds that technical expertise and bureaucratic organization should be subsumed under political leadership operating outside the parameters of legal-procedural authority. Although Weber saw legal-procedural rationality as the quintessential source of authority in bureaucratic organizations and the modern era at large, he neither saw it as possible nor normatively desirable to fully rationalize political decisions by this logic alone: 'in the last analysis political action cannot rationally justify its own premises' (Habermas, 1971: 63). In addition to legal-procedural authority and technical expertise, political action will always require an additional element of 'irrational' orientation to values, goals, needs and power instincts of political leaders. Based on this distinction, the decisionistic model introduces a clear division of labour between bureaucracy and political leadership. While this division of labour is often seen to rest on Weber's distinction between legal-procedural rationality and charismatic authority, it also invokes a broader ethical framework of contrast between two 'fundamentally different' and even 'irreducibly opposed' ethical maxims: *Gesinnungsethik* and *Verantwortungsethik* (Weber, 1921: 441). This pair generally translates into an ethics of conviction and an ethics of responsibility, but the span of meaning includes attitudes, intentions, passion and virtue vis-à-vis attention to consequences, results, context, perspective and a sense of proportion.

The decisionistic model as a normative framework

Weber's outline of the two principles is found in his infamous speech on 'Politics as Vocation' given at Munich University in 1918. The speech plays on the meaning of the German term *Beruf*, which implies not only vocation (*Politik als Beruf*), but also the quality of being truly called to politics (*'Beruf' zur Politik*) (Weber, 1921: 449). Following a brief history of the professional politician, which has earned the speech its central place in debates about the professionalization of politics, Weber draws a sharp contrast between the professional politician and the political leader truly 'called' to politics. The latter, in Weber's view, is defined by the ability to incarnate and mediate between the contrasting ethical principles of conviction and responsibility. Only the politician capable of this balancing act has a true calling for politics. This is what led Weber to his infamous definition of the political leader as a political 'hero' rising out of the grinding machinery of political life: 'Politics is a strong and slow boring of hard boards. It takes both passion and perspective' (Weber, 1921: 450).

The juxtaposition of the professional politician and the political leader truly called to politics is based on Weber's claim that politics has become increasingly and pervasively professionalized, not only in the immediate German context of the speech, but even more so in the United States. The result is a 'a leaderless democracy', based entirely on bureaucratic 'party machines' reducing politics to business and the rule of 'professional politicians without a calling, i.e. without the inner charismatic qualities that make a leader' (Weber, 1921: 434). In this respect, the critical tenor of Weber's analysis of professionalized politics is essentially an extension of his broader reservations about the dynamics of rationalization and bureaucratization, and true to his view that swimming against the currents of these dynamics would ultimately be impossible, Weber saw the leaderless mass democracy operated by party machines as a fact of political life that simply had to be accepted. However, he did see a fundamental choice between a leaderless democracy purely based on bureaucratic party machines operated by professional politicians and a 'plebiscitarian leadership democracy' introducing an element of true political leadership into this machinery (Weber, 1921: 434).

This is also where Weber enters into a terrain that has given the speech a dubious reputation. The German term for leadership democracy is *Führerdemokratie* (Weber, 1921: 450), and in light of the events that followed, coupled with Weber's support for strong executive power, this term has become key to an interpretation of Weber as someone on the wrong side of history (Stanton, 2016: 332). This is, however, a rather anachronistic and problematic interpretation (Kalyvas, 2002; Satkunanandan, 2014). Although Weber 'plebiscitarian leadership democracy' is certainly full of ambiguities, it nevertheless represents an attempt to outline a path of democratic development in less than favourable circumstances. Plebiscitarian leadership democracy, for Weber, is the only type of regime capable of transcending fully depoliticized professional politics without trying to fundamentally overturn it in the manner of radical democracy and revolutionary politics 'in the name of ending domination once and for all' (Breiner, 1996: 161). The latter, of course, is also a motivating concern ingrained in the historical context of Weber's speech. While this clearly invalidates Weber's argument if one is calling for radical democracy and revolutionary politics, it also 'introduces the struggle between party and administrative discipline and the offsetting discipline of charismatic leadership into a political framework that has the rudiments of parliamentary democracy' (Breiner, 1996: 161).

Indeed, this rudimentary outline of parliamentary democracy is the core of the decisionistic model. A key reason that this model is usually considered democratically problematic is Weber's emphasis on the charismatic authority as the basic of political leadership. Charismatic and personal authority is clearly premodern and anti-democratic in origin, invoking a form of domination exercised by warlords, feudal monarchs, resistance leaders and the like (Weber, 1921: 398). This ancestry of charismatic authority also leads Weber to support constitutional monarchy as a way to retain a charismatic element in politics. Nevertheless, charismatic authority can also survive the transition to a republican framework as a quality of freely elected leaders and in this way function as a source of authority compatible with popular sovereignty (Weber, 1978: 267). Charismatic authority is, however, insufficient in normative and ethical terms: the leadership of a politician truly called to politics still requires mediation between the opposing ethics of conviction and responsibility. The two principles thus represent a simple but decisive ethical framework for the exercise of political power more important than the possession of charismatic authority, even if the latter often gets the brunt of the attention.

Failure to mediate between the ethical principles of conviction and responsibility thus results in a distorted or even perverted form of politics. Political authority based on conviction without responsibility results in pure power politics reducing politics to a theatre and vanity show of noisy effects with the political leader in the starring role. This does not only reduce political decisions to an empty display of conviction and decisiveness, but also involves an attitude of indifference to the human consequences and potentially tragic effects of political actions (Weber, 1921: 437). Pure power politics thus represents a perverted form of the ethics of conviction in a cult of leadership where the political leader and the external symbols of power become the political cause in itself. Moreover, an ethics of conviction without responsibility involves a radical moralization of politics and an ideology of absolute ends, regardless of whether these ends are national, cultural, religious and so on (Weber, 1921: 437). Correspondingly, the political leader assumes a 'prophetic role' in relation to more or less revolutionary forms of mobilization (Weber, 1921: 443). Without the countervailing principle of responsibility, the radicalization of the ethics of conviction characteristic of moralized politics invariably ends in the well-know maxim of justification of any means necessary by the ultimate end.

These attributes of pure power politics and moralized politics are, of course, a more or less exact description of how populist politics, and populist political leaders in particular, operate. This point is all the more important to emphasize since plebiscitarian leadership democracy has to some degree been taken hostage in current debates about the populist challenge, meaning that it supposedly presents a model and a form of legitimization for populist politics (Caramani, 2017). This is, however, a problematic interpretation that disregards the ethical parameters proposed by Weber for a rather one-sided and somewhat superficial emphasis on the charismatic element in populist leadership. Indeed, it could be said that plebiscitarian leadership democracy and its decisionistic model, understood here as the basic scaffold of parliamentary democracy is intended specifically to *avoid* populism in the sense of political decisions based purely on an ethics of conviction, resulting in pure power politics and/or absolute moralization. More generally: Weber's outline of plebiscitarian leadership democracy as a possible way to transcend professionalized 'business' politics without revolutionary overturn or regime change is very much akin to the problem of breaking the vicious circle of technocratic depoliticization and populist repoliticization. For Weber, the one-sided reliance on the ethics of responsibility without the countervailing balance from the ethics of conviction is essentially the modus operandi of professionalized politics. Seen from the current state of affairs, we also recognize this approach as technocratic depoliticization and the politics of responsibility. Once subjected to this distinction between technocracy and bureaucracy, the decisionistic model and its potential degradation into a circle of technocracy and populism can be depicted as seen in Figure 3.

The decisionistic model is based on relationship between bureaucracy and political leadership, that is, the legal-procedural rationality and discipline of bureaucracy and the offsetting rationality and discipline of political leadership, which ideally incarnates both of these opposing ethical principles. Of course, legal-procedural rationality and administrative discipline still involve a strong principle of responsibility,

Figure 3: Technocracy and populism vs the decisionistic model

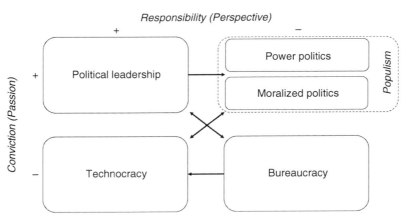

but such responsibility is both impersonal and politically neutral, at least for administrative officials, in direct contrast to the personal and political responsibility of political leadership. Whereas bureaucrats make decisions *sine ira et studio* based on an impersonal responsibility to rules and procedures, political leadership is based on *ira et studium* under ultimate personal responsibility (Weber, 1921: 415). The transition from the decisionistic model to the technocratic model originally identified by Habermas thus occurs when bureaucrats and/or politicians gravitate from the respective positions on the basic axis of the decisionistic model to the technocratic position (as techno-bureaucrats and technopols) of a pure ethics of responsibility that is neither impersonal nor personal, but supposedly an expression of pure technological-scientific rationality. The populist counter-reaction, in turn, can be seen as the gravitation of political leadership towards the pure ethics of conviction represented by the power politics and complete moralization, thus tilting the axis of the decisionistic model to a new axis of technocratic depoliticization and populist repoliticization. A return to the decisionistic model, correspondingly, requires a dual movement back to the original axis of political leadership and bureaucracy.

Political leadership

The responses available to mainstream political parties and their candidates are, of course, one of the more intensely debated topics in the overall search for answers to the populist challenge. However, Weber's normative archetype of the called politician provides a somewhat revised starting point for this issue. The imperative combination of the ethics of conviction and the ethics of responsibility has no immediate bearing on the question of whether to engage or ignore populist movements and parties, but rather suggests that the most essential answer lies in the avoidance of a regression to the populist form of politics *and* the technocratic form of politics. In this respect, the logic of political leadership ingrained in the decisionistic model can be seen as a broad guideline on how to stay the course of normal politics in a way that avoids the pitfalls of technocracy as well as populism. We could, of course, interpret this as a matter of avoiding too many economists and professional politicians in parliament, that is, increasing the representativeness and balance of national parliaments in response to the populist challenge. Although it would probably not hurt to have fewer economists or political scientists in parliament, however, the decisional model has no direct claims on equal representation or diversity in educational and occupational backgrounds. The balance between the contrastive ethical principles of conviction and responsibility is not a principle of equal representation of whatever groups society is composed of. Moreover, the composition of national parliaments ultimately is what it is, at least without radical reforms of electoral procedures that are highly problematic in themselves or voluntary changes in candidate recruitment and selection.

The ethical parameters of avoiding a complete regression to a pure ethics of responsibility has more to do with the style of political decision-making and ultimately pertains to how individual politicians exercise their popular mandate, irrespective of their background. A particularly important aspect of this problematic is knowing when to leave technical advice and scientific evidence aside. The switch from a decisionistic model to a technocratic model of decision-making occurs with the submission of political leadership to scientific and technical knowledge, and this submission presently occurs much too willingly and extensively. Avoiding a regression to a pure ethics of responsibility is very often a matter of daring to insist that science has its limits in politics. This is not easy in a climate where politicians will routinely fight over political decisions by pointing to the scientific evidence proving their necessity and throw model calculations of possible effects at each other. The problem here is not one of political instrumentalization or outright distortion of scientific knowledge, apparent and even rampant as it is, but more fundamentally that this climate of political debate suggests that scientific evidence is the only test and the true test of political proposals and decisions. The decisionistic model requires politicians to draw a line in the sand even when facts and calculations are presented honestly and properly. However, the very suggestion of drawing such a line is in itself enough to incur accusations of populist politics at present, which is certainly one way to get caught in vicious circle of technocracy and populism.

Although it is ultimately up to elected politicians to avoid this willing submission to expertise, the scientific experts do not get a free pass. Simply adopting the old technocratic pose of an exemption from politics and a claim to pure scientific rationality is as problematic as it ever was, even if the political stakes are not a reign of terror (of course, some would hold that it is). Simply claiming the safe harbour of having kept to standard scientific procedure and taken proper reservations is a highly debatable approach under current circumstances. At the very least, it is no excuse for avoiding a stronger commitment to a public discussion of what every scientist knows: that the 'best available' evidence is often not very good at all, and that there is ultimately no such thing as purely scientific rationality and knowledge inside the political system. Some might suggest that public debate about the limits of scientific evidence will play straight into the hands of the post-factual populist agenda and that this is not a time for public displays of scientific doubt. The vicious circle of technocracy and populism, however, suggests otherwise. Populists are largely correct in interpreting overextended claims to scientific certainty as a form of scientific arrogance, and maintaining such arrogance will do very little to alleviate current problems. Scientists may stay away from public debate about the limits of scientific knowledge and authority because of prestige, recognition, rewards or other understandable mechanisms, but fear of post-factualism should not be added to the list.

However, the ethical parameters of political leadership in the decisionistic model also emphasize that regression to pure power politics and moralized politics is untenable. This line of argument bears strong resemblance to the suggestion that mainstream politicians should avoid competition with populists by adopting their style of politics (Mudde & Kaltwasser, 2017). Populists follow an extreme and radicalized ethics of conviction about the truth and destiny of the people with populist leaders displaying all the hallmarks of power politicians and prophetic leaders. The temptation for mainstream politicians to follow this blueprint in order to take the wind of the populists' sails is apparent. However, it is an illusion to think that this can be done without effectively supporting and joining populist politics. On the other hand, the decisionistic model does suggest that mainstream politicians should incorporate the ethics of conviction in their approach to political life. Without submitting to extreme and even perverted form of the ethics of conviction expressed by pure power politics and extreme moralization, values, norms and even a form of virtue without any 'rational' justification should remain an operational part of mainstream politics. This is essentially a way to fill the hole in mainstream politics that often provides populists with their window of opportunity.

In defence of bureaucracy

The other side of the decisionistic model is the existence of a bureaucracy nullifying both the ethics of conviction *and* the ethics of responsibility through legal-procedural rationality and impersonal responsibility. Although Weber's normative archetype of the called politician is grounded in a critique of the bureaucratic tendency to produce leaderless democracy and depoliticized politics, plebiscitarian leadership democracy is still based on the existence of bureaucratic party machines and public administrations – the work of political and administrative officials. In the case of administrative officials, the core principle of the decisionistic model is, of course, political neutrality and a clear division of labour between political leadership and the ability of the major part of the public administration to serve alternating executives rather than political parties and factions. In the framework of the decisionistic model, neutrality simply means the simultaneous absence of the political ethics of conviction and responsibility. It does not mean, as some interpretations of neutrality and the division of labour between politics and administration suggest, that bureaucracy is a strictly apolitical machine for implementation of political decisions. Administrative officials can advise, develop and propose policy, indeed they are expected and required to. Administrative neutrality is simply an expression of a basic division of labour where legal-procedural rationality and political leadership negate each other in the decision-making process.

In a broader sense, the decisionistic model identifies a bureaucratic 'ethos' as a necessary supplement to the ethical parameters of political leadership. Strengthening the bureaucratic ethos in public administration is in this sense no less essential to the problem of breaking the vicious circle of technocracy and populism than the combined ethics of conviction and responsibility at the level of political leadership. In this respect, the problem of reining technocracy back in is much in line with mounting a 'defence of bureaucracy' against empirical and normative claims about the irrelevance of the bureaucratic model (Du Gay, 2000; Lynn et al, 2001; Suleiman, 2003; Lynn, 2011; Pollitt & Bouckaert, 2011; Fukuyama, 2014). This defence has been motivated not least by the advance of the new governance and its anti-bureaucratic stance (Du Gay, 2000; Olsen, 2006). In the context of the analysis presented here, the issue is essentially the inherent challenges of a techno-bureaucracy. Just as technopols are here to stay, techno-bureaucrats are also an integral part of public administrations. Strengthening the bureaucratic ethos, or bureaucracy more generally, correspondingly, is not a matter of a self-defeating attempt to repopulate public administrations entirely with lawyers and the odd humanist. The challenge is rather to find a workable form of techno-bureaucracy and operational guidelines for techno-bureaucrats rebuffing the anti-bureaucratic push of the new technocracy.

Such a model of techno-bureaucracy would to a large degree resemble what has been called the neo-Weberian state (NWS). As the creators of this label state, NWS is *'not … Weber plus NPM'* (Pollitt & Bouckaert, 2011: 119, original emphasis). However, the NWS could well be seen as Weber plus technocracy. Although intended as an empirically descriptive model rather than a normative framework, the NWS points exactly to the problem of the balance between bureaucracy and the pervasive effects of reforms guided by the new governance. States under the NWS label are thus characterized by a continued commitment to the role of the state, legal-procedural rationality, representative democracy and a public ethos, in conjunction with the following 'neo' elements: a professional culture oriented towards quality of service, a corresponding change in the role of civil servants such that 'bureaucrats' are no longer just rule-followers and 'experts in the law', new modes of consultation, more *ex post* control and a 'degree of performance management' (Pollitt & Bouckaert, 2011: 118). In addition to the link between the NWS and performance management highlighted here, we can add the 'neo' elements introduced by network management and risk management. More generally, the emphasis on professionalism in the NWS is an expression of a technocratic orientation towards technical expertise, less politics and 'the Progressive's vision of the administrative state' (Bourdeaux, 2008: 350).

The crucial attribute of the NWS, in this view, is that the technocratic influence is partially rebuffed and contained by politico-administrative systems based on a strong institutionalization of the bureaucratic ethos. Bureaucratic essentials such as formalization of administrative principles, proper procedure, equality before the law and legal scrutiny remain the bedrock of public administration, even if they are partially modernized. New standards of professional competence and expertise are added to, rather than supplanting bureaucratic ideas of civil service and a public ethos. The NWS thus represents a workable but fragile compromise between bureaucracy and technocracy. This compromise, crucially, is not simply a return to the techno-bureaucracy of the industrial state, but an apparatus based on bureaucratic resistance to the new technocracy and containment of new governance reforms. The difficulty is, however, that the new technocracy is clearly less likely to accept such a compromise due to the pervasive anti-bureaucratic stance ingrained in network organization, risk regulation and performance calculation. Bureaucratic resistance can be developed and nurtured through minor programmes, procedures and practices in public administration, but ultimately comes to down to the large-scale public sector reforms of administrative policy that have been firmly in the grip of the new governance for decades.

Correspondingly, current public administrations may look less like the NWS than neo-technocratic states (NTS). The tipping point from NWS to NTS can be said to appear when the professionalization of civil servants is no longer an extension of the public ethos to better public service and the ability to meet the needs and wishes of citizens, but rather intended to nurture a professional devoid of any basis in bureaucratic skills or ethos, when avenues of participation offered to citizens are less a matter of consultations supplementing representative democracy than involvement in scientific management requiring relevant knowledge and expertise from citizens and their organizations, and when we are no longer witnessing a moderate degree of performance management and *ex post* control but rather an extensive implementation of quantification and measurement systems that affect even the most mundane of administrative practices and routines. Steering administrative development towards NWS rather than NTS is not easy under the combined effects of network governance, risk regulation and performance calculation, and the job gets even more difficult where bureaucracy and the bureaucratic ethos are weakly developed and/or institutionalized to begin with. However, development of public administrations according to the principles of NWS seems the best available course of action in the attempt to rein technocracy back in and maintain the division of labour ingrained in the decisionistic model.

Beyond the decisionistic model?

To Habermas, the decisionistic model was neither normatively attractive, nor practically realizable after the gravitational shift in the logic of rationalization and bureaucratic domination involved in the shift to the technocratic model. Rather than going backwards, his suggestion was to move forwards to a 'pragmatic' model (Habermas, 1971: 66). Even if we maintain, contra Habermas, that the decisionistic model is a necessary and still viable blueprint of parliamentary democracy, this pragmatic model represents an important caveat: in order to mount a sufficiently strong democratic defence against the destructive circle of technocracy and populism, we will have to move beyond the parameters of the decisionistic model. The particular contribution of the pragmatic model in this respect is to ensure that the assumption of a clear division of labour in the decisionistic model does not preclude sound deliberation: 'the strict separation of the function of the expert and the politician is replaced by critical interaction ... reciprocal communication seems possible and necessary, through which scientific experts advise the decision-makers and politicians consult scientists in accordance with practical needs' (Habermas, 1971: 67).

As such, the pragmatic model serves as a deliberative corrective to the strict division of labour and functional separation of political leadership and technical expertise contained by bureaucratic principles. The pragmatic model prescribes a material relation between the political and scientific/technical horizons where 'communication between experts and agencies of political decision determines the direction of technical progress on the basis of tradition-bound self-understanding of practical needs ... inversely it measures and criticizes this self-understanding in light of the possibilities for gratification created by technology' (Habermas, 1971: 68). Though this feedback relation, scientific and technical knowledge are governed by the horizon of needs and value systems rooted in concrete traditions, situations and practical experiences, just as the social interests ingrained in this tradition-bound self-understanding of practical needs is regulated by being tested against technical possibilities and strategic means of gratification. This corrective to the decisionistic model not only pertains to the relation between politicians and technical experts, but also brings citizens and public into the equation. The emphasis on tradition-bound self-understanding of practical needs emphasizes that the political horizon is ultimately grounded in the value orientations of a given social lifeworld and thus that the 'successful transposition of technical and strategic recommendations into practice', according to the pragmatic model, is 'increasingly dependent on mediation by the public as a political institution' (Habermas, 1971: 68). In other words, the pragmatic model introduces the public sphere, public deliberation and public opinion as the missing link in the decisionistic model.

This argument is clearly a somewhat rudimentary outline of what would eventually become the fully developed model of deliberative democracy and communicative rationality in Habermas' work. Correspondingly, it is certainly possible to incorporate more refined deliberative standards into the basic contours of the pragmatic model. For the purposes at hand, however, the pragmatic model conveys the crucial point sufficiently: without a systematic and reciprocal test of political and technical horizons of decision making grounded in the political institution of the public sphere, the decisionistic model is bound to come up short, also as a means to rein technocracy back. Habermas pitted the pragmatic model directly against the technocratic model of complete rationalization and exclusion of the tradition-bound self-understanding of practical needs. However, the pragmatic model clearly also renders the populist rejection of scientific and technical standards untenable. Indeed, the pragmatic model is a one of deliberative democracy designed specifically to break the vicious circle of technocracy and populism through a reciprocal test of horizons that serves as a guideline for mainstream politicians, experts and citizens alike.

The pragmatic model also speaks to the critical role of the media alluded to in the discussion of short-term strategies. The relationship between public deliberation and the media is a contentious one, going back to Habermas' own reservations about the detrimental effects of modern media on the more ideal principles of the public sphere (Habermas, 1992). In the current reality of global informational networks and hybrid media systems, the practices and principles of public deliberation have certainly not become less complex. For some, new social media with little or no journalistic control represents a new infrastructure of freely flowing communication with significant democratic potential, policing, surveillance and intrusion of privacy notwithstanding. From the more narrow perspective of the paradigmatic model, however, it seems clear that new media have also been used to provide populism with a communicative infrastructure of 'alternative media', leaving it mostly to 'old media' – quality media and legacy media – to ensure and maintain the reciprocal test of scientific and technical knowledge vis-à-vis a horizon of needs and value systems rooted in concrete traditions, situations and practical experiences.

Conclusion

The search for responses to the new populist challenge constitutes one of the more pressing issues in political science and practical problems. Populism is showing no signs of abating, and the future of democracy very much depends on how the political system (and to a large degree also the media system) deals with populist parties and movements. The right-wing populist party Vox has had considerable national electoral success in Spain twice in 2019, a country previously highlighted as the one remaining exception to the rise of populism in Europe and a possible case for the value of integrating populism, or its host ideologies, into mainstream politics. The only thing clear in the current search for responses to the new populist challenge is that there is no single or simple solution. Hence, any attempt to provide input to this search should be understood as part of a multipronged fight for democracy, and we are in this fight for the long haul. In this spirit, my outline of some possible implications of an analysis focused on the interplay between technocratic depoliticization and populist repoliticization should be seen part of larger puzzle.

The first and most basic result of such an analysis is the claim that any attempt to deal with populism must carefully consider how to rein technocracy back in order to break out of the vicious circle of technocracy and populism. Recognizing this challenge is all the more essential since current responses often gravitate towards reinforcement of 'enlightened' and 'democratic' technocracy, which is more or less certain to exacerbate the problem. Fighting fire with fire does not work, and reinforcement of technocracy as a response to populism is the ultimate fight-fire-with-fire strategy. The temptation to pit more technocracy against populism is, of course, understandable and indeed in some sense a battle of enlightenment and counter-enlightenment. However, the scientific (and in the current state of affairs increasingly moralized) arrogance of technocracy is nevertheless rather certain to make the vicious circle spin even more out of control. Insisting on enlightenment is vital, but avoiding 'enlightenment blackmail' of those deemed less enlightened, irrational or downright hysterical and moronic is equally important.

In addition to more short-term strategies, I have outlined the reinforcement of a decisionistic-pragmatic model of democracy as the basic long-term strategy in the attempt to rein technocracy back in. This suggestion is made in recognition of the fact that techno-bureaucrats and technopols are an integral part of the political system. Simply dispensing with technocracy is neither possible nor normatively attractive. By returning to the key historical point of transition where technocracy seemed to gain decisive influence on the political system and political decisions, however, it is possible to conceive of the problem of how to rein technocracy back in as a return to the preceding model. The underlying assumption here is that a decisionistic model combined with pragmatic elements of deliberation provides rather clear-cut principles of resistance to technocratic impulses and influence on the level of political leadership (broadly understood) and public administration alike.

Conclusion: Technocracy at the End of the World

Any movement toward a more just and civil society can now be considered a meaningful climate action.

(Franzen, 2019)

The ultimate case for technocracy?

This book has been about a fundamental transformation in the art of government since the 1980s, which involves an attack on fundamental democratic and bureaucratic principles. Technocracy has always been difficult to disentangle from its main competitors, but the job has become particularly difficult with the new technocratic partnership with democracy against bureaucracy. Perhaps for this reason, technocracy had fallen of the radar for some time, but has now re-emerged as populism has pitted itself with increasing force against technocratic policy and politics. Indeed, as I have argued, it is necessary to rein technocracy back in if we are to curb populism and mount an effective defence of democracy in a wider sense. However, the question remains whether this attempt to solve one problem will not simply exacerbate a bigger and even more fundamental problem affecting politics, the economy, technology and ultimately the future of the human race: faced with the reality of accelerating climate change and global warming, one might reasonably ask whether this is really the time to rein in technocracy. Is what we need not *more* technocracy in the face of climate change and the impending end of the world as we know it? Would reining technocracy back in not simply leave the field open to climate change denial, interest capture and political opportunism? This is certainly a possible scenario, not entirely unlike the one we are already in, but let me conclude by suggesting that the decisionistic-pragmatic model is still a better option than pure technocracy.

In itself, the scientific evidence on climate change should obviously already have resulted in concerted political action nothing short of global mobilization, and at least beyond the meagre results so far. The scientific evidence on climate change has been steadily increasing and dutifully summarized by the IPCC since 1988. Political action, however, has been limited to ad hoc support for sustainable energy initiatives, at best inadequate and at worst rife with damaging side-effects (think bioethanol and biomass), minor modifications of transportation infrastructure, toying around with emission standards and Green New Deals suggesting, perhaps involuntarily, that we still have the problem under control. There are of course a variety of reasons for the wide gulf between scientific evidence and political (in)action, but it seems almost commonsensical that insufficient adherence to scientific knowledge and expertise is part of the problem. Indeed, one could argue that climate change makes the ultimate case for a technocratic model of political decision-making in its purest and simplest form: political leaders should submit completely and without reservation to the scientific evidence on climate change and take appropriate action.

Nevertheless, I still suggest that we need to take the destructive circle of technocratic depoliticization and populist repoliticization into account even in the extreme and difficult case of climate change, before calling for a fuller implementation of a technocratic regime. Indeed, the political stasis in relation to climate change is to some degree the result of the mutually reinforcing dynamics of technocratic depoliticization and populist repoliticization. The decisionistic-pragmatic model, I contend, still presents the best hope of blocking these dynamics and the mounting antagonism they produce. Given this very antagonism, it is probably worth emphasizing that an attempt to rein technocracy back within the parameters of the decisionistic-pragmatic model is *not* an argument against scientific expertise and evidence on climate change. On the contrary, I proceed from the rather discouraging interpretation, along with the recent comment by Jonathan Franzen in *The New Yorker* cited in the epigraph to this conclusion, that there is incontrovertible evidence of the fact that the global catastrophe of climate change has to some extent already happened. Even a concerted political effort on a scale hitherto unseen will only be able to moderate climate change, and climate change politics has to be seen as a matter of dealing with the effects of change as much as trying to reduce it.

Even under these circumstances, or perhaps particularly under such circumstances, we have to consider a retreat to the decisionistic-paradigmatic model rather than a better implementation of a fully technocratic model for the way ahead. By the terms of the former, this places a particular responsibility on political leadership for moving beyond scientific expertise instead of looking for the final piece of evidence on the right course of action. Although the core evidence on climate change comes from hard science, in contrast to the social science background of most evidence used to legitimize traditional welfare politics (in the broad sense), it is still complex, uncertain and open to contestation. Given the complexity of model simulations, margins of error and difficult CBAs, scientific expertise will never be able to be provide absolute proof of what appropriate political action should look like. In other words, further technocratic depoliticization will not bring us any closer to political solutions. Climate change mitigation will not be helped by more or better scientific evidence, but only by asserting a form of political leadership that at some point leaves science behind. Political leadership in the face of climate change should not await further scientific instructions, but consider itself sufficiently informed by its bureaucracy.

Reining technocracy back in under political leadership in this way amounts to a form of repoliticization, but not of the populist kind. Populist parties and movements have of course been key suppliers of climate change indifference, scepticism and outright denial. It should be clear by now, however, that no amount of scientific evidence and expertise will convert populists to climate change believers. The conflict between technocratic scientism and populist post-truth politics is played out with particular clarity in the case of climate change: IPCC reports and the underlying wealth of scientific documentation versus the everyday experience of the fact that the world is still here, seasons still change and a cold winter clearly shows that the Earth is not getting warmer. Difficult as it may be, however, the temptation to counter such sentiments with moralized technocratic enlightenment should be resisted. Simply insisting more on the authority of scientific evidence and the irrelevance of misinterpreted everyday experience will at best do nothing and at worst give a further push to populist repoliticization. More generally, the problem of tackling climate change without getting caught in the destructive spiral of technocracy and populism pertains both to technocratic organization, regulation and calculation.

Networks, risk and performance revisited

The argument of the book has been very much inside-out and top-down. Technocracy is a political regime in the very basic sense of the word, and my emphasis on reining technocracy back in ultimately comes down to a reinforcement of democracy and bureaucracy in the heart and head of the political system and its elite culture. This approach has offered little room to consider the question of political changes coming from below and from the outside-in – changes driven by citizen engagement, social movements and new forms of political participation. For the matters at hand, the main question is whether such forms of mobilization are capable of 'pushing technocracy back' without falling into the trap of populist repoliticization. Such forms of mobilization can be conceived as constructive 'project identities' build around a broad project of social transformation anchored in concrete life experiences (Castells, 2010b), a type of 'connective action' based on a logic of personalized public engagement trough mediated networks (Bennett & Segerberg, 2008), or the participatory logic of 'expert citizens' and 'everyday makers', engaging politics in order to sort out concrete issues and problems in a dynamic and creative way with more or less direct engagement of formal government (Bang, 2015).

Expert citizens, everyday makers, project identities and the new logic of collective action all point to connectivity from below as a driving force of democratic development and political participation in network society and the information age. Thus understood, the informational revolution has facilitated a new form of connective political mobilization, operating in a 'glocal' horizon defined by a new intimacy between local and global (or at least transnational) levels of action, often bypassing the political institutions of the nation-state. Examples of such connective and glocal political mobilization and action include, inter alia, local community groups, citizens working part time as unpaid policy professionals in relation to specific projects, the revolutionary moment of the Arab Spring, the Zapatistas, Podemos, the #MeToo campaign and, in particular of course, social movements forming around the problem of climate change. According to a rather widespread interpretation, popular mobilization around climate change, symbolically represented by global icon Greta Thunberg (as opposed to the tired face of Greenpeace) has become the prime example of popular engagement and mobilization applying pressure on a laggard political system bottom-up and outside-in through the avenues opened up by digital ICTs in the information age.

Although some glocal network organizations clearly gravitate towards populism, they also seem to hold the potential for a mode of repoliticization that resists the pitfalls of populism. Moreover, everyday makers, connective action and project identities seem to fly directly against my analysis of network organization in the information age as a vehicle of technocratic depoliticization, offering a more hopeful view of the democratic and emancipatory potential of the informational revolution and the network society. Even if this potential should clearly not be neglected, my analysis also emphasizes that the existence of network organization and connective action from below should not cloud the reality of technocratic depoliticization through network organization. The risk of such an approach comes to a head with the 'end-of-power' hypothesis that pits the nimble guerrilla warfare (both in the literal and not so literal sense) of the micropowers operating through network organization against the old and failing macropowers tied down by their continuing attachment to bureaucratic organizations (Naím, 2013). This is a highly skewed image that more or less completely disregards the considerable degree of network organization and connective action from above ingrained in the difficult but imperative transition to a network state.

Indeed, the question of how to moderate this transition is equally or more important than mobilizaiton around climate change from below. It has become truism in political science and practice that transnational problems need transnational solutions. This is the operative logic behind arguments for global and transnational governance in general and of an MLG system of governance in particular. A similar logic applies to the necessity of collaborative governance in response to complex problems. Climate change is both global and highly complex. However, continued and unwavering insistence on the need for yet another push in the direction of a network state may well pull us further away from adequate responses to climate change. At least, any insistence that the price of efficient climate change solutions is to give up on the nation-state is more than likely to exacerbate the problem of populist resistance. Climate change policies clearly demand internationally concerted action, but it is far from given that the technocratic project of network states enables such action in the current state of affairs. The technocratic inclination to view the incomplete realization of the network state as the a principal problem to be overcome in the pursuit of adequate solutions is as likely to result in conflict and inaction when faced with the reality of populist resistance.

A similar point can be made with respect to risk management. On the surface, climate change seems to present us with the ultimate vindication of risk society and risk management. Climate change is the quintessential global, manufactured and incalculable risk, and if we have indeed already reached the point of no return, it would seem that there is nothing left to do but prepare for coming catastrophe(s) and work to increase the resilience of citizens, infrastructures, cities, communities and so on. However, insistence on this regulatory approach and its underlying security grammar is, once again, likely to result in a problematic but not entirely unfounded pushback from populists. In effect, governance attempts to increase risk resilience following the maxim that 'everything is dangerous, nothing can be made safe and therefore you will have to change your entire way of life'. While it is true that we *will* have to change our entire way of life, the security grammar of risk management also holds that this has to take place entirely without political responsibility or security guarantees. Instead, risk management offers only reflexivity and irony. For one, this resilience approach inherently gravitates towards individualization vis-à-vis systemic intervention against the sources of climate change. Moreover, it limits political intervention to capacity building. In this respect, the problem of reining technocracy back in amounts to bringing climate change mitigation back to the security grammar of ordinary politics where burdens and benefits are decided according to some kind of reasonably transparent principle of (re)distribution.

Finally, of course, performance management brings us back to the fundamental problem of technocratic reliance on scientific evidence vs populist resistance. Although the problem of reinforced technocratic scientism should be clear by now, it is clearly exacerbated by the pervasive development of performance management systems, also in the case of climate change. While performance management systems geared towards public accountability may facilitate CBA and comparison of various climate change policies, they also potentially furnish political interventions with a legitimacy derived from simply following best practice. The moralized accountability demands advanced by populists may be highly problematic, but they are also motivated by the absence of a moral or ethical component missing from technocratic accountability. If nowhere else, the need for such a component at least appears straightforward in the case of climate change and global warming. Performance management geared more towards evaluation and experimentation can, of course, be seen as necessary instruments to ensure policy innovation, learning, diffusion and transfer in response to climate change. However, they also provide an interface with citizens, at least in the case of co-development and co-innovation, often designed as an outlet for expertise, educating and managing citizens. When used in this way, the reaction may well be more or less populist pushback, whereas an honest attempt at the arduous task of somehow connecting with the lived experience of everyday climate and environment could give experimental governance a more productive role in non-populist repoliticization. All of this, however, would also have to be done in the recognition that climate change and global warming also place a very definite limit on the very logic of experimental governance and incrementalism, even of the radical kind.

References

Aberbach, J.D., Putnam, R.D. & Rockman, B.A. (1981). *Bureaucrats and Politicians in Western Democracies*. Cambridge, MA: Harvard University Press.

Adair, D. (1970). The technocrats 1919–1967: a case study of conflict and change in a social movement. Master's thesis. Simon Frasier University, Vancouver.

Agamben, G. (1998). *Homo Sacer: Sovereign Power and Bare Life*. Trans. D. Heller-Roazen. Stanford, CA: Stanford University Press.

Agranoff, R. (2007). *Managing Within Networks: Adding Value to Public Organizations*. Washington, DC: Georgetown University Press.

Akin, W.E. (1977). *Technocracy and the American Dream: The Technocrat Movement, 1900–1941*. Berkeley: University of California Press.

Albertazzi, D. & McDonnell, D. (eds) (2008). *Twenty-First Century Populism: The Spectre of Western European Democracy*. Basingstoke: Palgrave Macmillan.

Albertazzi, D. & Mueller, S. (2013). Populism and liberal democracy: Populists in government in Austria, Italy, Poland and Switzerland. *Government and Opposition*, 48(3), 343–71.

Alder, K. (1997). *Engineering the Revolution: Arms and Enlightenment in France, 1763–1815*. Princeton, NJ: Princeton University Press.

Aldrich, D.P. & Meyer, M.A. (2014). Social capital and community resilience. *American Behavioral Scientist*, 59(2), 254–69.

Alexiadou, D. (2018). Technocratic government and economic policy. *Oxford Research Encyclopedia of Politics*. Oxford: Oxford University Press.

Allen, P. (2013). Linking pre-parliamentary political experience and the career trajectories of the 1997 general election cohort. *Parliamentary Affairs*, 66(4), 685–707.

Altheide, D.L. (2013). Media logic, social control, and fear. *Communication Theory*, 23(3), 223–38.

Andreas, J. (2009). *Rise of the Red Engineers: The Cultural Revolution and the Origins of China's New Class*. Stanford, CA: Stanford University Press.

Ansell, C. & Gash, A. (2008). Collaborative governance in theory and practice. *Journal of Administration Research and Theory*, 18(4), 543–71.

Ansell, C. & Torfing, J. (2014). *Public Innovation Through Collaboration and Design*. Abingdon: Routledge.

Arditi, B. (2004). Populism as a spectre of democracy: a response to Canovan. *Political Studies*, 52(1), 135–43.

Arendt, H. (1970). *On Violence*. New York: Harcourt Mifflin.

Armytage, W.H.G. (1965). *The Rise of the Technocrats: A Social History*. London: Routledge.

Askim, J., Karlsen, R. & Kolltveit, K. (2017). Political appointees in executive government: exploring and explaining roles using a large-N survey in Norway. *Public Administration*, 95(2), 342–58.

Bache, I. & Flinders, M. (2004). Multi-level governance and the study of the British state. *Public Policy and Administration*, 19(1), 31–51.

Bahadur, A. & Tanner, T. (2014). Transformational resilience thinking: putting people, power and politics at the heart of urban climate resilience. *Environment and Urbanization*, 26(1), 200–14.

Bang, H. (1998). David Easton's postmodern images. *Political Theory*, 26(3), 281–316.

Bang, H. (2003). A new ruler meeting a new citizen: culture governance and everyday making. In H. Bang (ed) *Governance as Social and Political Communication*. Manchester: Manchester University Press, pp 241–66.

Bang, H. (2015). Between democracy and governance. *British Politics*, 10(3), 268–307.

Bang, H. & Esmark, A. (2009). Good governance in network society: reconfiguring the political from politics to policy. *Administrative Theory & Praxis*, 31(1), 7–37.

Beck, U. (1992a). From industrial society to the risk society: questions of survival, social structure and ecological enlightenment. *Theory, Culture & Society*, 9(1), 97–123.

Beck, U. (1992b). *Risk Society: Towards a New Modernity*. Trans. M. Ritter. London: Sage.

Beck, U. (1994). The reinvention of politics: towards a theory of reflexive modernization. In U. Beck, A. Giddens & S. Lash (eds) *Reflexive Modernization: Politics, Tradition and Aesthetics in the Modern Social Order*. Cambridge: Polity Press, pp 1–55.

Beck, U. (1995). *Ecological Politics in an Age of Risk*. Trans. A. Weisz. Cambridge: Polity Press.

Beck, U. (1996). Risk society and the provident state. In S. Lash, B. Szerszynski & B. Wynne (eds) *Risk, Environment & Modernity: Towards a New Ecology*. London: Sage, pp 27–43.

Beck, U. (1998). Politics of risk society. In J. Franklin (ed) *The Politics of Risk Society*. Cambridge: Polity Press, pp 9–22.

Beck, U. (1999). *World Risk Society*. Cambridge: Polity Press.

Beck, U. (2006). Living in the world risk society. *Economy and Society*, 35(3), 329–45.

Beck, U. (2009). *World at Risk*. Trans. C. Cronin. Cambridge: Polity Press.

Beck, U. & Holzer, B. (2007). Organizations in world risk society. In C. Pearson, C. Roux-Dufort & J.A. Clair (eds) *The International Handbook of Organizational Crisis Management*. London: Sage, pp 3–24.

Beck, U., Giddens, A. & Lash, S. (1994). *Reflexive Modernization: Politics, Tradition and Aesthetics in the Modern Social Order*. Cambridge: Polity Press.

Becker, G.S. (1976). *The Economic Approach to Human Behavior*. Chicago: University of Chicago Press.

Behrent, M.C. (2010). Accidents Happen: François Ewald, the 'Antirevolutionary' Foucault, and the Intellectual Politics of the French Welfare State. *The Journal of Modern History*, 82(3), 585–624.

Bell, D. (1973). *The Coming of Post-Industrial Society: A Venture in Social Forecasting*. New York: Basic Books.

Bell, D. (1999). Introduction. In D. Bell, *The Coming of Post-Industrial Society: A Venture in Social Forecasting*, anniversary edn. New York: Basic Books, pp 1–46.

Bellamy, E. (1888). *Looking Backward 2000–1887*. Boston, MA: Ticknor & Co.

Bengali, S. (2017). Emmanuel Macron wanted to rule like Jupiter, but governing France has brought him quickly down to earth. Los Angeles Times, 3 October.

Bennet, W.L. & Entmann, R.M. (eds) (2011). *Mediated Politics: Communication in the Future of Democracy*. Cambridge: Cambridge University Press.

Bennett, W.L. & Segerberg, A. (2008). *The Logic of Connective Action: Digital Media and the Personalization of Contentious Politics*. Cambridge: Cambridge University Press.

Beran, M.K. (2017). Bacon's bastards: The folly of the technocratic elite. *National Review*, 2 January. Available from: www.nationalreview.com/2017/01/technocratic-elites-condescending-arrogant-foolish/

Berkes, F. & Folke, C. (1998). Linking social and ecological systems for resilience and sustainability. In F. Berkes & C. Folke (eds) *Linking Social and Ecological Systems: Management Practices and Social Mechanisms for Building Resilience*. Cambridge: Cambridge University Press, pp 1–26.

Berman, S. (2006). *The Primacy of Politics: Social Democracy and the Making of Europe's Twentieth Century.* New York: Cambridge University Press.

Berman, S. (2017). Populism is a problem. Elitist technocrats aren't the solution. *Foreignpolicy.com*, 20 December. Available from: https://foreignpolicy.com/2017/12/20/populism-is-a-problem-elitist-technocrats-arent-the-solution/

Bernauer, T. & Schaffer, L.M. (2012). Climate change governance. In D. Levi-Faur (ed) *The Oxford Handbook of Governance*, Oxford: Oxford University Press, pp 441–54.

Best, H. & Cotta, M. (eds) (2000). *Parliamentary Representatives in Europe 1848–2000: Legislative Recruitment and Careers in Eleven European Countries.* Oxford: Oxford University Press.

Best, H., Cromwell, V., Hausmann, C. & Rush, M. (2001). The transformation of legislative elites: the cases of Britain and Germany since the 1860s. *Journal of Legislative Studies*, 7(3), 65–91.

Bevir, M. (2006). Democratic governance: systems and radical perspectives. *Public Administration Review*, 66(3), 426–36.

Bevir, M. (2013). *A Theory of Governance.* Berkeley: The University of California Press.

Bickerton, C. & Accetti, C.I. (2017). Populism and technocracy: opposites or complements? *Critical Review of International Social and Political Philosophy*, 20(2), 186–206.

Bickerton, C. & Accetti, C.I. (2018). 'Techno-populism' as a new party family: the case of the Five Star Movement and Podemos. *Contemporary Italian Politics*, 10(2), 132–50.

Blanco, I. (2015). Between democratic network governance and neoliberalism: a regime-theoretical analysis of collaboration in Barcelona. *Cities*, 44, 123–30.

Blick, A. (2004). *People Who Live in the Dark: The History of the Special Adviser in British Politics.* London: Politico's.

Boin, A. & Van Eeten, M.J.G. (2013). The resilient organization. *Public Management Review*, 15(3), 429–45.

Boin, A., Rhinard, M. & Ekengren, M. (2014). Managing transboundary crises: the emergence of European Union capacity. *Journal of Contingencies and Crisis Management*, 22(3), 131–42.

Boix, C., Miller, M. & Rosato, S. (2013). A complete data set of political regimes, 1800–2007. *Comparative Political Studies*, 46(12), 1523–54.

Bouckaert, G. & Halligan, J. (2008). *Managing Performance: International Comparisons.* Abingdon: Routledge.

Bourdeaux, C. (2008). Politics versus professionalism: the effect of institutional structure on democratic decision making in a contested policy arena. *Journal of Public Administration Research and Theory*, 18(3), 349–73.

Bovaird, T. (2005). Public governance: balancing stakeholder power in a network society. *International Review of Administrative Sciences*, 71(2), 217–28.

Bovens, M. & Wille, A. (2017). *Diploma Democracy: The Rise of Political Meritocracy*. Oxford: Oxford University Press.

Braedley, S. & Luxton, M. (eds) (2010). *Neoliberalism and Everyday Life*. Montreal: McGill-Queens University Press.

Brandsen, T. & Pestoff, V. (2006). Co-production, the third sector and the delivery of public services. *Public Management Review*, 8(4), 493–501.

Breiner, P. (1996). *Max Weber and Democratic Politics*. Ithaca, NY: Cornell University Press.

Bressers, H.T.A. & O'Toole, L.J. Jr (1998). The selection of policy instruments: a network-based perspective. *Journal of Public Policy*, 18(3), 213–39.

Briguglio, L., Cordina, G., Farrugia, N. & Vella, S. (2009). Economic vulnerability and resilience: concepts and measurements. *Oxford Development Studies*, 37(3), 229–47.

Brunetta, G., Caldarice, O., Tollin, N., Rosas-Casals, M. & Morató, J. (eds) (2019). *Urban Resilience for Risk and Adaptation Governance: Theory and Practice*. Cham: Springer.

Bucchi, M. (2009). *Beyond Technocracy: Science, Politics and Citizens*. Trans. A. Belton. Dordrecht: Springer.

Bulkeley, H. & Betsill, M. (2003). *Cities and Climate Change: Urban Sustainability and Global Environmental Governance*. Abingdon: Routledge.

Bulmer, S. & Paterson, W.E. (2013). Germany as the EU's reluctant hegemon? Of economic strength and political constraints. *Journal of European Public Policy*, 20(10), 1387–405.

Burchell, G., Gordon, C. & Miller, P. (eds) (1991). *The Foucault Effect: Studies in Governmentality*. Chicago: University of Chicago Press.

Burnell, P. & Schlumberger, O. (eds) (2012). *International Politics and National Political Regimes*: Promoting Democracy – Promoting Autocracy. Abingdon: Routledge.

Burnham, J. (1941). *The Managerial Revolution: What Is Happening in the World*. New York: John Day.

Burnham, P. (2001). New Labour and the politics of depoliticisation. *The British Journal of Politics and International Relations*, 3(2), 127–49.

Burnham, P. (2014). Depoliticisation: economic crisis and political management. *Policy & Politics*, 42(2), 189–206.

Burris, B.H. (1993). *Technocracy at Work*. Albany, NY: State University of New York Press.

Buzan, B., Wæver, O. & de Wilde, J. (1998). *Security: A New Framework for Analysis*. Boulder, CO: Lynne Rienner Publishers.

Cairney, P. (2007). The professionalization of MPs: refining the 'politics-facilitating' explanation. *Parliamentary Affairs*, 60(2), 212–33.

Campbell, D.T. (1969). Reforms as experiments. *American Psychologist*, 24(4), 409–29.

Campbell, D.T. (1991). Methods for the experimenting society. *Evaluation Practice*, 12(3), 223–60.

Canovan, M. (1999). Trust the people! Populism and the two faces of democracy. *Political Studies*, 47(1), 2–16.

Capoccia, G. (2005). *Defending Democracy: Reactions to Extremism in Interwar Europe*. Baltimore, MD: Johns Hopkins University Press.

Capoccia, G. (2013). Militant democracy: the institutional bases of democratic self-preservation. *Annual Review of Law and Social Science*, 9(1), 207–26.

Caramani, D. (2017). Will vs. reason: the populist and technocratic forms of political representation and their critique to party government. *American Political Science Review*, 111(1), 54–67.

Castells, M. (2001) *Conversations with History: Manuel Castells – Identity and Change in Network Society*. Interviewer: H. Kreisler. University of California, Berkeley. University of California Television. Available from: www.uctv.tv/shows/Identity-and-Change-in-the-Network-Society-with-Manuel-Castells-Conversations-with-History-7234

Castells, M. (2005). The network society: from knowledge to policy. In M. Castells & G. Cardoso (eds) *The Network Society: From Knowledge to Policy*. Washington, DC: Johns Hopkins Center for Transatlantic Relations, pp 3–22.

Castells, M. (2007). Communication, power and counter-power in the network society. *International Journal of Communication*, 1, 238–66.

Castells, M. (2010a). *The Rise of the Network Society*, 2nd edn. The Information Age – Economy, Society, and Culture, Vol 1. Oxford: Wiley-Blackwell.

Castells, M. (2010b). *The Power of Identity*, 2nd edn. The Information Age – Economy, Society, and Culture, Vol. 2. Oxford: Wiley-Blackwell.

Centeno, M.A. (1993). The new Leviathan: the dynamics and limits of technocracy. *Theory and Society*, 22(3), 307–35.

Centeno, M.A. & Cohen, J.N. (2012). The arc of neoliberalism. *Annual Review of Sociology*, 38, 317–40.

Chadwick, A. (2013). *The Hybrid Media System: Politics and Power.* Oxford: Oxford University Press.

Chandler, D. (2014). *Resilience: The Governance of Complexity.* London: Routledge.

Chandler, D. & Coaffee, J. (2017). *The Routledge Handbook of International Resilience.* Abingdon: Routledge.

Chang, H.-J. (2010). *23 Things They Don't Tell You About Capitalism.* London: Allen Lane.

Chang, H.-J. (2014). *Economics: The User's Guide.* London: Pelican.

Chapman, T. (2016) Should engineers rule the world? Interviewer: R. Sweet. *Global Construction Review,* 6 October. Available from: www.globalconstructionreview.com/perspectives/should-engine7ers-rul7e-wo7rld/

Chomsky, N. (2011). *Profit over People: Neoliberalism and Global Order.* New York: Seven Stories Press.

Chow, C.C. & Sarin, R.K. (2002). Known, unknown, and unknowable uncertainties. *Theory and Decision,* 52(2), 127–38.

Christensen, T. (2014). New public management and beyond: the hybridization of public sector reforms. In G.S. Drori, M.A. Höllerer & P. Walgenbach (eds) *Global Themes and Local Variations in Organization and Management: Perspectives and Glocalization.* Abingdon: Routledge, pp 161–74.

Christensen, T. & Lægreid, P. (eds) (2007). *Transcending New Public Management: The Transformation of Public Sector Reforms.* Farnham: Ashgate.

Christensen, T. & Lægreid, P. (2011). *The Ashgate Research Companion to New Public Management.* Farnham: Ashgate.

Clegg, S.R. (1990). *Modern Organizations: Organization Studies in the Postmodern World.* London: Sage.

Comfort, L.K., Boin, A. & Demchak, C.C. (2010). *Designing Resilience: Preparing for Extreme Events.* Pittsburgh, PA: University of Pittsburgh Press.

Conklin, J. (2006). *Dialogue Mapping: Building Shared Understanding of Wicked Problems.* Hoboken, NJ: Wiley.

Connaughton, B. (2010). 'Glorified gofers, policy experts or good generalists': A classification of the roles of the Irish ministerial adviser. *Irish Political Studies,* 25(3), 347–69.

Considine, M. & Lewis, J.M. (2003). Bureaucracy, network or enterprise? Comparing models of governance in Australia, Britain, the Netherlands and New Zealand. *Public Administration Review,* 60(2), 131–40.

Corry, O. (2011). Securitisation and 'riskification': second-order security and the politics of climate change. *Millennium*, 40(2), 235–58.

Cotta, M. (2018). Technocratic government versus party government? Non-partisan ministers and the changing parameters of political leadership in European democracies. In A.C. Pinto, M. Cotta & P.T. de Almeida (eds) *Technocratic Ministers and Political Leadership in European Democracies*. Cham: Palgrave Macmillan, pp 267–88.

Couldry, N. & Hepp, A. (2013). Conceptualizing mediatization: contexts, traditions, arguments. *Communication Theory*, 23(3), 191–202.

Council of the European Union (2017). *The Rome Declaration: Declaration of the Leaders of 27 Member States and of the European Council, the European Parliament and the European Commission*. Available from: www.consilium.europa.eu/en/press/press-releases/2017/03/25/rome-declaration/

Crick, B. (2005). Populism, politics and democracy. *Democratization*, 12(5), 625–32.

Cristofoli, D., Meneguzzo, M. & Riccucci, N. (2017). Collaborative administration: the management of successful networks. *Public Management Review*, 19(3), 275–83.

Crouch, C. (2004). *Post-democracy*. Cambridge: Polity Press.

Crouch, C. (2011). *The Strange Non-death of Neo-liberalism*. Cambridge: Polity Press.

Crozier, M. (1964). *The Bureaucratic Phenomenon*. Chicago: University of Chicago Press.

Crozier, M. (2007). Recursive governance: contemporary political communication and public policy. *Political Communication*, 24(1), 1–18.

Culpepper, P.D. (2014). The political economy of unmediated democracy: Italian austerity under Mario Monti. *West European Politics*, 37(6), 1264–81.

Dahler-Larsen, P. (2012). *The Evaluation Society*. Stanford, CA: Stanford University Press.

Daniels, R.J., Kettl, D.F. & Kunreuther, H. (2006). *On Risk and Disaster: Lessons from Hurricane Katrina*. Philadelphia, PA: University of Pennsylvania Press.

Dardot, P. & Laval, C. (2013). *The New Way of the World: On Neoliberal Society*. Trans. G. Elliott. London: Verso.

Dargent, E. (2015). *Technocracy and Democracy in Latin America: The Experts Running Government*. Cambridge: Cambridge University Press.

Davis, A. (2017). The new *professional econocracy* and the maintenance of elite power. *Political Studies*, 65(3), 594–610.

Dawes, S.S. (2008). The evolution and continuing challenges of e-governance. *Public Administration Review*, 68(s1), S86–S102.

de la Torre, C. (2013). In the name of the people: democratization, popular organizations, and populism in Venezuela, Bolivia, and Ecuador. *European Review of Latin American and Caribbean Studies*, 95, 27–48.

De Vries, J. (2010). Is new public management really dead? *OECD Journal on Budgeting*, 10(1), 1–5.

Dean, M. (2010). *Governmentality: Power and Rule in Modern Society*. London: Sage.

Domínguez, J.I. (ed) (1997). *Technopols: Freeing Politics and Markets in Latin America in the 1990s*. University Park, PA: Pennsylvania State University Press.

Drexler, K.E. (1986). *Engines of Creation: The Coming Era of Nanotechnology*. New York: Anchor Press.

Du Gay, P. (2000). *In Praise of Bureaucracy: Weber, Organization, Ethics*. London Sage.

Duit, A. (2015). The four faces of the environmental state: environmental governance regimes in 28 countries. *Environmental Politics*, 25(1), 69–91.

Dunleavy, P., Margetts, H., Bastow, S. & Tinkler, J. (2006). New public management is dead – long live digital-era governance. *Journal of Public Administration Research and Theory*, 16(3), 467–94.

Dusek, V. (2012). Risk management in technocracy. In S. Roeser, R. Hillerbrand, P. Sandin & M. Peterson (eds) *Handbook of Risk Theory: Epistemology, Decision Theory, Ethics, and Social Implications of Risk*. Dordrecht: Springer, pp 1137–63.

Earle, J., Moran, C. & Ward-Perkins, Z. (2017). *The Econocracy: The Perils of Leaving Economics to the Experts*. Manchester: Manchester University Press.

Easton, D. (1965). *A Systems Analysis of Political Life*. Hoboken: John Wiley & Sons.

Edelenbos, J., Van Buuren, A. & Klijn, E.-H. (2013). Connective capacities of network managers. *Public Management Review*, 15(1), 131–59.

Eggers, W. (2005). *Government 2.0: Using Technology to Improve Education, Cut Red Tape, Reduce Gridlock, and Enhance Democracy*. Lanham, MD: Rowman & Littlefield.

Eichbaum, C. & Shaw, R. (2007). Ministerial advisers, politicization and the retreat from Westminster: the case of New Zealand. *Public Administration*, 85(3), 609–40.

Elliott, L. (2018) Macron's politics look to Blair and Clinton: the backlash was inevitable. *The Guardian*, 6 December. Available from: www.theguardian.com/commentisfree/2018/dec/06/macron-clinton-blair-backlash

Elsner, H.J. (1963). *Messianic Scientism: Technocracy, 1919–1960*. Ann Arbor, MI: University of Michigan.

Elsner, W., Heinrich, T. & Schwardt, H. (2015). *The Microeconomics of Complex Economies*. Oxford: Academic Press.

Esmark, A. (2008). The functional differentiation of governance: public governance beyond hierarchy, market and networks. *Public Administration*, 87(2), 351–70.

Esmark, A. (2017). Maybe it is time to rediscover technocracy? An old framework for a new analysis of administrative reforms in the governance era. *Journal of Public Administration Research and Theory*, 27(3), 501–16.

Esmark, A. (2018). Limits to liberal government: an alternative history of governmentality *Administration & Society*, 50(2), 240–68.

Esmark, A. (2019). Communicative governance at work: how choice architects nudge citizens towards health, wealth and happiness in the information age. *Public Management Review*, 21(1), 138–58.

Esping-Andersen, G. (1990). *The Three Worlds of Welfare Capitalism*. Cambridge: Polity Press.

Etzioni-Halevy, E. (1983). *Bureaucracy and Democracy: A Political Dilemma*. London: Routledge & Kegan Paul.

Etzioni-Halevy, E. (1993). *The Elite Connection: Problems and Potential of Western Democracy*. Cambridge: Polity Press.

European Commission (2018). *JRC Science for Policy Report: The Resilience of EU Member States to the Financial and Economic Crisis – What Are The Characteristics of Resilient Behaviour?* Available from: https://publications.jrc.ec.europa.eu/repository/bitstream/JRC111606/jrc111606_resilience_crisis_pilot_withidentifiers.pdf

Evans, J.St.B.T. & Stanovich, K.E. (2013). Dual-process theories of higher cognition: advancing the debate. *Perspectives on Psychological Science*, 8(3), 223–41.

Evans, M. & Davies, J. (1999). Understanding policy transfer: a multi-level, multi-disciplinary perspective. *Public Administration*, 77(2), 361–85.

Ewald, F. (1986). *L'Etat providence*. Paris: Grasset.

Fawcett, P., Flinders, M., Hay, C. & Wood, M. (eds) (2017). *Anti-Politics, Depoliticization, and Governance*. Oxford: Oxford University Press.

Feitsma, J.N.P. (2018). The behavioural state: critical observations on technocracy and psychocracy. *Policy Sciences*, 51(3), 387–410.

Fischer, F. (1990). *Technocracy and the Politics of Expertise*. London: Sage.

Fischer, F. (2000). *Citizens, Experts, and the Environment: The Politics of Local Knowledge*. Durham, NC: Duke University Press.

Fischer, R. (2008). European governance still technocratic? New modes of governance for food safety regulation in the European Union. *European Integration Online Papers*, 12(6). Available from: http://eiop.or.at/eiop/pdf/2008-006.pdf

Flinders, M. (2008). The future of the state. *The Political Quarterly*, 79(s1), 19–40.

Flinders, M. (2015). The general rejection? Political disengagement, disaffected democrats and 'doing politics' differently. *Parliamentary Affairs*, 68(s1), 241–54.

Flinders, M. & Buller, J. (2006). Depoliticisation: principles, tactics and tools. *British Politics*, 1(3), 293–318.

Flinders, M. & Wood, M. (2014). Depoliticisation, governance and the state. *Policy & Politics*, 42(2), 135–49.

Florida, R. (2012). *The Rise of the Creative Class – Revisited*. New York: Basic Books.

Foucault, M. (2007). *Security, Territory, Population: Lectures at the Collège de France, 1977–78*. Trans. G. Burchell. London: Palgrave Macmillan.

Foucault, M. (2008). *The Birth of Bio-Politics: Lectures at the Collège de France, 1977–78*. Trans. G. Burchell. London: Palgrave Macmillan.

Franzen, J. (2019). What if we stopped pretending? The climate apocalypse is coming. To prepare for it, we need to admit that we can't prevent it. *The New Yorker*, 8 September. Available from: www.newyorker.com/culture/cultural-comment/what-if-we-stopped-pretending

Freeland, C. (2010). Forget left and right. The real divide is technocrats vs. populists. *Reuters*, 5 November. Available from: http://blogs.reuters.com/chrystia-freeland/2010/11/05/forget-left-and-right-the-real-divide-is-technocrats-versus-populists/

Fukuyama, F. (2004). *State-Building, Governance and World Order in the 21st Century*. Ithaca, NY: Cornell University Press.

Fukuyama, F. (2014). *Political Order and Political Decay: From the Industrial Revolution to the Globalization of Democracy*. New York: Farrar, Straus and Giroux.

Fuller, C. & Geddes, M. (2008). Urban governance under neoliberalism: New Labour and the restructuring of state-space. *Antipode*, 40(2), 252–82.

Galbraith, J.K. (1967). *The New Industrial State*. Princeton, NJ: Princeton University Press.

Gantt, H.L. (1919). *Organizing for Work*. New York: Harcourt, Brace and Howe.

Gaxie, D. & Godmer, L. (2007). Cultural capital and political selection. In M. Cotta & H. Best (eds) *Democratic Representation in Europe: Diversity, Change, and Convergence*. Oxford: Oxford University Press, pp 106–35.

Geddes, M. (2005). Neoliberalism and local governance: cross-national perspective and speculations. *Policy Studies*, 26(3/4), 359–77.

Genieys, W. (2010). *The New Custodians of the State: Programmatic Elites in French Society*. New Brunswick, NJ: Transaction Publishers.

Giddens, A. (1991). *Modernity and Self-Identity: Self and Society in the Late Modern Age*. Stanford, CA: Stanford University Press.

Giddens, A. (1998). Risk society: the context of British politics. In J. Franklin (ed) *The Politics of Risk Society*. Cambridge: Polity Press, pp 23–34.

Giddens, A. (1999). Risk and responsibility. *The Modern Law Review*, 62(1), 1–10.

Gilardi, F. & Radaelli, C.M. (2012). Governance and learning. In D. Levi-Faur (ed) *The Oxford Handbook of Governance*. Oxford: Oxford University Press, pp 155–68.

Gitelman, L. (2006). *Always Already New: Media, History, and the Data of Culture*. Cambridge, MA: MIT Press.

Goldhammer, A. (2018). Macron's centrism is coming apart at the seams. *Foreign Policy*, 23 April.

Goldsmith, S. & Eggers, W.D. (2004). *Governing by Network: The New Shape of the Public Sector*. Washington, DC: The Brookings Institution.

Goldsmith, S. & Kettl, D.F. (2009). *Unlocking the Power of Networks: Keys to High-Performance Government*. Washington, DC: The Brookings Institution.

Goodwyn, L. (1978). *The Populist Movement: A Short History of the Agrarian Revolt in America*. Oxford: Oxford University Press.

Goplerud, M. (2013). The first time is (mostly) the charm: special advisers as parliamentary candidates and members of parliament. *Parliamentary Affairs*, 68(2), 332–51.

Graham, O.L. Jr (1976). *Toward A Planned Society: From Roosevelt to Nixon*. New York: Oxford University Press.

Grewal, D.S. (2008). *Network Power: The Social Dynamics of Globalization*. New Haven, CT: Yale University Press.

Gunderson, L.H. & Holling, C.S. (eds) (2002). *Panarchy: Understanding Transformations in Human and Natural Systems*. Washington, DC: Island Press.

Haack, S. (2003). *Defending Science – Within Reason: Between Scientism and Cynicism*. Amherst, NY: Prometheus Books.

Haber, S. (1964). *Efficiency and Uplift: Scientific Management in the Progressive Era, 1890–1920*. Chicago: University of Chicago Press.

Habermas, J. (1971). *Toward a Rational Society: Student Protest, Science and Politics*. London: Heinemann.

Habermas, J. (1992). *The Structural Transformation of the Public Sphere*. Cambridge: Polity Press.

Hajer, M.A. (2009). *Authoritative Governance: Policy-Making in the Age of Mediatization*. Oxford: Oxford University Press.

Halpern, D. (2015). *Inside the Nudge Unit: How Small Changes Can Make a Big Difference*. London: W.H. Allen.

Hardt, M. & Negri, A. (2000). *Empire*. Cambridge, MA: Harvard University Press.

Harvey, D. (2005). *A Brief History of Neoliberalism*. Oxford: Oxford University Press.

Hawkins, K.A., Kaltwasser, C.R. & Andreadis, I. (2018). The activation of populist attitudes. *Government and Opposition*, ahead of print: https://doi.org/10.1017/gov.2018.23

Hay, C. (2007). *Why We Hate Politics*. Cambridge: Polity Press.

Hay, C. (2014). Depoliticisation as process, governance as practice: what did the 'first wave' get wrong and do we need a 'second wave' to put it right? *Policy & Politics*, 42(2), 293–311.

Hay, C. & Stoker, G. (2009). Revitalising politics: have we lost the plot? *Representation*, 45(3), 225–36.

Hayek, F.A. (1955). *The Counter-Revolution of Science: Studies in the Abuse of Reason*. New York: The Free Press.

Head, B.W. & Alford, J. (2015). Wicked problems: implications for public policy and management. *Administration & Society*, 47(6), 711–39.

Helbing, D. (2013). Globally networked risks and how to respond. *Nature*, 497(7447), 51–9.

Hepburn, C. (2010). Environmental policy, government, and the market. *Oxford Review of Economic Policy*, 26(2), 117–36.

Héritier, A. & Lehmkuhl, D. (2008). The shadow of hierarchy and new modes of governance. *Journal of Public Policy*, 28(1), 1–17.

Hermansen, M. & Röhn, O. (2017). Economic resilience: the usefulness of early warning indicators in OECD countries. *OECD Journal: Economic Studies*, 2016(1), 9–35.

Higley, J. & Burton, M. (2006). *Elite Foundations of Liberal Democracy*. Lanham, MD: Rowman & Littlefield.

Hobbs, A.H. (1953). *Social Problems and Scientism.* Harrisburg, PA: Stackpole Press.

Hoffmann, E.P. & Laird, R.F. (1985). *Technocratic Socialism: The Soviet Union in the Advanced Industrial Era.* Durham, NC: Duke University Press.

Holling, C.S. (1973). Resilience and stability of ecological systems. *Annual Review of Ecology and Systematics*, 4, 1–23.

Hood, C. (1991). A public management for all seasons? *Public Administration*, 69(1), 3–19.

Hood, C. (2010). *The Blame Game: Spin, Bureaucracy, and Self-Preservation in Government.* Princeton, NJ: Princeton University Press.

Hood, C. & Dixon, R. (2015). *A Government that Worked Better and Cost Less? Evaluating Three Decades of Reform and Change in UK Central Government.* Oxford: Oxford University Press.

Hood, C. & Margetts, H. (2014). Cyber-bureaucracy: If information technology is so central to public administration, why is it so ghetto-ized? In J. Pierre & P.W. Ingraham (eds) *Comparative Administrative Change and Reform: Lessons Learned.* Montreal: McGill–Queens University Press, pp 114–37.

Hood, C., Rothstein, H. & Baldwin, R. (2001). *The Government of Risk: Understanding Risk Regulation Regimes.* Oxford: Oxford University Press.

Hooghe, L. & Marks, G. (2001). *Multi-level Governance and European Integration.* Lanham, MD: Rowman & Littlefield.

Hooghe, L. & Marks, G. (2003). Unraveling the central state, but how? Types of multi-level governance. *American Political Science Review*, 97(2), 233–43.

Hounshell, D.A. (1985). *From the American System to Mass Production, 1800–1932: The Development of Manufacturing Technology in the United States*, 2nd edn. Baltimore, MD: Johns Hopkins University Press.

Howlett, M. (2009). Government communication as a policy tool: a framework for analysis. *The Canadian Political Science Review*, 3(2), 23–37.

Hustedt, T. & Salomonsen, H.H. (2017). Political control of coordination? The roles of ministerial advisers in government coordination in Denmark and Sweden. *Public Administration*, 95(2), 393–406.

IPCC (Intergovernmental Panel on Climate Change) (2014). *AR5 Synthesis Report: Climate Change 2014.* Available from: www.ipcc.ch/report/ar5/syr/

Jessop, B. (2002). Liberalism, neo-liberalism and urban governance: a state-theoretical perspective. *Antipode*, 34(3), 452–72.

Jessop, B. (2011). Metagovernance. In M. Bevir (ed) *The Sage Handbook of Governance*. London: Sage, pp 106–23.

John, P. (2013). All tools are informational now: how information and persuasion define the tools of government. *Policy & Politics*, 41(4), 605–20.

John, P. (2016). Behavioral approaches: how nudges lead to more intelligent policy design. In G.B. Peters & P. Zittoun (eds) *Contemporary Approaches to Public Policy: Theories, Controversies and Perspectives*. Basingstoke: Palgrave Macmillan, pp 113–32.

John, P., Cotterill, S., Moseley, A., Richardson, L., Smith, G., Stoker, G. & Wales, C. (2013). *Nudge, Nudge, Think, Think: Experimenting with Ways to Change Civic Behaviour*. London: Bloomsbury Academics.

Joignant, A. (2011). The politics of technopols: resources, political competence and collective leadership in Chile 1990–2010. *Journal of Latin American Studies*, 43(3), 517–46.

Judis, J.B. (2016). *The Populist Explosion: How the Great Recession Transformed American and European Politics*. New York: Columbia Global Reports.

Jun, U. (2003). The political class in the United Kingdom: from the prevalence of the amateur to the dominance of the professional politician. In J. Borchert & J. Zeiss (eds) *The Political Class in Advanced Democracies: A Comparative Handbook*. Oxford: Oxford University Press, pp 164–86.

Kahneman, D. (2011). *Thinking, Fast and Slow*. New York: Farrar, Straus and Giroux.

Kaltwasser, C.R. (2012). The ambivalence of populism: threat and corrective for democracy. *Democratization*, 19(2), 184–208.

Kaltwasser, C.R. (2017). Populism and the question of how to respond to it. In C.R. Kaltwasser, P. Taggart, P.O. Espejo & P. Ostiguy (eds) *The Oxford Handbook of Populism*. Oxford: Oxford University Press, pp 489–507.

Kaltwasser, C.R., Taggart, P., Ochoa Espejo, P. & Ostiguy, P. (eds) (2017). *The Oxford Handbook of Populism*. Oxford: Oxford University Press.

Kalyvas, A. (2002). Charismatic politics and the symbolic foundations of power in Max Weber. *New German Critique*, 85, 67–103.

Katz, R.S. & Mair, P. (1995). Changing models of party organization and party democracy: the emergence of the cartel party. *Party Politics*, 1(1), 5–28.

Katz, R.S. & Mair, P. (2009). The cartel party thesis: a restatement. *Perspectives on Politics*, 7(4), 753–766.

Keast, R.L., Mandell, M. & Brown, K.A. (2006). Mixing state, market and network governance modes: the role of government in 'crowded' policy domains. *International Journal of Organization Theory and Behavior*, 9(1), 27–50.

Keller, S. (1963). *Beyond the Ruling Class: Strategic Elites in Modern Society*. New York: Random House.

Kelley, D.R. (1986). *The Politics of Developed Socialism: The Soviet Union as a Post-industrial State*. New York: Praeger.

Khanna, P. (2016). *Connectography: Mapping the Future of Global Civilization*. New York: Random House.

Khanna, P. (2017). *Technocracy in America: Rise of the Info-State*. NP: author.

Khanna, P. (2019). *The Future is Asian*. New York: Simon & Schuster.

Kickert, W.J.M. (1997). Public governance in the Netherlands: an alternative to Anglo-American 'managerialism'. *Public Administration*, 75(4), 731–52.

Kickert, W.J.M. (2011). Steering emergent and complex change processes. In S. Groeneveld & S. Van de Walle (eds) *New Steering Concepts in Public Management*. Bingley: Emerald Group, pp 71–89.

Klijn, E.H. & Edelenbos, J. (2007). Meta-governance as network management. In E. Sørensen & J. Torfing (eds) *Theories of Democratic Network Governance*. Basingstoke: Palgrave Macmillan, pp 199–214.

Klijn, E.H. & Koppenjan, J. (2000). Public management and policy networks: foundations of a network approach to governance. *Public Management*, 2(2), 135–58.

Klijn, E.H. & Koppenjan, J. (2015). *Governance Networks in the Public Sector*. Abingdon: Routledge.

Kooiman, J. (2003). *Governing as Governance*. London: Sage.

Koppenjan, J. & Klijn, E.-H. (2004). *Managing Uncertainties in Networks*. Abingdon: Routledge.

Kriesi, H. (2014). The populist challenge. *West European Politics*, 37(2), 361–78.

Kuhlmann, S. (2010). New public management for the 'classical continental European administration': modernization at the local level in Germany, France and Italy. *Public Administration*, 88(4), 1116–30.

Kuisel, R.F. (1981). *Capitalism and the State in Modern France: Renovation and Economic Management in the Twentieth Century*. Cambridge: Cambridge University Press.

Kurki, M. (2011). Human rights and democracy promotion: reflections on the contestation in, and the politico-economic dynamics of, rights promotion. *Third World Quarterly*, 32(9), 1573–87.

Laclau, E. (2005). *On Populist Reason*. London: Verso.

Laclau, E. (2008). Populism: what's in a name? In F. Panizza (ed) *Populism and the Mirror of Democracy*. London: Verso, pp 32–50.

LaPorte, T.R. & Consolini, P.M. (1991). Working in practice but not in theory: theoretical challenges of 'high-reliability organizations'. *Journal of Public Administration Research and Theory*, 1(1), 19–48.

Lash, S. (2002). *Critique of Information*. London: Sage.

Layton, E. (1962). Veblen and the engineers. *American Quarterly*, 14(1), 64–72.

Layton, E.T. Jr (1976). American ideologies of science and engineering. *Technology and Culture*, 17(4), 688–701.

Lee, K.-H. & Raadschelders, J.C.N. (2008). Political-administrative relations: impact of and puzzles in Aberbach, Putnam, and Rockman, 1981. *Governance*, 21(3), 419–38.

Leggett, W. (2014). The politics of behaviour change: nudge, neoliberalism and the state. *Policy & Politics*, 42(1), 3–19.

Leonard, M. (2011). Four scenarios for the reinvention of Europe. ECFR/43. Available from: www.ecfr.eu/page/-/ECFR43_REINVENTION_OF_EUROPE_ESSAY_AW1.pdf

Levi-Faur, D. (ed) (2012). *The Oxford Handbook of Governance*. Oxford: Oxford University Press.

Levitsky, S. & Way, L. (2002). The rise of competitive authoritarianism. *Journal of Democracy*, 13(2), 51–65.

Lijphart, A. (1999). *Patterns of Democracy: Government Forms and Performance in Thirty-Six Countries*. New Haven, CT: Yale University Press.

Linz, J.J. (2000). *Totalitarian and Authoritarian Regimes*. Boulder, CO: Lynne Rienner.

Lippmann, W. (1937). *An Inquiry into the Principles of the Good Society*. Boston, MA: Little, Brown and Company.

Lodge, M. & Gill, D. (2011). Toward a new era of administrative Reform? The myth of post-NPM in New Zealand. *Governance*, 24(1), 141–66.

Loeb, H. (1933). *Life in a Technocracy: What It Might Be Like*. New York: Viking Press.

Loewenstein, K. (1937). Militant democracy and fundamental rights, I. *The American Political Science Review*, 31(3), 417–32.

Luhmann, N. (2005). *Risk: A Sociological Theory*. New Brunswick, NJ: Transaction Publishers.

Lynn, L.E. Jr (2011). The persistence of hierarchy. In M. Bevir (ed) *The Sage Handbook of Governance*. London: Sage, pp 218–36.

Lynn, L.E. Jr, Heinrich, C.J. & Hill, C.J. (2001). *Improving Governance: A New Logic for Empirical Research*. Washington, DC: Georgetown University Press.

Madrian, B.C. (2014). Applying insights from behavioral economics to policy design. *Annual Review of Economics*, 6, 663–88.

Mair, P. (2002). Populist democracy vs party democracy. In Y. Mény & Y. Surel (eds) *Democracies and the Populist Challenge*. Basingstoke: Palgrave Macmillan, pp 81–98.

Mair, P. (2013). *Ruling the Void: The Hollowing-Out of Western Democracy*. London: Verso.

Majone, G. (1996). *Regulating Europe*. London: Routledge.

Malkopoulou, A. & Kirshner, A.S. (eds) (2019). *Militant Democracy and Its Critics: Populism, Parties, Extremism*. Edinburgh: Edinburgh University Press.

Mann, M. (2013). *The Sources of Social Power, Volume 4: Globalizations, 1945–2011*. New York: Cambridge University Press.

Marcussen, M. & Torfing, J. (eds) *Democratic Network Governance in Europe*. Basingstoke: Palgrave Macmillan.

Martin, S. (2005). 'Deliberative', 'independent' technocracy vs democratic politics: will the globe echo the EU? *Law and Contemporary Problems*, 68(3), 341–56.

Mathur, N. & Skelcher, C. (2007). Evaluating democratic performance: methodologies for assessing the relationship between network governance and citizens. *Public Administration Review*, 67(2), 228–37.

McCarthy, J. (2007). *Partnership, Collaborative Planning and Urban Regeneration*. Farnham: Ashgate.

McDonnell, D. & Valbruzzi, M. (2014). Defining and classifying technocrat-led and technocratic governments. *European Journal of Political Research*, 53(4), 654–71.

McGuire, M. & Agranoff, R. (2011). The limitations of public management networks. *Public Administration*, 89(2), 265–84.

Meadows, D.H., Meadows, D.L., Randers, J. & Behrens, W.W. III (1972). *The Limits to Growth: A Report for The Club of Rome's Project on the Predicament of Mankind*. New York: Universe Books.

Mellors, C. (1978). *The British MP: A Socio-economic Study of the House of Commons*. Farnborough: Saxon House.

Metz, J. (2015). *The European Commission, Expert Groups, and the Policy Process: Demystifying Technocratic Governance*. Basingstoke: Palgrave Macmillan.

Meuleman, L. (2008). *Public Management and the Metagovernance of Hierarchies, Networks and Markets: The Feasibility of Designing and Managing Governance Style Combinations.* Heidelberg: Springer.

Meynaud, J. (1968). *Technocracy.* New York: Free Press.

Mintzberg, H. (1980). Structure in 5's: a synthesis of the research on organizational design. *Management Science*, 26(3), 322–41.

Mirowski, P. & Plehwe, D. (2009). *The Road from Mont Pèlerin: The Making of the Neoliberal Thought Collective.* Cambridge, MA: Harvard University Press.

Mischen, P.A. (2015). Collaborative network capacity. *Public Management Review*, 17(3), 380–403.

Moore, M.H. (1995). *Creating Public Value: Strategic Management in Government.* Cambridge, MA: Harvard University Press.

Morozov, E. (2013). *To Save Everything, Click Here: The Folly of Technological Solutionism.* New York: PublicAffairs.

Mudde, C. (2004). The populist zeitgeist. *Government and Opposition*, 39(4), 541–63.

Mudde, C. & Kaltwasser, C.R. (2017). *Populism: A Very Short Introduction.* New York: Oxford University Press.

Müller, J.-W. (2016). *What Is Populism?* Philadelphia, PA: University of Pennsylvania Press.

Müller, W.C. & Saalfeld, T. (eds) (1997). *Members of Parliament in Western Europe: Roles and Behaviour.* London: Frank Cass.

Naím, M. (2013). *The End of Power: From Boardrooms to Battlefields and Churches to States, Why Being in Charge Isn't What It Used to Be.* New York: Basic Books.

Nelson, D.R. (2011). Adaptation and resilience: responding to a changing climate. *Wiley Interdisciplinary Reviews: Climate Change*, 2(1), 113–20.

Nelson, D.R., Adger, W.N. & Brown, K. (2007). Adaptation to environmental change: contributions of a resilience framework. *Annual Review of Environment and Resources*, 32, 395–419.

Neocleous, M. (2008). *Critique of Security.* Edinburgh: Edinburgh University Press.

Norris, P. (ed) (1997). *Passages to Power: Legislative Recruitment in Advanced Democracies.* Cambridge: Cambridge University Press.

Norris, P. & Lovenduski, J. (1995). *Political Recruitment: Gender, Race and Class in the British Parliament.* Cambridge: Cambridge University Press.

O'Flynn, J. & Wanna, J. (eds) (2008). *Collaborative Governance: A New Era of Public Policy in Australia?* Canberra: ANU Press.

OECD (2015). *Economic Resilience: What Role for Policies?* Available from: www.oecd-ilibrary.org/economics/economic-resilience-what-role-for-policies_5jrxhgf61q5j-en

OECD (2016). *Strengthening Economic Resilience: Insights from the Post-1970 Record of Severe Recessions and Financial Crises.* Available from: www.oecd-ilibrary.org/economics/strengthening-economic-resilience_6b748a4b-en

Oliver, A. (ed) (2013). *Behavioural Public Policy.* Cambridge: Cambridge University Press.

Olsen, J.P. (2006). Maybe its time to rediscover bureaucracy. *Journal of Public Administration Research & Theory*, 16(1), 1–24.

Olson, R.G. (2016). *Scientism and Technocracy in the Twentieth Century: The Legacy of Scientific Management.* Lanham, MD: Lexington Books.

Osborne, D. & Gaebler, T. (1992). *Reinventing Government: How the Entrepreneurial Spirit Is Transforming the Public Sector.* New York: Plume.

Osborne, S.P. (ed) (2000). *Public–Private Partnerships: Theory and Practice in International Perspective.* London: Routledge.

Osborne, S.P. (ed) (2010). *The New Public Governance? Emerging Perspectives on the Theory and Practice of Public Governance.* Abingdon: Routledge.

Osborne, S.P. & Brown, K. (2005). *Managing Change and Innovation in Public Service Organizations.* Abingdon: Routledge.

Page, E.C. & Wright, V. (eds) (1999). *Bureaucratic Elites in Western European States: A Comparative Analysis of Top Officials.* Oxford: Oxford University Press.

Parkin, J. (1994). *Public Management: Technocracy, Democracy, and Organizational Reform.* Aldershot: Avebury.

Pastorella, G. (2015). Technocratic governments in Europe: getting the critique right. *Political Studies*, 64(4), 948–65.

Perrow, C. (1984). *Normal Accidents: Living with High-Risk Technologies.* New York: Basic Books.

Perrow, C. (2007). *The Next Catastrophe: Reducing Our Vulnerabilities to Natural, Industrial, and Terrorist Disasters.* Princeton, NJ: Princeton University Press.

Pestoff, V. & Brandsen, T. (2008). *Co-production: The Third Sector and the Delivery of Public Services.* Abingdon: Routledge.

Peters, G.B. & Pierre, J. (1998). Governance without government? Rethinking public administration. *Journal of Administration Research and Theory*, 8(2), 223–43.

Pettit, P. (2004). Depoliticizing democracy. *Ratio Juris*, 17(1), 52–65.

Pinto, A.C., Cotta, M. & de Almeida, P.T. (eds) (2018). *Technocratic Ministers and Political Leadership in European Democracies.* Cham: Palgrave Macmillan.

Plehwe, D., Walpen, B. & Neunhöffer, G. (eds) (2006). *Neoliberal Hegemony: A Global Critique*. Abingdon: Routledge.

Pollitt, C. (1995). Justification by works or by faith? Evaluating the new public management. *Evaluation*, 1(2), 133–54.

Pollitt, C. & Bouckaert, G. (2011). *Public Management Reform: A Comparative Analysis – New Public Management, Governance, and the Neo-Weberian State*, 3rd edn. Oxford: Oxford University Press.

Pollitt, C., Girre, X., Lonsdale, J., Mul, R., Summa, H. & Waerness, M. (1999). *Performance or Compliance? Performance Audit and Public Management Reform in Five Countries*. Oxford: Oxford University Press.

Porter, T.M. (1995). *Trust in Numbers: The Pursuit of Objectivity in Science and Public Life*. Princeton, NJ: Princeton University Press.

Poulain, A. (2019) Macron vowed to fight the populists. Now he's being engulfed by them. Interviewer: M. Bell. CNN, 11 January, updated 14 January. Available from: https://edition.cnn.com/2019/01/11/europe/france-macron-yellow-vests-populism-intl/index.html

Power, M. (1999). *The Audit Society: Rituals of Verification*, 1st paperback edn. Oxford: Oxford University Press.

Power, M. & McCarty, L.S. (2002). Trends in the development of ecological risk assessment and management frameworks. *Human and Ecological Risk Assessment*, 8(1), 7–18.

Purdy, J. (2016). America's rejection of the politics of Barack Obama. *The Atlantic*, 25 July.

Putnam, R.D. (1973). The political attitudes of senior civil servants in Western Europe: a preliminary report. *British Journal of Political Science*, 3(3), 257–90.

Putnam, R.D. (1976). *The Comparative Study of Political Elites*. Englewood Cliffs, NJ: Prentice-Hall.

Putnam, R.D. (1977). Elite transformation in advanced industrial societies: an empirical assessment of the theory of technocracy. *Comparative Political Studies*, 10(3), 383–412.

Putnam, R.D. (2000). *Bowling Alone: The Collapse and Revival of American Community*. New York: Simon & Schuster.

Rauh, C. (2016). *A Responsive Technocracy? EU Politicisation and the Consumer Policies of the European Commission*. Colchester: ECPR Press.

Raymond, A. (1933). *What Is Technocracy?* New York: Whittlesey House, McGraw-Hill.

Regan, P.M. & Bell, S.R. (2010). Changing lanes or stuck in the middle: why are anocracies more prone to civil wars? *Political Research Quarterly*, 63(4), 747–59.

Reich, R. (1983). *The Next American Frontier*. New York: Crown.

Reinhoudt, J. & Audier, S. (2018). *The Walter Lippmann Colloquium: The Birth of Neo-liberalism*. Cham: Palgrave Macmillan.

Renn, O. (2008). *Risk Governance: Coping with Uncertainty in a Complex World*. Abingdon: Earthscan.

Renn, O. & Walker, K.D. (eds) (2008). *Global Risk Governance: Concept and Practice Using the IRGC Framework*. Dordrecht: Springer.

Rhodes, R.A.W. (1996). The new governance: governing without government. *Political Studies*, 44(4), 652–67.

Rhodes, R.A.W. (2007). Understanding governance: ten years on. *Organization Studies*, 28(8), 1243–64.

Rice, R.E. & Atkin, C.K. (eds) (2013). *Public Communication Campaigns*, 4th edn Los Angeles, CA: Sage.

Richardson, G.E. (2002). The metatheory of resilience and resiliency. *Journal of Clinical Psychology*, 58(3), 307–21.

Ridley, F.F. (1966). French Technocracy and comparative government. *Political Studies*, 14(1), 34–52.

Rifkin, J. (2011). *The Third Industrial Revolution: How Lateral Power Is Transforming Energy, the Economy and the World*. New York: Palgrave Macmillan.

Rittel, H.W.J. & Webber, M.M. (1973). Dilemmas in a general theory of planning. *Policy Sciences*, 4(2), 155–69.

Robbins, L. (1935). *An Essay on the Nature and Significance of Economic Science*, 2nd edn. London: Macmillan & Co.

Rogers, P. (2015). Researching resilience: an agenda for change. *Resilience*, 3(1), 55–71.

Rogers, P. (2017). The etymology and genealogy of a contested concept. In D. Chandler & J. Coaffee (eds) *The Routledge Handbook of International Resilience*. Abingdon: Routledge, pp 13–25.

Rosanvallon, P. (2008). *Counter-Democracy: Politics in an Age of Distrust*. Cambridge: Cambridge University Press.

Rosanvallon, P. (2011). The metamorphoses of democratic legitimacy: impartiality, reflexivity, proximity. *Constellations*, 18(2), 114–23.

Rose, N. (1996). Governing 'advanced' liberal democracies. In A. Barry, T. Osborne and N. Rose (eds) *Foucault and Political Reason: Liberalism, Neo-liberalism and Rationalities of Government*. Chicago: University of Chicago Press, pp 37–64.

Rose, N. (1999). *Powers of Freedom: Reframing Political Thought*. Cambridge: Cambridge University Press.

Rossides, D.W. (1998). *Social Theory: Its Origins, History, and Contemporary Relevance*. Dix Hills, NY: General Hall.

Roth, A.E. (2002). The economist as engineer: game theory, experimentation, and computation as tools for design economics. *Econometrica*, 70(4), 1341–78.

Rummens, S. (2017). Populism as a threat to liberal democracy. In C.R. Kaltwasser, P. Taggart, P. Ochoa Espejo & P. Ostiguy (eds) *The Oxford Handbook of Populism*. Oxford: Oxford University Press, pp 554–70.

Ryan, A. (2012a). *The Making of Modern Liberalism*. Princeton, NJ: Princeton University Press.

Ryan, A. (2012b). *On Politics: A History of Political Thought from Herodotus to the Present*. New York: W.W. Norton.

Sabel, C.F. (2012). Dewey, democracy, and democratic experimentalism. *Contemporary Pragmatism*, 9(2), 35–55.

Sabel, C.F. & Zeitlin, J. (2008). Learning from difference: the new architecture of experimentalist governance in the EU. *European Law Journal*, 14(3), 271–327.

Sabel, C.F. & Zeitlin, J. (2010). *Experimentalist Governance in the European Union: Towards a New Architecture*. Oxford: Oxford University Press.

Sabel, C.F. & Zeitlin, J. (2012). Experimentalism in the EU: common ground and persistent differences. *Regulation & Governance*, 6(3), 410–26.

Salamon, L.M. (ed) (2002). *The Tools of Government: A Guide to the New Governance*. Oxford: Oxford University Press.

Sanderson, I. (2002). Evaluation, policy learning and evidence-based policy making. *Public Administration*, 80(1), 1–22.

Satkunanandan, S. (2014). Max Weber and the ethos of politics beyond calculation. *American Political Science Review*, 108(1), 169–81.

Schedler, A. (1997). Expected stability: defining and measuring democratic consolidation. *ISH Political Science Series*, Working Paper 50. Vienna: IHS (Institut für Höhere Studien [Institute for Advanced Studies]).

Schlesinger, A.M. (1957). *The Colonial Merchants and the American Revolution 1763–1776*, first pub. 1918. New York: Frederick Ungar.

Schmidt, V.A. (2013). Democracy and legitimacy in the European Union revisited: input, output *and* 'throughput'. *Political Studies*, 61(1), 2–22.

Schudson, M. (2006). The trouble with experts – and why democracies need them. *Theory and Society*, 35(5/6), 491–506.

Scott, H. (1965). *History and Purpose of Technocracy*. Rushland, PA: Technocracy Inc. Available from: https://archive.org/details/HistoryAndPurposeOfTechnocracy.howardScott

Segal, H.P. (1985). *Technological Utopianism in American Culture*. Chicago: Chicago University Press.

Segal, H.P. (1997). Foreword to the reissue of *Life in a Technocracy*. In H. Loeb, *Life in a Technocracy: What It Might be Like*. Syracuse, NY: Syracuse University Press.

Self, P. (1975). *Econocrats and the Policy Process: The Politics and Philosophy of Cost-Benefit Analysis*. London: Macmillan.

Shafir, E. (ed) (2013). *The Behavioral Foundations of Public Policy*. Princeton, NJ: Princeton University Press.

Shahbaz, A. (2018). From Brussels to Silicon Valley, coping with the failures of technocratic rule. *Freedom at Issue Blog*, 1 May. Available from: https://freedomhouse.org/blog/brussels-silicon-valley-coping-failures-technocratic-rule

Shrivastava, P. & Hart, S. (1995). Creating sustainable corporations. *Business Strategy and the Environment*, 4(3), 154–65.

Siems, M. & Schnyder, G. (2014). Ordoliberal lessons for economic stability: different kinds of regulation, not more regulation. *Governance*, 27(3), 377–96.

Skaaning, S.-E. (2006). Democracy besides elections, an inquiry into the (dis)respect for civil liberty in Latin American and post-communist countries after the third wave. PhD thesis. University of Aarhus, Aarhus.

Smyth, W.H. (1921). *Technocracy: First, Second and Third Series*, reprints. Berkeley, CA: np. Available from: https://archive.org/details/technocracyfirst00smyt

Sochor, Z.A. (1981). Soviet Taylorism revisited. *Soviet Studies*, 33(2), 246–64.

Sorell, T. (1991). *Scientism: Philosophy and the Infatuation with Science*. London: Routledge.

Stabe, M. (2016). Democracy is dying as technocrats watch. *Foreign Policy*, 23 December.

Sørensen, E. & Torfing, J. (eds) (2007). *Theories of Democratic Network Governance*. Basingstoke: Palgrave Macmillan.

Sørensen, E. & Torfing, J. (2009). Making governance networks effective and democratic through metagovernance. *Public Administration*, 87(2), 234–58.

Sørensen, E. & Torfing, J. (2016). Collaborative innovation in the public sector. In J. Torfing & P. Triantafillou (eds) *Enhancing Public Innovation by Transforming Public Governance*. Cambridge: Cambridge University Press, pp 117–38.

Stabile, D.R. (1987). Veblen and the political economy of technocracy: the herald of technological revolution developed an ideology of 'scientific' collectivism. *The American Journal of Economics and Sociology*, 46(1), 35–48.

Stanton, T. (2016). Popular sovereignty in an age of mass democracy: politics, parliament and parties in Weber, Kelsen, Schmitt and beyond. In R. Bourke & Q. Skinner (eds) *Popular Sovereignty in Historical Perspective*. Cambridge: Cambridge University Press, pp 320–58.

Stein, M. & Turkewitsch, L. (2008). The concept of multi-level governance in studies of federalism. Paper presented at the International Political Science Association Conference, Montreal, 2 May. Available from: www.semanticscholar.org/paper/The-Concept-of-Multi-level-Governance-in-Studies-of-Stein-Turkewitsch/2dfe4 1d5aadf66cd6919b1d5b2b8afda5983565f

Stephens, P. (2019). Emmanuel Macron receives a lesson on populist politics. *Financial Times*, 23 January.

Stetler, H. (2016). With Emmanuel Macron, technocrats can have their revolution too. *The New Republic*. Available from: https://newrepublic.com/minutes/135082/emmanuel-macron-technocrats-can-revolution-too

Stoker, G. (1998). Governance as theory: five propositions. *International Social Science Journal*, 50(155), 17–28.

Stoker, G. (2006a). Public value management: a new narrative for networked governance? *The American Review of Public Administration*, 36(1), 41–57.

Stoker, G. (2006b). *Why Politics Matters: Making Democracy Work*. Basingstoke: Palgrave.

Stoker, G. (2010). Translating experiments into policy. *The Annals of the American Academy of Political and Social Science*, 628(1), 47–58.

Stoker, G. (2017). *Why Politics Matters: Making Democracy Work*, 2nd edn. London: Palgrave.

Stoker, G. (2019). Can the governance paradigm survive the rise of populism? *Policy & Politics*, 47(1), 3–18.

Stoker, G. & John, P. (2009). Design experiments: engaging policy makers in the search for evidence about what works. *Political Studies*, 57(2), 356–73.

Straussman, J.D. (1978). *The Limits of Technocratic Politics*. New Brunswick, NJ: Transaction Books.

Stritzel, H. (2007). Towards a theory of securitization: Copenhagen and beyond. *European Journal of International Relations*, 13(3), 357–83.

Suleiman, E.N. (1978). *Elites in French Society: The Politics of Survival*. Princeton, NJ: Princeton University Press.

Suleiman, E.N. (2003). *Dismantling Democratic States*. Princeton, NJ: Princeton University Press.

Sullivan, H. & Skelcher, C. (2002). *Working Across Boundaries: Collaboration in Public Services*. Basingstoke: Palgrave Macmillan.

Sunstein, C.R. (2002a). *The Cost-Benefit State: The Future of Regulatory Protection*. Chicago: American Bar Association.

Sunstein, C.R. (2002b). *Risk and Reason: Safety, Law, and the Environment*. Cambridge: Cambridge University Press.

Sunstein, C.R. (2015). Nudging smokers. *New England Journal of Medicine*, 372(22), 2150–1.

Sunstein, C.R. (2018). *The Cost-Benefit Revolution*. Cambridge, MA: MIT Press.

Svallfors, S. (2016). Politics as organised combat: new players and new rules in the game in Sweden. *New Political Economy*, 21(6), 505–19.

Syrett, M. & Devine, M. (2012). *Managing Uncertainty: Strategies for Surviving and Thriving in Turbulent Times*. London: Profile Books.

Szaszi, B., Palinkas, A., Palfi, B., Szollosi, A. & Aczel, B. (2018). A systematic scoping review of the choice architecture movement: toward understanding when and why nudges work. *Journal of Behavioral Decision Making*, 31(3), 355–66.

Szyszczak, E. (2006). Experimental governance: the open method of coordination. *European Law Journal*, 12(4), 486–502.

Taggart, P. (2017). Populism in Western Europe. In C.R. Kaltwasser, P. Taggart, P. Ochoa Espejo & P. Ostiguy (eds) *The Oxford Handbook of Populism*. Oxford: Oxford University Press, pp 248–64.

Tao, J., Cheung, A.B.L., Painter, M. & Li, C. (eds) (2010). *Governance for Harmony in Asia and Beyond*. Abingdon: Routledge.

Taylor, F.W. (1967). *The Principles of Scientific Management*, first pub. 1911. New York: W.W. Norton.

Thaler, R.H. (2015). *Misbehaving: The Making of Behavioral Economics*. New York: W.W. Norton.

Thaler, R.H. & Sunstein, C.R. (2009). *Nudge: Improving Decisions about Health, Wealth, and Happiness*, 2nd edn. New York: Penguin.

Tilman, R. (2014). *Thorstein Veblen and His Critics, 1891–1963: Conservative, Liberal, and Radical Perspectives*. Princeton, NJ: Princeton University Press.

Torfing, J., Peters , B.G., Pierre , J. & Sørensen, E. (2012). *Interactive Governance: Advancing the Paradigm*. Oxford: Oxford University Press.

Torfing, J., Sørensen, E. & Røiseland, A. (2019). Transforming the public sector into an arena for co-creation: barriers, drivers, benefits, and ways forward. *Administration & Society*, 51(5), 795–825.

Trottier, D. & Fuchs, C. (eds) (2015). *Social Media, Politics and the State: Protests, Revolutions, Riots, Crime and Policing in the Age of Facebook, Twitter and YouTube*. Abingdon: Routledge.

Ulibarri, N. & Scott, T.A. (2016). Linking network structure to collaborative governance. *Journal of Public Administration Research and Theory*, 27(1), 163–81.

Union of Concerned Scientists (2016). *Toward Climate Resilience: A Framework and Principles for Science-Based Adaptation. Union of Concerned Scientists*, 1 August. Available from: www.ucsusa.org/resources/toward-climate-resilience

United Nations (1987). *Our Common Future: Report of the World Commission on Environment and Development* (Brundtland Report). Available from: www.un-documents.net/wced-ocf.htm

United Nations (2015). *Transforming Our World: The 2030 Agenda for Sustainable Development*. Available from: https://sustainabledevelopment.un.org/content/documents/21252030%20Agenda%20for%20Sustainable%20Development%20web.pdf

Urbinati, N. (2013). The populist phenomenon. *Raisons politiques*, 51, 137–54.

Urbinati, N. (2018). Political theory of populism. *Annual Review of Political Science*, 22, 111–27.

van Dijk, J.A.G.M. (2006). *The Network Society: Social Aspects of New Media*, 2nd edn. London: Sage.

Van Dooren, W., Bouckaert, G. & Halligan, J. (2015). *Performance Management in the Public Sector*, 2nd edn. Abingdon: Routledge.

Veblen, T. (1921). *The Engineers and the Price System*. New York: B.W. Huebsch.

Vedung, E. & van der Doelen, F.C.J. (1998). The sermon: information programs in the public policy process – choice, effects and evaluation. In M.-L. Bemelmans-Videc, R.C. Rist & E. Vedung (eds) *Carrots, Sticks and Sermons: Policy Instruments and Their Evaluation*. New Brunswick, NJ: Transaction Publishers, pp 102–28.

Walker, B., Holling, C., Carpenter, S.R. & Kinzig, A. (2004). Resilience, adaptability and transformability in social-ecological systems. *Ecology and Society*, 9(2), art. 5. Available from: www.ecologyandsociety.org/vol9/iss2/art5/

Wallace, W. & Smith, J. (1995). Democracy or technocracy? European integration and the problem of popular consent. *West European Politics*, 18(3), 137–57.

Weber, E.P. & Khademian, A.M. (2008). Wicked problems, knowledge challenges, and collaborative capacity builders in network settings. *Public Administration Review*, 68(2), 334–49.

Weber, M. (1921). Politik als Beruf. In M. Weber (ed) *Gesammelte Politische Schriften*. Munich: Drei-Masken Verlag, pp 396–450.

Weber, M. (1978). *Economy and Society*. Los Angeles: University of California Press.

Weick, K.E. (2012). *Making Sense of the Organization, Volume 2: The Impermanent Organization*. New York: John Wiley & Sons.

Weyland, K. (2001). Clarifying a contested concept: populism in the study of Latin American politics. *Comparative Politics*, 34(1), 1–22.

Wiener, N. (1961). *Cybernetics, or Control and Communication in the Animal and the Machine*, 2nd edn. New Orleans, LA: Quid Pro Books.

Wildavsky, A. (1988). *Searching for Safety: Social Theory and Social Policy*. New Brunswick, NJ: Transaction Books.

Wilkinson, I. (2002). *Anxiety in a Risk Society*. London: Routledge.

Williams, D. (2006). On and off the 'net: scales for social capital in an online era. *Journal of Computer-Mediated Communication*, 11(2), 593–628.

Williamson, J. (1994). In search of a manual for technopols. In J. Williamson (ed) *The Political Economy of Policy Reform*. Washington, DC: Institute for International Economics, pp 9–48.

Willke, H. (1992). *Ironie des Staates: Grundlinien einer Staatstheorie polyzentrischer Gesellschaft*. Frankfurt am Main: Suhrkamp.

Wolin, S.S. (2004). *Politics and Vision: Continuity and Innovation in Western Political Thought*, expanded edn. Princeton, NJ: Princeton University Press.

Yang, K. & Bergrud, E. (2008). *Civic Engagement in a Network Society*. Charlotte, NC: Information Age Publishing.

Young, M.D. (1958). *The Rise of the Meritocracy, 1870–2033: An Essay on Education and Equality*. London: Thames & Hudson.

Zeitlin, J. (2015). *Extending Experimentalist Governance? The European Union and Transnational Regulation*. Oxford: Oxford University Press.

Index